Regulatory Economics and Quantitative Methods

THE CRC SERIES ON COMPETITION, REGULATION AND DEVELOPMENT

Series Editors: Paul Cook, *Professor of Economics and Development Policy, Institute for Development Policy and Management, Director of the Centre on Regulation and Competition (CRC) and Director, Competition Research Programme in the CRC, University of Manchester, UK* and Martin Minogue, *Senior Research Fellow, Institute for Development Policy and Management and Director of the Regulatory Governance Research Programme, CRC, University of Manchester, UK*

Titles in the series include:

Leading Issues in Competition, Regulation and Development
Edited by Paul Cook, Colin Kirkpatrick, Martin Minogue and David Parker

The Politics of Regulation
Institutions and Regulatory Reforms for the Age of Governance
Edited by Jacint Jordana and David Levi-Faur

Regulating Development
Evidence from Africa and Latin America
Edited by Edmund Amann

Regulatory Governance in Developing Countries
Edited by Martin Minogue and Ledivina Cariño

Regulatory Economics and Quantitative Methods
Evidence from Latin America
Edited by Omar O. Chisari

Regulation, Markets and Poverty
Edited by Paul Cook and Sarah Mosedale

Competitive Advantage and Competition Policy in Developing Countries
Edited by Paul Cook, Raul Fabella and Cassey Lee

Regulatory Impact Assessment
Towards Better Regulation?
Edited by Colin Kirkpatrick and David Parker

Regulatory Economics and Quantitative Methods

Evidence from Latin America

Edited by

Omar O. Chisari

Center for Advanced Research (Universidad Argentina de la Empresa) and Argentine Council of Research (CONICET)

Edward Elgar

Cheltenham, UK • Northampton, MA, USA

Published by
Edward Elgar Publishing Limited
Glensanda House
Montpellier Parade
Cheltenham
Glos GL50 1UA
UK

Edward Elgar Publishing, Inc.
William Pratt House
9 Dewey Court
Northampton
Massachusetts 01060
USA

A catalogue record for this book
is available from the British Library

ISBN: 978 1 84542 961 4

Printed and bound in Great Britain by MPG Books Ltd, Bodmin, Cornwall

Contents

Contributors

Alvaro Bustos is a PhD candidate in Economics at Princeton University. He holds a BA in Civil Industrial Engineering and an MSc in Economics from the University of Chile.

Omar O. Chisari is a Graduate in Economics and a Doctor in Economics at the Universidad de Buenos Aires. He is Director of the Center for Advanced Research at the Universidad Argentina de la Empresa. He is also President of the Argentine Economic Association and a consultant of the World Bank on regulated sectors and infrastructure.

Antonio Estache holds a Licence en Sciences Economiques (BA in Economics) Université Libre de Bruxelles, Belgium and a PhD in Economics (Focus on Regulation/Industrial Organization/Public Economics), Université Libre de Bruxelles, Belgium. He is Senior Economic Advisor to the Vice President for Infrastructure and to the Vice President for Growth and Poverty Reduction (PREM) at the World Bank. In addition he is a Fellow at the ECARES research center, Université Libre de Bruxelles, a Member of the Research Advisory Board of the World Bank, and a Member of the Advisory Board, Journal of Network Industries (2003–date), Utilities Policy (2003–date), World Bank Economic Review (2000–04). Dr Estache has advised governments in Asia, Latin America and West Africa on infrastructure regulation as well as public sector reforms. He teaches and publishes extensively in this area.

Alexander Galetovic is Commercial Engineer and Master in Economics at the Universidad Católica de Chile and has a PhD in Economics from Princeton University. He is Associate Professor at the Universidad de los Andes. He specialized in Industrial Organization and Regulation of the electrical sector. He has been Associate Researcher, Centro de Estudios Públicos and member of the expert panel of consultants of ADERASA (Association of Water and Sewage Regulators of America) and Director of Sociedad de Economía de Chile.

Andrés Gómez-Lobo Echenique has an MSc in Environmental and Resource Economics and a PhD in Economics from University College London. He has worked on regulatory issues throughout Latin America as a consultant to Oxford Economic Research Associates and the World Bank. He currently holds a research and teaching position in the Department of Economics of the University of Chile.

Maria Manuela González is Assistant Professor of Microeconomics and Macroeconomics at the University de Las Palmas de Gran Canaria. She is a specialist in the study of efficiency, regulation and performance applied to the transport sector. She has consulted for the World Bank and the Spanish government. She has recently published in *World Development*.

Paula Margaretic is a Graduate Magna Cum Laude in Economics at Universidad de Buenos Aires (UBA). She has a Masters in Economics from Universidad Torcuato Di Tella (UTDT). She is a Researcher at Centro de Estudios Económicos de la Regulación (CEER) of Universidad Argentina de la Empresa (UADE) and an Economist at the Comisión Nacional de Defensa de la Competencia, participating in the evaluation of the economic impact of mergers and concentration operations. She is also Professor at UADE and the Universidad de Buenos Aires.

María Fernanda Martínez graduated in Economics at University of Buenos Aires. She received her Masters in Economics, Universidad T.S. Di Tella. She is now a researcher at the National Regulatory Gas Agency of Argentina.

Diego Petrecolla has a PhD in Economics from the University of Illinois at Urbana-Champaign. He is Director of the Centre for the Studies on Economic Regulation and Competition Policy at Universidad Argentina de la Empresa. He is a consultant for the World Bank, the IBD and UNCTAD on Competition Issues and Economic Regulation of Infrastructure. He was President and Commissioner at the National Competition Commission in Argentina.

Carlos Romero graduated in Economics from the Universidad de Buenos Aires (UBA). He is a Master in Economics, Universidad Torcuato Di Tella (UTDT), a Master of Science in Economics, Warwick and a PhD candidate in Economics, Universidad Nacional de La Plata (UNLP). Carlos Romero is also a Researcher at the Centro de Estudios Económicos de la Regulación (CEER) and the Instituto de Economía de Universidad Argentina de la Empresa (UADE), and a Professor at UADE where he specialized in economics of energy and computable general equilibrium models.

Martín Rossi graduated in Economics from the Universidad de Buenos Aires (UBA). He holds a Master in Political Economy, UBA and a PhD in Economics, Oxford University. He held the post of Assistant Professor,

Master in Economics, Oxford University, 2002–2004 and he has been an External Consultant since 1999 at the World Bank and an External Consultant of Centro de Estudios Económicos de la Regulación (CEER-UADE).

Lourdes Trujillo is Associate Professor of Microeconomics at the University de Las Palmas de Gran Canaria. She has consulted for the Spanish Government, the European Commission, the OECD and the World Bank. She advises governments in Latin America on transport and water sector reform. Her areas of specialization include pricing theory, efficiency measurement, demand forecasting and regulatory design for network industries. She has recently been published in the areas of *Transportation*, *World Development*, *Transport Policy* and *Utility Policy*.

Preface

This book is a welcome contribution to the Edward Elgar Series on Regulation, Competition and Development. It consists of a set of contributions by leading researchers working on issues relating to regulation in Latin America. The chapters focus on regulation in infrastructure industries and attempt to show how quantitative analysis can contribute to more effective regulation. In particular, central issues relating to the measures used for benchmarking natural monopolies and incentives used in the regulatory environment and the impact of regulation and regulatory reforms are dealt with in the various chapters. The analysis throughout the book is both theoretical and applied, with numerous illustrations drawn from various infrastructure sectors such as electricity, water, telecommunications and ports. An innovative feature of the contributions is the link they make to solving the practical problems faced by regulators in various sectors and in helping them to improve the design of policy.

The issues covered in this book are central to the research being conducted by the Centre on Regulation and Competition (CRC), which was established in 2001 with core funding from the UK Department of International Development, to conduct research into competition, regulation and regulatory governance in developing countries. The series aims to be a focal point for the dissemination of research findings in these areas.

Paul Cook
Martin Minogue
CRC, University of Manchester, UK

1. Introduction and overview
Omar O. Chisari

Private sector participation in infrastructure in Latin America was dynamic and in the 1990s it took several forms, from privatisation to concessions. Although there has been controversy over the income and welfare distribution implications arising from the growth of the private sector, their participation has helped to provide the much needed investment that has fostered growth during the last decade. In most cases private sector participation has contributed to increased efficiency and productivity in the production process and the organisational structure and the quality of investment decisions. In some cases new investments have alleviated short term balance of payments and public deficits but have created future obligations that not all countries have been capable of managing consistently.

Private participation was accompanied by the development of new regulatory institutions and competition policy agencies, needed to supervise natural monopolies with potential opportunities to exert market power. Government agencies, international institutional and private firms have sought the advice of economists on a wide range of issues concerning regulation and regulatory governance. It was apparent that in economics, where mainstream thinking on regulatory economics had developed, there were significant differences in market processes and the institutions for regulation. As a result, economists in international institutions, government officials, private company managers and academics in Latin America have devoted time and effort to adapt available knowledge on regulation to local specificities. However, the achievements have gone beyond those expected and new perspectives on the design of cost effective regulation and regulatory supervision have been introduced that will benefit regulators.

This book includes chapters that summarise some of these ideas and perspectives that have been developed from cases in Latin America. The chapters have a common element, in the use of quantitative methods and economic and financial measures to aid regulation. What then constitutes these 'new perspectives or ideas'?

- **Benchmarking of regulated firms** If measurement is necessary for good regulation then there is a need for clear instructions on what to measure, how to do it, and how to reassess the information that was provided in the legal and institutional framework in countries that gave birth to price-cap and cost-plus methods of regulation. Two of the chapters in this book review the advantages and disadvantages of the efficient-firm method, which has been used to benchmark natural monopolies. A further two chapters present adaptations of the econometric approaches used to estimate efficient frontiers for electricity distribution companies by examining technical efficiency and productivity.

- **Incentives and renegotiation** A further chapter explores the possibility of using methods of benchmarking to assess the relative efficiency of competition policy agencies in three countries within the region.
- **Income distribution and regulatory performance** Privatisation and subsequent regulation have created controversy in Latin America. The salient feature for the region is the significant size of the privatised and concessioned sectors with respect to the whole economy. The extent to which efficiency and productivity gains have been good or bad for economies, and especially for the poor, is uncertain. This question is addressed in one of the chapters which summarises the results from Computable General Equilibrium models that have been applied to two countries in Latin America (Argentina and Uruguay).
- **Macroeconomics and the regulatory process** The CGE model helps to understand different links of interaction between the regulatory framework and the macroeconomy. Price-cap and cost-plus methods could have very different impacts on trade balance. Governments could become shareholders of concession firms through the profits tax. But on the other hand, macroeconomic shocks could hide or offset productivity gains obtained with effective regulatory institutions.

Following the introductory chapter, the book is organised into eight chapters. In Chapter 2 Andrés Gómez-Lobo provides an interesting study comparing two benchmarking applications in the United Kingdom and Chilean water sectors. Gomez-Lobo emphasises a different perspective and maintains that the power of benchmarking (yardstick competition with a real firm or other firms) helps to overcome asymmetries of information by providing adequate dynamic incentives. A direct comparison of the average cost of each firm allows the regulator to make relative efficiency judgements and to set tariffs. Therefore, a company that is relatively inefficient would have to reduce costs during each pricing period to obtain a normal rate of return on its assets; and a relatively efficient company would obtain above normal returns since its tariff would be set above its average cost. Thus, the advantage of this method is not the information it gives to the regulator, but rather the dynamic incentives it creates because the firm will try to beat the industry average by reducing costs. In practice, benchmarking is not a simple method because firms are not directly comparable, and exogenous factors can affect their costs.

In the UK, regulators set tariffs using a 'top-down' approach and impose price caps every five years. Prices are capped by the $RPI - X$ formula. The initial price level and the efficiency gain factor X, are determined by the revenue required to cover operations, maintenance and investment expenditure. Computations are reviewed every five years. The regulator projects future expenditures by considering two elements: that companies can reduce their costs as a consequence of general productivity increases and that, what determines each X factor is the relative efficiency of each firm. The latter consideration leads to a multi-step procedure that consists of the collection of data from each operator, the estimation of multivariate regressions models for different cost categories, the presentation of benchmarking results and tariff proposals for consultation with interested parties and finally, the publication of the regulator's final decision concerning the initial tariff levels, efficient costs and the X for each company.

In contrast, in Chile, tariffs are capped for five years but the X does not exist explicitly and the approach is 'bottom-up'. Tariffs are based on the operational and maintenance costs and on an optimal investment programme of a hypothetically efficient company designed to satisfy the projected demand. The procedure that leads to final tariffs includes the publication of guidelines to be followed in the design of the efficient company by both the regulator and the company, the presentation of both studies, a negotiation process in order to arrive at an agreement regarding the tariffs and the intervention of an Expert Committee (that finally sets tariffs, at least for water and sewerage).

The author concludes that no regulatory system is flawless. Both price cap regulation and comparative efficiency and efficient-firm standard approaches have advantages and disadvantages. He suggests the use of both methods in order to achieve a more adequate classification of the companies. However, he believes that, if asymmetry of information is to be considered as the main problem, then the efficient-firm method should not be implemented. He argues that the efficient-firm method obliges the regulator to 'micro-manage' an ideal company in the presence of significant information asymmetries that can lead to implicit 'capture' of the regulator through the black-box model that has been created by engineers and consultants in an attempt to design the ideal company.

The main objectives of privatisation in Argentina over the last decade were to increase the efficiency in the supply of services through the transfer of ownership from public to private and the adoption of more powerful incentive schemes. It is therefore pertinent to ask whether or not they really worked.

In this context, two of the more well known approaches to the estimation of efficiency are presented in Chapters 3 and 5.

Efficiency measures are an important tool for regulators, as they enable regulators to evaluate the performance of utilities. In particular, the frontier methodology aims to develop objective measures to screen the functioning and the operation of different natural monopolies through time in order to promote competition, provide incentives to cost minimisation and ensure that eventually, users benefit from cost reductions. Additionally the efficiency measurement is useful for price reviews.

Both Chapter 3 and Chapter 5 focus on the measurement of the relative efficiency of a set of firms in the electricity distribution sector. In Chapter 3 the sample set includes distributors from Latin America, while in Chapter 5 the authors concentrate only on Argentina. Both chapters discuss the methodological implications of estimating the relative efficiency of firms under public regulation, considering the peculiarities of the sector under analysis. They provide two different but complementary approaches to the issue. Martín Rossi in Chapter 3 focuses on labour productivity, while Paula Margaretic and Carlos Romero in Chapter 5 concentrate on the estimation of productive efficiency.

The construction of the efficiency frontier can be broadly classified in terms of the type of specification of the frontier (a production function, or a cost function) and the estimation methodology. Implicit in the first dimension is another choice regarding the type of efficiency to estimate. Rossi estimates an input requirement function to derive measures of labour productivity. Margaretic and Romero estimate a cost function to provide measures of productive efficiency (which includes technical and efficiency in allocation). The rationale for the former approach relates to labour being treated as an endogenous factor since capital inputs (distribution lines and transformer capacity) are treated as exogenous variables.

In comparison, Rossi concentrates on physical variables, while the estimation of a cost function requires monetary variables, i.e. input prices. Regarding the estimation methodology, Rossi obtains the efficiency scores through econometric techniques while Margaretic and Romero apply non-parametric techniques for the measurement of relative efficiency. In addition, both consider the possibility that the measures vary over time, distinguishing between shifts in the frontier reflecting efficiency gains at the sectoral level and catching-up effects at the firm level. Therefore the two chapters constitute complementary approaches to the measurement of efficiency in utilities. In this sense they provide a regulatory application that contributes to a reduction in information asymmetry between firms and regulators.

In Chapter 3 Rossi provides an estimate of the growth of labour productivity for the electricity distribution sector in Latin America between 1994 and 2001. The author presents a model of electricity distribution that contains three outputs (number of final customers, total energy supplied to final customers and area served), and one input, labour (number of employees). The concept of efficiency used is labour use efficiency: a firm is inefficient if, given the capital inputs, it uses more labour to produce a given bundle of outputs than would an otherwise efficient firm. In order to identify technical change over time, a parametric labour requirement function is estimated, using a translog functional form. He finds an annual rate of labour productivity change in the electricity distribution sector in Latin America for the period 1994–2001 of about 6 per cent. To check the robustness of the results, he estimates an alternative specification including time-fixed effects to reach a similar conclusion.

Rossi tries to establish whether final consumers have benefited from this increase in labour productivity, by exploring whether or not the increases in labour productivity led to lower prices for final consumers. A comparison of the changes in prices and labour productivity reveals that in most cases, final prices to customers did not fall to reflect the huge gains in labour productivity that were achieved during the period under analysis. However, he argues that the results are not in any sense conclusive, since the quality of the service improved and the final price is influenced, not only by efficiency in the distribution activity, but also by generation and transmission. Further research and a longer time period after the reforms came into place are needed before definitive conclusions can be drawn on whether final customers benefited from privatisation in the electricity sector.

In Chapter 5 Margaretic and Romero build an efficiency frontier applying a Data Envelopment Analysis (DEA) methodology in a regulatory context. The estimation of the efficiency of firms is based on a cost function. This measure is obtained under different assumptions regarding the type of technology and the environment within which firms operate. The authors use a dataset of 17 firms that specialise in electric distribution in Argentina for the years between 1993 and 2001. The variables used for the estimation are sales, clients, employment, area, lines, structure (proportion of residential sales to total sales) and density (ratio of the number of clients to area). A single frontier is constructed for the whole period, treating each observation in the panel as independent, and the relative efficiency of each firm is measured in terms of this single frontier. A linear envelopment programme is solved to estimate the efficiency frontiers. Several models are estimated under the assumptions of constant and variable returns to scale. They also construct a model with non-increasing returns to scale and compare the results obtained by each model in terms of their efficiency scores.

The authors find that private firms tend to perform better on average than publicly-owned firms. Further results on how relevant the role of ownership is are obtained through programme evaluation that focuses on the performance of groups of units rather than on individual performance.

In Chapter 4, Alvaro Bustos and Alexander Galetovic, present the basic elements of public utility regulation in Chile. The model of the efficient-firm is defined as a hypothetical firm that produces the quantity demanded at the lowest cost technically feasible. They present an analytical model, discuss the advantages and limitations of the methodology, compare price-cap and rate-of-return regulation and summarise sectoral applications. The chapter is important because the efficient-firm method provides an alternative to methodologies that have been developed in countries with legal traditions that are much more effective than those found in Chile. In the chapter the authors analyse the foundations of 'efficient-firm' regulation and the formulas that are used to set prices for water and sanitation, electric power distributors and the dominant phone companies. The authors show that efficient-firm regulation implies setting prices equal to long-run average cost, which is optimal when the firm is required to be self-financing (the present value of cash flows generated by the assets invested by the regulated firm should cover the costs of the investment). Furthermore, they show that in both efficient-firm and price-cap regulation, the fixed and exogenous period that is maintained between price-setting processes stimulates productive efficiency. This characteristic is absent in regulation based upon rate of return.

Nevertheless, the authors highlight the most important disadvantage of this system, notably information asymmetry. They argue that the price-setting formulas and procedures used assume that the regulator has sufficient information to determine the costs of a hypothetical efficient firm, without the need for information from the real firm. Nonetheless, modern regulatory theory and practice shows that the firm knows its cost and demand parameters more precisely than the regulator, in other words information is asymmetric. This means that there is a clear conflict of interest, since the firm will not wish to admit that its costs are lower or demand is higher if this results in lower prices being set.

The model developed in this chapter is used to discuss the potential gains from replacing efficient-firm regulation by a price cap. Contrary to the argument that the intensity of asymmetry could be moderated by replacing efficient-firm regulation with a price cap (since it would not be necessary to redesign the efficient firm every time prices were set), the authors show that the price-cap mechanism requires assets to be valued at historic cost, which stimulates overinvestment and cost activation just as in case regulation by rate of return.

In Chapter 6 Lourdes Trujillo and Maria Gonzalez examine efficiency in Mexican ports. In spite of the large consensus on the multiproduct nature of the port industry, many studies of port efficiency rely on an aggregate measure of port output. In practice, when the multiproduct nature of the port sector has been addressed explicitly, it has been done through DEA. There are only three multi-output parametric distance functions applications in the port sector. The chapter examines the efficiency of Mexican ports through the use of distance function, to capture the multi-output features of the sector.

The empirical application had three objectives. First, to measure the technical efficiency of port infrastructure service provision in the main Mexican Port Administration (Administraciones Portuarias Integrales, API). Second, to evaluate the impact of port reforms on efficiency levels. Third, to determine whether external factors, such as geographic location (Atlantic and Pacific cost), could influence the efficiency of the system. The results show that the annual average technical efficiency of the Mexican ports between 1996–1999 was 55.76 per cent. At the same time, the evidence suggests that the variation in performance across ports is quite high, ranging from 4.3 per cent in Ensenada in 1996 to 93.7 per cent in Salina Cruz. From an overall policy viewpoint, the results confirm that the expected gains from reform are becoming a reality.

Chapter 7 summarises the results obtained by Omar Chisari, Antonio Estache and Carlos Romero in their applications of Computable General Equilibrium models to regulatory economics. Their use is relevant when infrastructure sectors under regulation represent a high proportion of GDP or they contribute to price formation in a critical way. The authors present the analytical structure and the adaptations needed to represent regulatory regimes in a general equilibrium environment, applying the model to Argentina and Uruguay.

The authors offer the following lessons. First, the design of good regulatory rules should take into account how regulated sectors are linked through the input-output matrix, and their substitutability or complementarity at the consumption level. Second, the effectiveness of regulatory rules and agencies is an important element for income distribution. Transfer of rents must be anticipated and minimised by regulatory authorities. Efficient regulatory action can reduce the transfer of rents, and this is important for the poor who receive most of the benefits in the form of lower prices rather than higher factor prices. Third, the public sector might be an implicit 'shareholder' of regulated sectors through the tax system. Infrastructure sectors contribute to total revenue significantly in less developed countries; their contribution can be channelled mainly through the profits tax – as in Argentina – or be collected directly from prices of services paid by customers – as in Uruguay. Both cases illustrate the temptation of governments to pursue collection objectives rather than welfare, maximising strategies when choosing regulations and pricing regimes. Fourth, macroeconomic shocks might jeopardise the gains in efficiency and productivity obtained from successful macroeconomic reforms. Despite the relevance of regulated sectors for the whole economy, macroeconomic shocks due to changes in interest rates or commodity prices could reduce, or even reverse, the efficiency and productivity gains obtained from privatisation and good regulation in fragile economies, as is the case in Latin America. This is important when results of privatisation are evaluated. Fifth, price-cap and cost-plus regimes might have differential effects on the trade balance. The simulations show that the gains and losses of each regime must be balanced by taking into account their effects on capital flows and the implicit stress on the objective of equilibrating the trade balance. This is important for a less developed country that faces a recurrent trade account crisis, where infrastructure sectors represent a high proportion of GDP and where transfers of their profits abroad represent an important burden on the total trade surplus.

The extended process of structural reforms in Latin America during the 1990s not only included privatisation and regulation, but also deregulation. As a consequence, the design of competition law and its implementation and performance became important issues. Different models were adopted for competition agencies. In Chapter 8, Paula Margaretic, Maria Martinez and Diego Petrecolla focus on competition policy in Argentina, Chile and Peru. They examine the implementation and enforcement of the legal framework for competition policy. Their aim is to compare and contrast the three countries for the period 1995–2003, considering not only the qualitative, but also the quantitative dimension. They find that antitrust policy has been affected by the instability of criteria used to assess competition cases and the lack of a clear pattern of objectives. However there have been some changes in the legal framework aimed at improving the effectiveness of legal enforcement, with differing degrees of success.

As mentioned, their objective is not only to compare and contrast the main features of each legal framework from a theoretical point of view, but also to provide performance indicators to assess the relative effectiveness of each agency to enforce competition law. In order to measure this effectiveness they construct partial productivity indexes. They also apply the frontier estimation approach to measure and compare the performance of the antitrust agencies, and test whether the conclusions derived from the partial productivity analysis can be confirmed when considering a broader analysis based on the estimation of a production frontier for the competition agency. The methodology provides an interesting approach that aims to improve the quantitative analysis on competition and increase the information a policy maker has in order to assess the implications of any political decision.

From the comparison between the partial productivity indexes and the analysis of the frontier estimation, there are six main conclusions. First, the Argentinean and Chilean agencies can be described as small agencies in terms of personnel. Second, in terms of budget, the Chilean agency is proportionately bigger than its Argentinean counterpart. This is confirmed by the index budget per employee. Third, considering indexes such as 'cases solved to budget' and 'cases solved per employee' one can conclude that the Argentinean agency is relatively more efficient in completing a determined number of cases with the given resources, personnel and budget. Fourth, in regard to the information on fines given to total cases solved, it seems that Peru tends to impose considerably more sanctions than the rest of the agencies under analysis. However, the real impact that these fines have on markets is not so significant. Fifth, from the comparison between countries on the evolution of fines imposed and their impact on markets, the authors conclude that the performance of Argentina and Chile is better than Peru. The main difference between the first two is that Chile tends to impose less significant sanctions, while Argentina tends to impose high-impact fines in leading cases. Finally, regarding the efficiency scores obtained from the different models that applied the frontier methodology, their descriptive statistics are comparable and quite similar. Through the frontier estimation, they conclude that Argentina has the highest score and thus, is relatively more efficient, than Chile and Peru.

2. Bottom-up or top-down benchmarking in natural monopoly regulation: The case of Chile and the United Kingdom
Andrés Gómez-Lobo

1. INTRODUCTION

Tariff regulation is the most important activity of natural monopoly regulators. Tariffs must be set so that the projected revenues cover expected operational costs, asset depreciation, and a 'normal' rate of return on investments. This revenue requirement applies both to private as well as public firms, although in the latter case it is not unusual for a government to subsidise capital costs (by funding a firm's investment) and sometimes even operational costs (by transferring resources to a loss making public firm).

When a regulated firm is operationally inefficient or has a sub-optimal asset configuration, the question arises as to what costs should projected revenues cover. One option is to use a company's real costs and historical asset valuations. This guarantees that revenues will be sufficient to cover current 'business as usual' operating costs and provide a normal return on the resources effectively invested in the company. However as is well known, setting tariffs according to real or historical costs does not provide firms with an incentive to improve efficiency and optimise their asset configuration. In the end customers will end up paying higher than necessary prices.

Ideally, tariffs should be set so that revenues are sufficient to cover a firm's efficient costs – that is, the costs that a company could reasonably achieve if it were to operate efficiently and with an optimal asset configuration. However these potential costs are hypothetical and thus not observable.

The main regulatory difficulty in setting tariffs then is to ascertain what costs a company can achieve if it were operated efficiently. In this task the regulator is at a disadvantage vis-à-vis the managers of the regulated company since he or she does not have access to detailed information regarding the operating conditions of the company, existing inefficiencies, potential areas of improvement, and other information that can be used to

11

project potential costs. This problem, known in the literature as the asymmetry of information problem, is compounded by the evident lack of incentives managers and company owners have to reveal this information to the regulator.

When setting tariffs regulators need some type of tool to overcome this asymmetry of information problem and determine a company's efficient costs. This tool should also provide the company with the correct incentives to become more efficient through time. The use of comparisons between companies, or benchmarking, is a powerful instrument in this respect. By comparing companies with their peers, a regulator can ascertain the relative efficiency of operators and generate valuable information to be used in the tariff setting process. Furthermore by setting tariffs based on the costs of peers (for example, operators in different regions), a system of yardstick competition (Shleifer 1985) is introduced that generates the required incentives for efficiency improvements.

In this chapter we analyse two benchmarking experiences in natural monopoly regulation: the United Kingdom and Chilean water sectors. There are important differences between the philosophy and techniques used in both cases. In the case of the UK, the regulator compares the real costs of regional water and sewerage companies, and for the most part compares aggregate cost categories for different services. This experience is more akin to the classical idea of 'yardstick competition'.

In contrast, in Chile the peers used in the tariff setting process of a company are not a set of comparable real operators, but rather a fictitious company created by consultants, of an efficient operator (efficient company cost standard). This economic-engineering model is built up from a very detailed model of the infrastructure, personnel, buildings and materials required to operate in the company's concession zone. That is, efficient costs for highly disaggregated categories and functions are determined and are then aggregated to determine the efficient cost of each service.

The use of an efficient company standard in Chile is a 'bottom-up' exercise whereas the UK approach is more 'top-down'. As will be discussed later, there are other important differences between each method; mainly the efficiency incentive they provide, the ease of implementation and informational requirements and the way both systems deal with the ever thorny issue of capital expenditure regulation.

The review of these experiences is important for several reasons. First, in Chile the efficient company cost standard model is used in the tariff regulation of all public utility sectors. In addition, it has been emulated in other Latin American countries, in particular in the Peruvian electricity sector and to some extent in the Brazilian electricity sector. Second, there is a trend towards the use of an efficient company cost standard in developed countries, for example in the telecommunications sector in the United States (Weisman

2000). In both cases, a critical review of this method and its comparison with the UK's price-cap regime may provide policymakers with useful information when deciding whether to adopt such a system.

In the next section we present a very simple cash-flow analysis of tariff determination that will later be used to illustrate the differences between the two regulatory regimes. We then discuss in more detail the logic behind the use of yardstick competition in natural monopoly regulation. In the following two sections we present a description of the systems used to set tariffs in the UK and the Chilean water sectors, followed by a discussion of the advantages and disadvantages of each method. We conclude with some very preliminary empirical evidence regarding the use of each regulatory system.

2. A CASH FLOW DESCRIPTION OF THE TARIFF DETERMINATION

As mentioned above, tariffs must be set in order to generate sufficient revenue to cover three types of costs: operation and maintenance costs, depreciation and a normal rate of return on investments. If we define c_t as operating and maintenance cost for year t, D_t depreciation, ρ as the cost of capital and K_t as the asset base (value of assets net of depreciation), then revenues should cover the following annual costs:

$$Costs_t = c_t + D_t + \rho K_{t-1} \tag{2.1}$$

If tariffs must be set in year zero to cover costs from year one to year T, then the cash flow requirement to cover costs during the period is:

$$R(p) = \sum_{t=1}^{T} \frac{c_t}{(1+\rho)^t} + \sum_{t=1}^{T} \frac{D_t}{(1+\rho)^t} + \sum_{t=1}^{T} \frac{\rho \cdot K_{t-1}}{(1+\rho)^{t-1}} \tag{2.2}$$

That is, tariffs must be set so that projected revenues generate a cash flow (in present value terms) equivalent to expression 2.2. Using the simple identity $K_t = K_{t-1} + I_t - D_t$ it is easy to show that the above expression is equivalent to:[1]

$$R(p) = K_{t-1} + \sum_{t=1}^{T} \frac{c_t + I_t}{(1+\rho)^t} - \frac{K_T}{(1+\rho)^T} \tag{2.3}$$

This last formula, save for some adjustments for taxes, is included in all of the sectoral regulatory laws in Chile (electricity, telecommunications and water) as the required income that tariffs must generate in present value terms. In the UK the same formula is used when calculating required revenues of a regulated company except that it is more common for regulators to express this requirement on a yearly basis and in a disaggregated form as in equation 2.1.

The value K_{t-1} is the opening regulatory asset base, K_T is the closing regulatory asset base, and T is the length of the regulatory period. As will be discussed further below, the difference between tariff regulation in Chile and in the United Kingdom boils down to four elements. First, how to calculate the c_t and I_t values to use in the above formula, the length of time, T, used to calculate revenue requirements, how the regulated asset base is calculated and, something that is implicit in the left-hand side of equation 2.3, the evolution of tariffs over time used to generate the required net present value of revenues.

3.   BENCHMARKING IN NATURAL MONOPOLY REGULATION

In this section we present the intuition behind the use of benchmarking to determine the efficient operating, maintenance and capital expenditure costs values to be used in the above revenue requirement formula.

A simple way to gauge the efficiency or inefficiency of a regulated company could be to compare its reported costs with those of a larger set of companies. This could be undertaken by comparing the average cost (measure of cost divided by measure of output) of each firm. For example, in the water sector one could compare the average operating cost per cubic meter of water produced or some other indicator. If we want to determine whether company i is relatively efficient we could compare its average cost to the average of this measure over a set of peers, for example companies of the same industry but ones that operate in different regions:

$$c_i \Leftrightarrow \frac{\sum\limits_{\substack{j \neq i}}^{N-1} c_j}{N-1}$$

where N is the total number of firms in the industry. If the average cost of firm i is larger than the industry average, excluding company i, then it can be classified as relatively inefficient, while the reverse can be said if it has costs below the industry average.

It is important to note that the simple benchmarking procedure described above can be used to make relative efficiency judgements between companies, but does not allow a regulator to determine the absolute level of costs that operators could attain if they operated efficiently. For example, if all firms are to some extent inefficient, then the procedure indicates which firms are more or less inefficient but does not tell the analyst what the efficient cost level is.[2] As will be discussed later, the emphasis placed on relative efficiency in a yardstick competition regime versus absolute efficiency in the efficient company cost standard is an important difference between both methods.

Using the information provided by the benchmarking exercise, a regulator could set tariffs for each firm based on the average cost of all the other firms. Thus a firm that is relatively inefficient would have to reduce costs during the pricing period in order to obtain a normal rate of return on its assets. On the other hand, a relatively efficient firm would obtain above normal returns since its tariff would be set above its average cost.

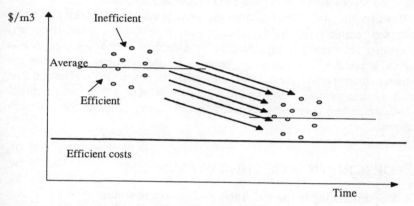

Figure 2.1   Yardstick competition and efficiency

From a regulatory point of view, the great advantage of a yardstick competition method is not the information generated on the relative efficiency of companies per se, but rather the dynamic incentives it creates. Since companies regulated under this method know that their tariffs do not depend on their realised costs, they have every incentive to try to 'beat' the industry average by reducing costs.[3] In essence each firm is competing against the industry's average. However if all companies behave this way, with time the industry average will decrease until all firms reach their efficient cost level, as illustrated by Figure 2.1. The regulator only needs to generate the dynamic incentives so that with time firms reveal their efficient cost level, rather than project or estimate the efficient costs of each firm, something they could only do imperfectly and at a cost given the asymmetry of information problem.

In practice, the benchmarking example presented above is too simplistic. First, in multi-output industries, outputs would somehow have to be aggregated in order to define an average cost measure. Second, firms are not directly comparable. One needs to first strip out cost differences among operators that are caused by differences in their operating environment, scale of operation, input cost variations, and other exogenous factors that affect costs but are not under the control of managers. One alternative that is used by the UK water regulator is to specify costs as a function of exogenous factors and then use multivariate regression techniques to estimate the parameters of this cost function. The residuals of this regression, that is, the variations in costs not explained by the exogenous factors, are then used to evaluate the relative efficiency of firms. There are many other techniques other than simple average cost comparisons or traditional regression models which can be used to determine the relative efficiency of firms. The best know are Stochastic Frontiers and Data Envelope Analysis.[4]

However the main message from the average cost benchmarking exercise presented earlier still holds when more sophisticated techniques and procedures are used. Namely, the great advantage of a yardstick competition system is not the information it generates for the regulator, but rather the dynamic incentives it creates for companies to reveal their efficient cost levels as time passes. This way the regulators overcome their informational disadvantage and eventually set tariffs based on the efficient costs of each company.

4.   DESCRIPTION OF THE TWO SYSTEMS

4.1 Benchmarking in the UK water and sewerage sector

In the UK, OFWAT sets tariffs for water and sewerage companies in England and Wales every five years ($T = 5$). These tariffs are set with reference to the efficiency gains that the regulator judges each company can reasonably make during the next regulatory period. Specifically, prices are capped by the well known $RPI - X$ formula:

$$P_{t+1} = P_t \cdot \left(1 + \pi_t - X\right)$$

where P_{t+1} is the price in year $t+1$, π_t is the inflation rate measured by the Retail Price Index and X is an efficiency gain factor. If X is positive, tariffs decrease in real terms between price reviews. The firm must be able to reduce costs by more than this X factor in order to gain above normal profits. In some sense this X factor acts as a 'competitor' to the regulated company between price reviews.

The initial price level and the X factor for each company are determined by the revenue requirements of the firm as expressed by equations 2.1 or 2.3 above. Thus to determine these values the regulator must project efficient operating and maintenance costs and investments. This section focuses on how this is done.

Future operating, maintenance and investment expenditure for the next five years are projected based on two underlying considerations. First, it is expected that all companies can reduce operating costs as a consequence of general productivity increases in the water industry or the economy as a whole. It is a well documented fact that the total factor productivity (TFP) of an economy or industry increases continually due to technological change, innovations in management and other general influences on the economy. This implies that companies should be able to reduce operating costs at least by this rate of general productivity increase. In the 1999 price review, when tariffs were set for the 2000–2004 period, OFWAT determined this productivity gain to be 1.4 per cent per year, both for the water and sewerage sectors (OFWAT, 1999). This value was based on estimates from specific TFP studies and expert opinion and was set after consultation with the regulated companies.

The second consideration that enters the determination of each X factor is the relative efficiency of each operator in the industry. Companies deemed to be relatively inefficient are set a higher X factor, since they have the potential to significantly reduce costs and 'catch-up' with the more efficient operators.

It is this last procedure that generates the incentives associated with a system of yardstick competition. But how does the regulator evaluate the relative efficiency of each operator? There are several steps involved in this benchmarking procedure.

The first stage is the collection of information from each operator. The usefulness of the efficiency comparisons depends crucially on the quality of the data used. As the well known saying 'garbage in, garbage out' eloquently expresses, no matter how sophisticated the benchmarking technique, if the data is of poor quality, in terms of its precision and comparability between companies, the results may not be very reliable. Thus the regulator in the UK spends a great deal of effort in the regular collection and analysis of industry data, including cost information, physical outputs and inputs, and measures of the operating environment.[5] The data collected is not just limited to cost, it includes demand variables and the topological characteristics of the network (such as the average pumping head) among other variables.

In a second stage, the regulator edits the cost data to strip out unusual or atypical expenditures incurred by each operator during the period under analysis. In the third stage, the regulator, with the aid of consultants, specifies and estimates multivariate regression models for different cost categories.[6] Once estimated and statistically validated, these models are then used to evaluate the relative efficiency of each operator for each of the cost categories and then aggregated to obtain a global efficiency evaluation for each company. The robustness of these results can be examined by using techniques other than multiple regression analysis.[7]

In the fourth stage, OFWAT presents the results of its benchmarking exercise, global efficiency evaluations and preliminary tariff proposals, for consultation. In this process any interested party can participate, including experts, operators and the general public. At this stage, the onus is on the operators to present proof that their relative efficiency ranking as presented by the regulator is incorrect or incomplete. Once the consultation process is over, the regulator collects any additional information provided, relevant criticisms and suggestions and makes revisions to the original analysis. At this stage, the regulator may adjust the analysis to take into account the different levels of quality offered by operators. The regulator will generally allow higher operating costs for companies deemed to offer a higher than average quality service.

Finally, the regulator publishes the final determination regarding efficient costs, initial tariff levels for that pricing period and the X factor for each company. Companies can appeal against the regulator's final decision to the Monopoly and Mergers Commission.

The actual models applied by OFWAT have evolved with each pricing review process. In the 1999 price review, 18 different operating and maintenance cost categories were modelled and estimated. Before presenting the models it will be useful to discuss in more detail how these models are used to make comparative efficiency judgments.

As mentioned above, costs can differ among operators due to various factors that are not under the control of management and thus should not be attributed to differences in efficiency. Econometric cost models control for these factors by specifying a relation between observed costs and the level of these exogenous variables. For example, assume that water distribution costs depend on the density of consumers in the concession area, something that in general is outside the control of the firm. Thus the following relation can be specified between costs and density:

$$C = \alpha_0 + \alpha_1 \cdot D$$

where C are distribution costs and D is the density level, while α_0 and α_1 are unknown parameters that define the exact relation between these two variables. Using statistical techniques it is possible to estimate α_0 and α_1 using data from different companies. OFWAT uses a well known technique called ordinary least squares (OLS) which, in simple terms, chooses the values of these parameters so that for each value of the exogenous factor the model predicts, with certain valuable statistical properties, the mean, or expected value, of the cost variable. Figure 2.2 illustrates this idea using a hypothetical example.[8] Distribution costs per client are measured on the vertical axis while the horizontal axis measures the density of clients. Each point on the figure represents a data point for each operator and the line represents the model estimated by OLS.

The model indicates the cost differences that can legitimately be attributed to exogenous factors such as the operating environment and other influences. For the same level of exogenous factors, the distance between the cost predicted by the model and the real costs of a given operator can be taken as a measure of relative efficiency. Thus in Figure 2.2, Firm *B* is relatively inefficient since its real costs are above the expected value of costs for that level of density. On the other hand, Firm *A* is relatively efficient for the density of clients it serves, even though the absolute level of costs (per client) for this company is above that of *B*.

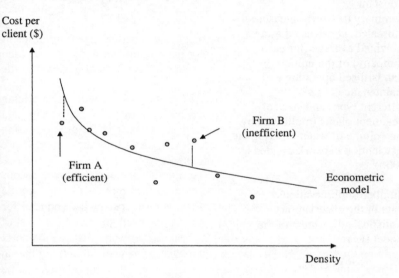

Figure 2.2   Relative efficiency

Tables 2.1 to 2.4 present the four models used by OFWAT during the 1999 pricing review to determine the operating costs of water production and distribution. Each table presents the definition of the cost variable (dependent variable) and the explanatory variables (independent variables) for each model. In addition the estimated coefficients are presented along with the date of the data used to estimate the model, the number of observations and the 'fit' of the model (which is called R^2 in the technical literature). This last parameter varies from zero to one, and measures the extent to which the independent variables account for the variations in the dependent variable. Thus a value close to zero indicates that much of the variation in the cost being modelled is not explained by variations in the exogenous factors, while a value close to one indicates that much of the variation in the cost variable is related to variations in the exogenous variables.

Table 2.1　Operating cost model for water resources and treatment

Modelled cost:	Resources and treatment functional expenditure less power expenditure, less Environmental Agency service charges (£ million), divided by distribution input

Explanatory variables	Coefficient
Constant	4.70
Summary treatment measure (unscaled) constructed as a weighted average (for each company) of the unitary standardised operating and maintenance costs of the different types and sizes of treatment plants (multiplied by the volume of water entering the distribution network divided by 1000)	3.87
Number of observations	25
Date of the observations	December 1997
Statistical adjustment of the model (R^2)	0.59

Source: OFWAT (1998)

Table 2.5 summarises the models used in the 1999 price review to model operating costs for sewerage collection and treatment.[9] In addition, OFWAT used four additional models for maintenance costs of water production and distribution infrastructure, and four further models for the maintenance cost of sewerage collection and treatment infrastructure.[10]

In order to determine the efficient level of capital expenditure for each company during the pricing period, the regulator also utilises a system of comparative efficiency. The regulator solicits information from companies on the budgets for different investment projects. Using this information the regulator estimates the average cost per type of project, which is then used to evaluate the expenditure proposed by companies for the investment plans during the five year period.[11] Benchmarking for the case of investment expenditure is less developed than for operating and maintenance expenditure.

Table 2.2   Operating cost model for water distribution

Modelled cost:	Log to base *e* of distribution functional expenditure excluding power expenditure (£million), divided by distribution input less total leakage (megalitres per day (Ml/d))
Explanatory variables	Coefficient
Constant	-3.74
Log to base *e* of total connected properties (000's) divided by distribution input less total leakage (ml/d)	0.68
Number of observations	28
Date of the observations	December 1997
Statistical adjustment of the model (R^2)	0.12

Source: OFWAT (1998)

Table 2.3   Power expenditure model

Modelled cost:	Log to base *e* of power expenditure (£ million)
Explanatory variables	Coefficient
Constant	-8.64
Distribution input (ml/d) times the average pumping head (meters)	0.92
Number of observations	28
Date of the observations	December 1997
Statistical adjustment of the model (R^2)	0.99

Source: OFWAT (1998)

How does the regulator use the results from the models to make a general judgment regarding the relative performance of firms? First, it is important to recognise that any empirical benchmarking exercise requires prudence and judgment in applying the exact numerical results. The quantitative results cannot always be taken at face value since there are measurement errors in the data used, and there are unaccounted for exogenous factors that affect costs between companies which were not controlled for in the model. In a particular quantitative exercise it is not unusual to find the results for some firms to be unbelievably high or low. For example, the results might indicate that a particular operator is 70 per cent inefficient. That is, for the particular cost being modelled, the operator could feasibly reduce costs by 70 per cent. Although one cannot discard this as a real possibility, in most cases it will be obvious that this result is in part driven by factors other than operational inefficiency.

Table 2.4   Business activity expenditure in water services

Modelled cost: Log to base *e* of business activities expenditure less local authority rates (£m)	
Explanatory variables	Coefficient
Constant	-3.93
Log to base of number of billed properties (000's)	0.92
Number of observations	28
Date of the observations	December 1997
Statistical adjustment of the model (R^2)	0.94

Source: OFWAT (1998)

In the UK as a first step to evaluate the efficiency of operators the results of the different models are aggregated by service (operational expenditure in water production and distribution, operational expenditure for sewerage collection and treatment, maintenance expenditure on water production and distribution infrastructure and maintenance expenditure on sewerage collection and treatment infrastructure). This is done by calculating the expected cost for each company, as indicated by each econometric model, adding them up and comparing the total to the aggregate real cost borne by each firm for that service. A simple argument based on the law of large numbers shows that this procedure reduces the influence of measurement error and other factors that potentially affect each of the individual models.[12]

As a second step, the regulator uses the results to classify each firm in one of five categories for each service: i) Very efficient: operators whose costs are 15 per cent below the expected costs for that service, ii) Efficient: operators whose costs are between 5 per cent and 15 per cent below expected costs, iii) Average: operators whose costs are between 5 per cent below or 5 per cent above expected costs, iv) Inefficient: operators whose costs are between 5 per cent and 15 per cent above expected costs and v) Very inefficient: operators whose costs are above 15 per cent of expected costs. Thus the regulator does not use the exact quantitative results of the benchmarking exercise but rather uses these numbers to infer the relative efficiency of each operator in more general terms.

Table 2.5   Summary of sewerage service models

Sub-service	Model type	Explanatory variables
Sewerage network	Log linear	Sewer length, critical sewer length, area, resident population, holiday population
Sewerage network: power	Log linear	Volume of sewage collected, average pumping head
Large sewage treatment works	Log linear	Total load, use of biological treatment, use of activated sludge, tight effluent consent for suspended solids and BOD, own sludge expenditure included, sludge centre expenditure included
Small sewage treatment works	Unit cost	Works size, works type, load
Sludge treatment and disposal	Unit cost	Weights of dry solids, disposal route
Business activities	Unit cost	Billed properties

Source: OFWAT (1998)

Finally the regulator compares the classification of each company in each of the four services (operating and maintenance cost for water and sewerage respectively). If a company is classified as inefficient or very inefficient in several services, then the projected c_t and I_t used in equation 2.3 are more demanding implying a higher X factor for that company. If the company has a mixed valuation across services, projected costs and investments are closer to current levels and the final X factor set by the regulator will be lower. The X factor will be lower still if the company is classified as efficient or very efficient across most or all services.

It is worth mentioning that in the UK, benchmarking is undertaken for relatively aggregate cost categories. As described above, models for 18 cost categories are specified and estimated in the case of operating and maintenance expenditure. The procedure for capital expenditure is not as well developed, as the projected budget for each investment project is benchmarked against the average budget as reported by firms in the industry.

Yardstick competition can be a very powerful regulatory tool to overcome the asymmetry of information problem faced by regulators and to provide operators with the right incentives for undertaking cost reducing efforts. However, as is illustrated by the UK example, it requires transparency and flexibility in its application. The regulator can only arrive at a reasonably informed judgment as to the relative efficiency of operators after a long process of data analysis, consultation with experts and interested parties, and due consideration to the particular circumstances and idiosyncratic factors that may affect each operator. Benchmarking techniques cannot be applied mechanically and thus require some flexibility in order to take into account quantitative as well as qualitative information. In turn this requires the regulator to exercise some discretion when setting tariffs, as is the case in the UK where the numerical results of the benchmarking exercise are used in a rather loose form and the exact X values for each company are determined in an ad-hoc manner by the regulator. However this discretion could be risky in countries where the regulator does not have political independence, as is the case in many Latin American countries. In this context a trade-off exists between giving regulators the required discretion to effectively apply yardstick competition methods and the risk that this discretion may be used opportunistically for political ends.

Finally it is also important to stress that a regulatory accounting system is a prerequisite to apply a UK type benchmarking approach since it requires comparable and high quality data among operators.

4.2 The efficient company standard, Chilean style

Chile has followed a somewhat different approach to the UK in setting tariffs for regulated public utilities, including water and sewerage sector. [13] As in the UK, tariffs are capped for a five year period and are indexed to past inflation.[14] However in Chile there is no explicit X factor as in the UK's *RPI – X* formula.

Tariffs are set based on the operational and maintenance costs, initial capital expenditure, and an optimal ongoing investment programme of a hypothetical efficient company designed to satisfy the projected demand for the next 35 years. Thus although prices are capped for five years, the tariff level is determined based on the average annual cost of the firm over a 35 year period which, in turn, is calculated using equation 2.3 with $T = 35$.

In practice the regulator, with the help of outside consultants, builds this efficient company based on engineering studies and criteria that determine the infrastructure, personnel, offices and other physical requirements of the ideal firm. It then multiplies these physical units by appropriate 'efficient' input prices to arrive at efficient costs and capital expenditures.[15] The efficient company then is a scale model, usually in a spreadsheet format along with several volumes of accompanying reports, of a company designed to operate in the regulated company's area.

As of December 2003, there were 49 urban water companies in Chile, most of them privatised or concessioned after 1998.[16] There is a separate price review process for each one, and the procedure, enshrined in law, is as follows. One year before the new prices are to come into effect, the regulator (SISS) publishes the guidelines that are to be followed in designing the efficient company model. These contain details on methodology, critical parameters and criteria that must be followed in projecting demand, estimating the cost of capital and designing the efficient company. It also specifies the costs, infrastructure and other information that the company must provide the regulator with in order to undertake its study. The regulated company has 60 days to make comments, criticisms and suggestions, after which SISS publishes the definitive guidelines. Based on these guidelines the company and the regulator build their own efficient company models.

Five months before the new tariffs come into effect, the company and the regulator exchange their respective studies. Once the company has analysed the differences between both studies, there is a 15 day period in which the company and the regulator can negotiate and arrive at a consensual set of tariffs. However in the vast majority of cases, especially with the larger companies, both studies arrive at irreconcilably different tariffs and the negotiation process does not lead to an agreement. In this case, an Expert Committee is set up with one member nominated by each party and a third member by mutual accord. This committee has 30 days to analyse each point of disagreement and opt for one of the two positions (not a value in between). The committee's determination, by majority voting, is binding. Thus in the end, it is the Expert Committee and more specifically the member nominated by mutual accord, who determines water and sewerage tariffs in Chile.

According to the tariff law and regulations, the efficient company model must be an 'optimised replacement' project. What this means is that the model must be of a new firm, built from scratch and in the most efficient form possible, to meet current and projected demand. Thus in theory, the model company should be built without reference to the existing real company. Perhaps a better way to understand this idea is to consider that the efficient company is an answer to the following question: if we were to build today a company from scratch to meet demand in the concession area, and for a given quality level, how would we do it to minimise operational, maintenance and capital expenditure? The operational costs and investments of this hypothetical company are then used in equation 2.3 which results in final tariffs.[17] Among other consequences to be discussed below, the approach adopted in Chile implies a very clear treatment of stranded assets. These would not form part of the efficient company and thus do not enter the regulatory asset base when calculating tariffs.

The regulator is forced to design the efficient company model in considerable detail. According to the regulations, the model must specifically consider the geographical, topological, and demographic characteristics of the concession area. It must also specify the physical characteristics and the configuration of the infrastructure used by the efficient company (pipe network, water sources, production and treatment plants) as well as an administrative layout. In practice, the model must determine the number and size of customer service offices, number of computers, the number and types of workers, wages for each type, office space needed, the rental or property values of buildings and many other detailed physical and monetary quantities that make up the efficient company. It is not surprising that the end result of these studies are several large volumes of text, presenting and justifying assumptions, data and intermediate results, along with very complex computer (often spreadsheet) models.

The large number of cost categories defined in the studies are aggregated to arrive at the operational, maintenance and capital costs for each service. In this sense, the efficient company model, which can be taken to be the benchmark against which the real company is competing, is built from the 'bottom-up' as opposed to the more 'top-down' approach used in the UK. Another important difference is the use of real cost data to arrive at the benchmarked costs in the UK as opposed to the use of the consultant's knowledge in Chile.

One of the most important differences between these regulatory schemes is the treatment of capital expenditure, or Capex regulation as is known in the literature. In the UK the depreciation allowance and the 'normal' return on investments required to set tariffs are determined by reference to the 'Regulatory Asset Base' (RAB), which is determined following a very simple accounting procedure. The regulatory asset base used in the last pricing review is carried forward by summing annual investments made during the last five years, I_t, and subtracting the depreciation allowances that were established for those years in the last price review, D_t:

$$K_{t+1} = K_t - D_t + I_t .^{18}$$

By contrast, in Chile the initial value of assets used to set tariffs is the value of the investments required to set up the efficient company model to meet the initial demand. The value of the company's real assets are not considered. This implies, as mentioned above, that stranded assets are immediately removed from the regulatory asset base, since the efficient company does not need them. In addition, any obsolescence of assets is immediately reflected in the asset base. In the UK stranded assets can still be part of the asset base, although the regulator does have discretion to remove these in part or totally from the RAB.

In theory this difference between the Chilean and the UK regulatory systems should not, by itself, affect tariffs in the long term, since the cost of capital ought to increase to compensate for the added risk that investors face in the Chilean case.[19] However, as will be discussed below, it does make a practical difference when there is asymmetric information. In order to understand the practical difficulties faced by the Chilean efficient company model it is useful to explain how asset values are determined in practice in the regulator's model.

As a first step the regulator gathers information from the regulated firm on its existing infrastructure. This information is not easy to validate, especially with underground assets. In part this difficulty stems from an unexpected consequence of the efficient company model. Because in theory the system decouples tariffs from real company costs, until recently regulators have not placed much emphasis on developing a regulatory accounting system to track the company's infrastructure or real costs. Companies therefore have room to strategically manipulate the information provided to the regulator. As an example, during a price review it is not unusual for the company to present information which is inconsistent with information provided just a few years earlier.

The regulator must also project future demand. Since prices per unit of consumption (cubic metre) are fixed during the pricing period and usually there are economies of scale, the company also has incentives to strategically understate future growth in demand.[20] Since average costs are decreasing when there are economies of scale, tariffs will be higher when demand projections are low. Any ex-post increase in demand will lower average costs and result in extraordinary profits for the company. Thus demand projections are another contentious issue during a price review.

Based on the infrastructure information and the current state of the infrastructure as informed by the companies, the regulator and his (or her) consultants 'optimise' the infrastructure of the real company in order to obtain an efficient configuration of assets. This optimisation may involve the elimination of stranded assets from the regulatory asset base or the use of engineering optimisation models to establish the optimal size and type of assets needed to satisfy demand. Once the efficient asset configuration is established, each element is valued at its replacement cost and the associated operational and maintenance expenditures are determined. These values are then used in the revenue requirement formula.

5.   ADVANTAGES AND DISADVANTAGES OF EACH SYSTEM

Each of the regulatory systems just described has advantages and disadvantages for the regulation of natural monopolies. For example, yardstick competition as applied in the UK has several drawbacks. First, companies are usually not directly comparable since they differ in size, quality of service, operating environment, demand characteristics and many other factors, some of which are not quantifiable. Some of these factors are taken into account in the cost regression models used by the regulator, but many others are not. These omissions may create biases that could affect the benchmarking results.

Second, individual efficiency estimates of quantitative benchmarking methods often result in unrealistically high or low efficiency values which cannot be taken at face value. In addition, the results in general are quite sensitive to the empirical benchmarking techniques used, the chosen sample and the variables included in the analysis. Thus as mentioned earlier, benchmarking results cannot be used mechanically and some flexibility and discretion must be exercised by the regulator in interpreting the results and evaluating the relative efficiency of operators. In countries such as Chile where the laws and regulations give the regulator very little discretion, such methods could not be applied without formidable legislative changes. In addition, giving regulators ample discretion to set tariffs, such as in the UK, may not be advisable in some countries owing to the increased risk of political opportunism in setting tariffs.[21]

Another drawback of yardstick competition is the requirement of a sufficient number of peers to undertake the analysis. If in a given country, there are only a small number of companies in a particular sector (as common in telecommunications), then the application of this method may not be viable. The same can occur if there are many companies but they differ significantly in size or another dimension. For example in Chile there is only one large sized water company with over a million clients, while the next largest is less than 42 per cent its size in terms of clients. In this context it may be unreasonable to benchmark this company to the other smaller operators.

In addition, when there are only a small number of comparators, the risk of tacit collusion among those companies rises. In this case yardstick competition looses some of its power as an incentive mechanism. Furthermore the application of yardstick competition may generate incentives for companies to take decisions to differentiate themselves from their peers, for example with respect to technology. By making companies less comparable, these incentives, besides generating distortions in investment decisions, also lower the power of yardstick competition.

The small number problem could in principle be overcome by undertaking an international benchmarking study. Although there are studies that compare the relative efficiency of productive units across countries, international benchmarking is fraught with difficulties.[22] First, there is the impact of exchange rate movements on monetary values. The relative cost efficiency between companies in different countries will depend on the exchange rate of the year or the period in which the comparison is based. If in order to avoid comparing monetary values, the analysis is limited to technical efficiency there is the further problem of the comparability of data definitions across countries. Finally, all the problems associated with idiosyncratic factors that make some companies not directly comparable within one country are compounded in an international context. Tax laws, regulatory institutions, climate and consumer behaviour, among other factors, may differ across countries in ways that are difficult to control for in an empirical study.

In summary, yardstick competition, although generally recommended by regulatory economists, does have a number of practical drawbacks relating to the comparability of firms, the number of peers available and the institutional flexibility required for its application.

In contrast to classical benchmarking, the efficient company standard can be applied even if there are no comparators. In addition it is a method better suited when geographic, topological, technical and other conditions differ widely across firms. However it must be borne in mind that an efficient company study is generally more expensive than a yardstick comparison. It must be undertaken for each regulated firm, and with a great deal of detail.[23]

According to Bustos and Galetovic (Chapter 4) there are several other advantages to the efficient cost standard model of regulation. Since tariffs are set to finance a company optimally designed to start from scratch, rather than one based on historical investments, the incentives for over-investing are reduced. Capital expenditures that become obsolete are wiped out from the regulated asset base.

In addition under price-cap regulation, as in the UK, the regulator has discretion to eliminate or reduce the value of stranded or obsolete assets from the regulatory asset base. This requires the regulator to continually evaluate the capital requirements of the regulated company and judge the efficient configuration of assets. This 'investment approval' activity can be criticised as representing a return to the practices of rate of return regulation. However this investment approval task is exactly what the efficient company method is concerned with, albeit in a more extensive form, since all assets of the firm are examined. Therefore as far as investment regulation is concerned, there is no clear advantage of the efficient company standard over traditional price-cap regulation.

Another point raised by Bustos and Galetovic (Chapter 4) is that the efficient company standard, as applied in Chile, guarantees an optimal time path of tariffs from a resource allocation point of view. Tariffs are set based on the average annuity required to fund the optimal replacement of the company, considering a time horizon of 35 years. Owing to the long time horizon, the depreciation rule adopted to estimate the residual value of assets at the end of the 35 years has only a marginal impact on tariffs. Therefore assuming that demand, technology and input prices do not change significantly between price reviews, water tariffs ought to be relatively constant through time. In contrast, water tariffs in the UK are quite sensitive to the depreciation rule adopted, since the time horizon in the tariff setting process is only five years, after which the residual value of the RAB is passed on to the next review. The depreciation rules commonly adopted, such as accelerated or straight line, will not result in an optimal time path of tariffs.

However it is not clear whether this issue constitutes a fundamental advantage of the efficient company standard compared to a price-cap system. In principle a regulator could adopt a depreciation rule that makes the time path of tariffs relatively constant under a price-cap system. However this is uncommon in practice.

Furthermore, under price-cap regulation the depreciation rule can be used by the regulator to 'time-sculpt' the evolution of tariffs.[24] This may be a useful instrument if the regulator wants to maintain certain financial indicators of the regulated firm within reasonable bounds during the pricing period. Thus the method used in Chile results in a time path of tariffs that is more efficient from an allocative point of view, but gives the regulator less flexibility to pursue other objectives when setting tariffs.

There is also the issue of how important it really is to optimise the time path of tariffs. As Newbery (1989) commented on the British experience: '...it is not difficult to argue that it is far more important to ensure that costs are minimised than that prices are set at the correct level. Suppose the elasticity of demand facing a nationalised industry is unity; then, roughly speaking, the welfare cost of setting the price 20 per cent too high or too low is no greater than the welfare gain of cutting production costs by 2 per cent; whilst if price elasticities are lower than unity, pricing errors are less costly'.[25] Therefore allocative efficiency, although important, might be considered of second order importance when compared to the cost reducing incentives of a regulatory scheme.

The most important criticism of the efficient company standard is that it is not designed to address the asymmetry of information problem between the regulator and the company (Goméz-Lobo and Vargas 2001; Weisman 2000). This asymmetry is simply passed to the consultants that built the efficient company model on behalf of the regulator. The asymmetry of information problem is exacerbated under this regulatory scheme, since the efficient company model requires detailed information on disaggregate cost items. The regulated company can always selectively present real information on input prices and technical requirements to counter the regulator's proposals in the appeals or conflict resolution stage of the process.

By forcing the regulator to specify how an efficient company ought to be designed and operated, the efficient company standard forces the regulator to 'micro-manage' the regulated company, a task the regulator is not able to undertake effectively due to the information asymmetry problem. This represents a fundamental difference compared to the benchmarking approach adopted in the UK, where the regulator does not attempt to determine the absolute efficient costs of a company but rather introduces an incentive mechanism so that companies reveal this information through time.

The detailed nature of the engineering approach to the efficient company standard also creates several practical problems. The amount of information that must be analysed, the number of variables and parameters that must be included, the complexity of the optimisation routines and computer programmes, imply that the model is a 'black-box' only understood by its creator, if at all. It is thus very difficult to know exactly what drives the results in these models. In addition, due to their complexity, it is close to impossible for an outside analyst to review a pricing review, making the regulatory process less transparent.[26]

Finally, there is a certain paradox to the efficient company standard. If the regulator were able to determine the minimum costs of an efficient company that starts from scratch in the regulated firm's concession area, and the cost of capital was correctly calculated, then the real owners could never earn a normal rate of return on their investments. The real company will always have a sub-optimal configuration of assets since past investments, however optimal and efficient they were when undertaken, will be sub-optimal ex-post. Due to the sunk cost nature of these investments it will generally not be optimal or efficient for owners to adopt the efficient company's asset configuration.

An example will serve to illustrate this last point. Suppose a company invests in a water production plant to serve a given area and that ex-post demand was higher than expected. At the next review, the efficient company model would establish that a bigger plant ought to be built to serve the total demand of the area. However for the real company, this would no longer be a realistic option and a second smaller sized plant would most likely be the recommended investment to undertake. If there are economies of scale in water production, then the real company, although making efficient decisions in each period of time, will still have costs above the efficient company model.

The efficient company standard, by starting from scratch, does not face any of the restrictions imposed by history and sunk costs, and should always have costs below those of the real company. In practice then, under this regulatory scheme, investors earn a fair rate of return only if the regulator makes mistakes in the design of the efficient company standard.

6.   SOME EVIDENCE REGARDING THE PERFORMANCE OF BOTH SYSTEMS IN PRACTICE

What can be said regarding the performance of each regulatory system? First, it must be recognised that natural monopoly regulation is more of an art than a science. Thus all regulatory systems will be far from perfect in practice. For example in the United Kingdom, the water regulator estimated that the operating costs of operators would increase by 3 per cent in real terms during the first pricing period starting in 1994, as a consequence of European Union environmental directives coming into effect. Ex-post operating expenditures actually declined by 12 per cent during this period. In the 1999 review period (starting in the year 2000), this reduction in operating costs was clawed backed to consumers in the form of lower tariffs. In addition, during this review process, the regulator considered that during the next five years operators could increase productivity by 2.4 per cent a year on average in the water sector and 3.1 per cent a year on average in the sewerage sector. Therefore although the first pricing review resulted in large rents for the owners of water and sewerage companies, these rents were eliminated in the following review process.[27]

The Chilean experience shows that firms regulated by the efficient company standard earned above normal profits during most of the 1990s.[28] The average rate of return of the electricity distribution companies between 1989 and 2000 was 18.2 per cent, with rates of return above 30 per cent a year for many companies during this period (Serra 2002). These returns more than doubled those earned by electricity generating companies. These latter companies operate in a competitive environment, face higher risks, and therefore, in theory, should have a higher cost of capital relative to distribution companies. In the telecommunications sector, the three companies offering fixed telephone services earned on average a rate of return of 23.2 per cent between 1989 and 1998 (Fisher and Serra 2002). In the long distance market, before the introduction of a competitive multi carrier system, the companies regulated by the efficient company method earned rates of return above 50 per cent for several years (Fisher and Serra 2002). Clearly these high rates of return signal a persistent regulatory failure. The water sector was the exception to this pattern. However until 1998 all the relevant water companies were in public hands and the aim of regulation during this period was to increase tariffs to a cost recovery level.

It is very difficult to judge whether the high rates of return in the Chilean telecommunications and electricity sectors during the 1990s were an inexorable consequence of the use of the efficient company method or, instead, the result of some idiosyncratic factor in its application in Chile or the particular features of the tariff laws and regulations in these sectors. For example, in electricity distribution the law states that final tariffs are to be set taking a weighted average of the costs of the regulator's efficient cost model (with a weight of two thirds) and the costs of the regulated companies' study (with weight of one third). Naturally this procedure gives the regulated companies the ability to partially set their own tariffs by declaring high costs.[29] In fact during the 1990s, the operating expenditures of the efficient company model presented by one distribution company were superior to its real operating costs during the previous years (Ministerio de Economía 2000). It is close to impossible to disentangle the effects of the features of the laws on the apparent regulatory failures encountered in Chile during the 1990s from the use of an efficient company standard per se.

The tariff setting laws and regulation in the water sector are probably the most perfected among all the utility sectors in Chile, owing to the fact that they were written several years after the electricity and telecommunications laws were passed and thus the accumulated experience of these last two sectors could be incorporated. In the water sector rates of return were low, below 6 per cent until 1998 (Arredondo and Mancilla 2000). However since most companies were in public hands during this period it is not clear how the regulatory system will fare under privitisation.[30]

Another piece of evidence regarding the performance of the efficient company standard is provided by Grifell-Tatjé and Lovell (2003), albeit using data from Spain. Using Data Envelope Analysis techniques they compare the costs of efficient company models for the Spanish electricity sector with the real costs of the regulated companies. They find that the engineers that built the model companies reduced the infrastructure requirements and used lower input prices compared to the real companies. However the relative input mix defined by the consultants in these studies was not optimal given the relative input prices used. In contrast, the managers of the real companies were much better at using the cost minimising relative input mix given the input prices they faced.

The results of Grifell-Tatjé and Lovell (2003) are illustrated using Figure 2.3. Q_0^r show the isoquant (alternative input combinations that produce a given level of output) of the real company. Q_0^m is the isoquant of the efficient company standard as conceived by the consultants. This curve is closer to the origin since the engineers that built the efficient company model assumed that less of each input was required to produce the same level of output as the real company.

The straight lines are isocost lines, that is the combination of inputs that given the input prices (p_1 y p_2) result in the same total production cost. The closer these lines are to the origin, the lower are costs. Costs are minimised when inputs are chosen so that they are on the lowest isocost line but still can produce the given level of output. It is easy to see that this occurs on the point where the isocost line is tangent to the isoquant.

What Grifell-Tatjé and Lovell (2003) find is that the total costs of the efficient company standard are lower than for the real companies given that the consultants used less inputs and at lower prices than their effective values. However, given the set of input prices, the consultants were unable to choose the cost minimising input mix. Rather they designed the company at a point such as *A* in Figure 2.3, with costs higher than the cost minimising point *B*. Managers on the other hand, optimised the input mix and, although they used more inputs, they were able to operate at a tangency point such as *C*. This result shows the difficulty that external agents have in designing an efficient company model of a regulated firm.

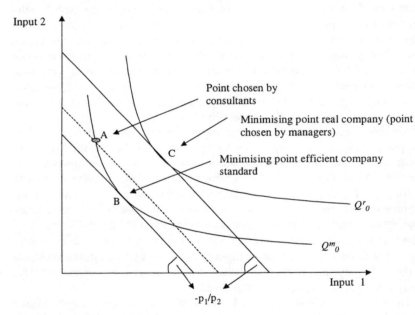

Figure 2.3   Cost minimisation

7.   CONCLUSIONS

No regulatory system is perfect. Price-cap regulation and comparative efficiency as used in the UK water sector and the efficient company standard as used in the Chilean water sector have advantages and disadvantages. Therefore perhaps the most reasonable conclusion that one can make is that a regulator should try to use both methods when possible.

An example could be the following. Using comparative efficiency techniques and an efficient company standard, companies could be classified in one of three groups. If a company is classified as inefficient by both methods then tough cost targets should be set during the price review process. When both methods dictate that a company is efficient, then tariffs should be set according to current real costs. When both methods give contradictory results then a more careful analysis should be undertaken on a case by case basis.

The above suggestion may be expensive to implement. If only one system can be used, which one is preferable? Although each method has its pros and cons, if asymmetry of information is considered to be an important issue, as will usually be the case in natural monopoly regulation, then the efficient company standard should be avoided. This system exacerbates the asymmetry of information problem. If the high rates of return regulated companies earned during the 1990s in Chile can be partially attributed to the use of the efficient company standard, then perhaps a system such as that used in the United Kingdom may be preferable in order to avoid these large regulatory errors.

NOTES

1. See Green and Rodriguez Pardina (1999) for example.
2. This is also true if the benchmarking exercise is done using more sophisticated techniques, such as stochastic frontiers or Data Envelope Analysis, rather than just comparing average costs between companies.
3. Unless companies collude to keep costs high. The risk of collusion under a yardstick competition system may be one reason why regulators may not want to approve mergers between regulated companies that reduce the number of peers in an industry.
4. Coelli, Estache, Perelman and Trujillo (2003) present these and other techniques and their use in a natural monopoly regulatory setting.
5. This is exemplified by the system of regulatory accounting adopted by OFWAT. All operators must submit each year ('July Returns') a dataset containing variables previously defined by the regulator.
6. Details of some of these models are presented further below.
7. At least on one occasion OFWAT has used Data Envelope Analysis to conduct an alternative benchmarking exercise.
8. Coelli, et al. (2003) present other estimation methods and their use in a regulatory context.
9. The estimated coefficients as well as other parameters for these models can be found in OFWAT (1998).
10. Since maintenance expenditure is less stable from year to year as compared to operating expenditure, the data used to estimate these models was the average expenditure during the last five years for each company.
11. The actual need to undertake each investment project is evaluated separately based on specialised studies and consultants' opinions.

12. If these influences are independent across models, then aggregating the results will average them out. For example, if a company was ranked as relatively inefficient in one cost model due to a random influence (for example, measurement errors in the data) but relatively efficient in another model also due to random influences, when costs are aggregated these two opposing influences will tend to cancel each other.

13. All utility sectors in Chile are regulated using an efficient company standard. However, there are differences in the details used in each sector. Here we describe the particular features of the water sector regulations.

14. The price index used to periodically adjust tariffs is not the Consumer Price Index (IPC), the Chilean counterpart to the *RPI*, but instead a specially designed index based on the cost structure of the efficient firm that tracks the prices of inputs used by the firm. The *IPC* is one component of this latter index, but it also combines a foreign exchange price index and other price indices.

15. This mainly 'engineering' approach in general will not result in the optimal input combination since input price ratios are ignored when determining the optimal configuration of assets and other physical input use. Further below we will present evidence from the Spanish electricity industry regarding this point.

16. However, the same type of tariff regulation was undertaken before privatization when most companies were public. This is an interesting case where publicly owned companies were subjected to regulation by another public agency (the water regulator) in a scheme mimicking the interplay of a private company and a public regulator. The evolution of tariffs, efficiency improvements and general performance of these companies during this period indicates that this scheme worked quite well in the case of Chile.

17. In reality, the tariff setting procedure is a bit more involved. First, long-run incremental costs are calculated for each service. Equation 2.3 is then used to make an adjustment to these marginal costs in order to guarantee full cost recovery. The water law implies that this adjustment should be of a Ramsey type, but in practice marginal costs for all services are increased by the same proportion in order to meet the budget constraint.

18. It is interesting to note that if the regulator uses the investment expenditures actually made by the company during the last five years, the company has no incentives to save on its investment programme. On the other hand, if the regulator uses the investment projections made during the last price review, and which were used to set tariffs, the company has incentives to over-declare the investment program at each price review. In practice, in the UK regulator takes a pragmatic stance and, when investments actually made are below those projected during the last price review, the regulator uses a value in between to update the regulatory asset base. Thus, companies have some incentives to try to find ways to reduce investments during the pricing period (without affecting service quality) but without an excessive incentive to over-declare future investment programs.

19. See Bustos and Galetovic (in this volume) for a demonstration of this result.

20. In the UK this is avoided by adopting a revenue cap instead of a price cap in some regulated sectors. If effective demand during a pricing period differs from the level projected when tariffs were set, an adjustment is made at the end of the year to maintain required revenues constant.

21. As Spiller and Savedoff (1999) convincingly argue, this risk is highest in the water sector, where sunk costs are high. Thus companies continue to operate even if quasi-rents are expropriated. Since consumption is widespread, the short-run political rewards from lowering tariffs are high.

22. See, for example, Estache, Rossi and Ruzzier (2004) for a study of electricity distribution companies in Latin America and Carrington, Coelli and Groom (2002) for an international benchmarking application to the gas distribution industry.

23. In Chile, an efficient company study for a large water company can easily cost over US$150.000 excluding the personnel time and other costs incurred by the regulatory agency.

24. See Green and Rodriguez Pardina (1999).

25. Newbery (1989), page 40.

26. In the 1999 pricing review for Aguas Andinas, the largest water company in Chile, the company's study amounted to nine volumes in total, each of several hundred pages. The regulator's model included six volumes of information.
27. Past rents were also taken away from owners by the retroactive windfall tax introduced by the new Labour government in 1997.
28. Ministerio de Economía (2000) presents a review of all pricing processes conducted during the 1990s in each public utility sector.
29. Knowing this, the regulator has the incentive to underestimate costs in their study in order for the average to be closer to the regulator's belief of the true efficient tariffs. Thus, both studies are manipulated and lose credibility as a source of information.
30. During the first price review under privatization in 1999, tariffs for the largest company, Aguas Andinas, increased by 20 per cent in real terms.

REFERENCES

Arredondo, M. and L. Mancilla (2000), 'Características de la Industria Sanitaria', in Oxman and Oxer (eds), *Privatización del Sector Sanitario Chileno: Análisis de un proceso inconcluso*, Ediciones CESOC, Santiago.

Carrington, R., T.J. Coelli and E. Groom (2002), 'International Benchmarking for Monopoly Price Regulation: The Case of Australian Gas Distribution', *Journal of Regulatory Economics*, **21** (2), 191–216.

Coelli, T., A. Estache, S. Perelman and L. Trujillo (2003), *A Primer on Efficiency Measurement for Utilities and Transport Regulators*, WBI Development Studies, World Bank Institute, The World Bank, Washington D.C.

Estache, A, M. Rossi and C. Ruzzier (2004), 'The Case for International Coordination of Electricity Regulation: Evidence from the Measurement of Efficiency in South America', *Journal of Regulatory Economics*, Vol. 25(3), May, pp. 271–295.

Fisher, R. and P. Serra (2002), 'Evaluación de las Regulación de las Telecomunicaciones en Chile', *Perspectivas*, **6** (1), 45–78.

Gómez-Lobo, A. and M. Vargas (2001), 'La regulación de las empresas sanitarias en Chile: una revisión del caso de EMOS y una propuesta de reforma regulatoria', Documento de Trabajo N° 177, Departament of Economics, University of Chile.

Green, R. and M. Rodriguez Pardina (1999), *Resetting Price Controls for Privatized Utilities: A Manual for Regulators*, EDI Development Studies, Economic Development Institute, The World Bank, Washington D.C.

Grifell-Tatjé, E. and C.A.K. Lovell (2003), 'The Managers versus the Consultants', *Scandinavian Journal of Economics*, Vol. 105(1), March, pp. 119-138.

Ministerio de Economía (2000), *Experiencias regulatorias de una década: balance y propuestas para el futuro*, División de Desarrollo de Mercados, Colección Sin Norte, Santiago.

Newbery, D. (1989), 'Energy Policy Issues after Privatization', in D. Helm, J. Kay and D. Thompson (eds), *The Market for Energy*, Oxford: Clarendon Press.

OFWAT (1998), 'Assessing the scope for future improvements in water company efficiency: A technical paper', Office of Water Services, Birmingham, April.

OFWAT (1999), 'Future water and sewerage charges 2000–05: Final Determination', Office of Water Regulation, Office of Water Services, Birmingham, November.

Serra, P. (2002), 'Regulación del Sector Eléctrico Chileno', *Perspectivas*, **6** (1), 11–43.

Shleifer, A. (1985), 'A Theory of Yardstick Competition', *Rand Journal of Economics*, **16**, 319–327.

Spiller, P. and W.D. Savedoff (1999), 'Government Opportunism and Water Supply', in Spiller and Savedoff (eds), *Spilled Water: Institutional Commitment in the Provision of Water Services*, Inter-American Development Bank, Washington D.C.

Weisman, D.L. (2000), 'The (in)efficiency of the "Efficient Firm" cost standard', *The Antitrust Bulletin*, Vol. XLV, Spring, pp. 195-211.

3. Labour productivity change estimates as an input for X-factors
Martín A. Rossi

1. INTRODUCTION

For decades rate of return regulation has been the dominant approach to regulating utilities. Though such regulation avoids the welfare losses that result from monopoly pricing, it provides few incentives for regulated firms to minimise costs. In recent years many regulators have developed and adopted stronger incentive schemes (see Crew and Kleindorfer 1986 and 2002; Laffont and Tirole 1993; Armstrong, Cowan, and Vickers 1994; Sappington 1994 and Vogelsang, 2002). Incentive regulation can take various forms, the most common of which involves price-cap regulation.

Price-cap regulation requires the regulator to adjust the utility's prices in line with some general index of prices—such as the consumer price index (CPI)—minus an efficiency factor X. This scheme is usually called CPI-X. The X-factor represents the real cost reduction the firm is expected to achieve. If the firm's cost reduction is greater than the expected reduction, it can keep the difference and earn above normal profits—at least while the price cap applies. This is the main incentive of this method.

A central issue in CPI-X regulation is how X-factors should be set. This decision is critical to the long term viability of any price-cap regulation. If too low an X-factor is imposed, the regulated firm's information rents will be excessive. If the X-factor is too high, the firm's financial viability can be threatened.[1]

In empirical applications the value of X is generally based on the regulator's assessment of the potential productivity growth of the regulated firm, which is based on assessments of the firm's current efficiency and past rates of productivity growth in the industry.

In this chapter we provide an estimate of labour productivity growth for the electricity distribution sector in Latin America, in the period 1994 to 2001, which can be used by regulators in the region as an input in the calculation of X-factors for the utilities in the sector.

2. LATIN AMERICAN ELECTRICITY DISTRIBUTION SECTOR

The Latin American electricity market has undergone a major transformation over the past 20 years. Reform in the region started in Chile with the privatisation of major electric utilities between 1986 and 1989. Argentina followed Chile's example in 1992; shortly thereafter Bolivia, Colombia, and Peru followed suit. During the second half of the 1990s, Panama, El Salvador, Guatemala, Nicaragua, Honduras, and Brazil also adopted reforms. The main missing players in the process of transforming the electricity sectors have been Costa Rica, Ecuador, Mexico, Paraguay, Uruguay and Venezuela, although Costa Rica, Ecuador, Mexico and Venezuela recently initiated actions toward restructuring.

Despite the diversity in the size of countries and power demand in the region – Brazil has a population of 160 million and an installed capacity of 58000 MW, while Honduras has 4.4 million people and 396 MW – all appear to have followed a similar path for reforms. The reform processes in the region have been based on a central change in the paradigm for the electrical business. The paradigm has evolved from a stated owned, vertically integrated electricity monopoly, to one in which different economic characteristics are recognised in the generation, transmission and distribution stages. Competition among private operators is established in generation, with the state regulating transmission and distribution activities.

As shown in Table 3.1 however, in many Latin American countries the state still controls sizeable amounts of the generation, transmission and distribution segments.[2] The average percentages of private participation are roughly 41 per cent, 22 per cent, and 51 per cent for generation, transmission and distribution—with a much lower variance for generation than for the other segments of the business. Generation has remained fully public only in Paraguay and Uruguay while transmission is mostly private only in Argentina, Bolivia and Chile. The largest diversity of organisational arrangements is found in distribution; the distribution activity has remained fully public in three countries (Mexico, Paraguay and Uruguay) and it has been fully transferred to the private sector in two countries (El Salvador and Guatemala). In most of the countries in the region public and private operators share the distribution market. From the viewpoint of efficiency concerns, this diversity is useful since it allows some degree of competition by comparison.

3. DATA

Data on firms were collected from several sources. Data for South America in the period 1994–2000 were mostly compiled from CIER (Comisión de Integración Energética Regional, a commission that coordinates the different participants in the electricity sector in South America) reports: Datos Estadísticos. Empresas Eléctricas. Año 1994; Datos Estadísticos. Empresas Eléctricas. Años 1995–1996–1997; Información Económica y Técnica de Empresas Eléctricas. Datos 1998–1999; and Información Económica y Técnica de Empresas Eléctricas, Datos 2000. Data for Argentina in the year 2001 were provided by ADEERA (Asociación de Distribuidores de Energía Eléctrica de la República Argentina, an institution that coordinates firms in the Argentine electricity sector). Other South American data corresponding to the year 2001 were obtained from firms' balance sheets. Data for Costa Rica were provided by the energy department of ARESEP (Autoridad Reguladora de los Servicios Públicos, the regulator of public services in Costa Rica). Data for Panama were obtained from the firm's balance sheet. Data for Mexico were provided by CFE (Federal Commission of Electricity). Data for El Salvador were provided by SIGET (Superintendencia General de Electricidad y Telecomunicaciones, the regulator of the electricity and telecommunication sectors in El Salvador).

Table 3.1   Share of private sector participation in selected countries (in per cent)

	Generation	Transmission	Distribution
Argentina	60	100	70
Bolivia	90	90	90
Brazil	30	10	60
Chile	90	90	90
Colombia	70	10	50
Costa Rica	10	0	10
Dominican Republic	60	0	50
Ecuador	20	0	30
El Salvador	40	0	100
Guatemala	50	0	100
Mexico	10	0	0
Paraguay	0	0	0
Peru	60	20	80
Uruguay	0	0	0
Venezuela	20	10	40

Source: Espinasa (2001).

Most of the data were checked using information provided by regulators and governmental agencies. In this respect we used information provided by ADEERA, ENRE (Ente Nacional Regulador de la Electricidad, the regulator of the electricity sector in Argentina), ANEEL (National Agency of Electrical Energy, Brazil), CONELEC (Consejo Nacional de Electricidad de Ecuador, governmental agency in charge of the electricity sector in Ecuador), CTE (Electricity Tariffs Commission, Peru) and URSEA (Unidad Reguladora de Servicios de Energía y Agua, regulator of the service of water and energy in Uruguay).

The database includes the following variables:

1. sales to final customers in GWh. Sales to final customers were calculated as total sales minus sales to other electric companies, in order to isolate the distribution activity in the case of integrated firms;
2. number of final customers;
3. service area in square kilometers;
4. total distribution lines, in kilometers (including high and low voltage power lines);
5. total transformer capacity in mega volt ampere, MVA; and
6. number of employees. Data on number of employees include information on part time and full time employees. Part time employees were counted as half time employees. In vertically integrated firms there is information on the number of employees employed by each department: generation, transmission, distribution, billing and collection and administrative. For these firms the number of employees of firm j was calculated as follows:

$$l_j = l_{1j} + l_{2j} + \left[\sum_{k=1}^{2} l_{kj} \Big/ \sum_{k=1}^{4} l_{kj} \right] l_{5j},$$

where l_{1j} = distribution (proper); l_{2j} = billing and collection; l_{3j} = generation; l_{4j} = transmission; and l_{5j} = administrative and general.

The sample is representative of the electricity distribution sector in the region. It covers the following countries: Argentina (29 firms supplying electricity to approximately 80 per cent of the total number of customers in the country), Bolivia (2, 31 per cent), Brazil (4, 19 per cent), Chile (2, 18 per cent), Colombia (4, 30 per cent), Costa Rica (4, 91 per cent), Ecuador (12, 61 per cent), Mexico (1, 79 per cent), Panama (1, 62 per cent), Paraguay (1, 100 per cent), Peru (11, 97 per cent), Uruguay (1, 100 per cent) and Venezuela (8, 92 per cent).

Summary statistics of the unbalanced panel are presented in Table 3.2. A total of 352 observations are available for estimation.

3.1   The variables

Electricity distributors use their network and transformer capacity, together with labour, to deliver a number of electrical units to a specified set of customers in a given geographical area. Our electricity distribution model reflects this: it includes three outputs (the number of final customers, the total energy supplied to final customers and the service area), a labour input (the number of employees) and two capital inputs (transformer capacity and kilometres of distribution network).[3]

Table 3.2   Sample summary statistics

Variable	Mean	Standard deviation	Maximum	Minimum
Sales (in GWh)	5962	21628	175498	61
Number of customers	868 290	2 592 453	19 760 000	17 782
Service area (in km²)	107 558	302 328	1 889 910	78
Distribution lines (in km)	29 748	89 861	595 170	380
Transformer capacity (in MWA)	1790	4475	33 078	38
Number of employees	2151	5929	41 063	95

Latin American electricity distribution firms have the obligation to meet demand; therefore we consider the amount of electricity supplied to final customers (in gigawatt hours, GWh) and the number of final customers served as exogenous outputs.

We include the service area (in square kilometres) as an output, since an increase in the service area either increases the use of resources or reduces the supply of other products (Førsund and Kittelsen, 1998). Although there is an occasional redrawing of boundaries due to merger and takeover, for practical purposes the firm has little direct control over the size of its service territory and hence the service area may be considered an exogenous variable.

We use two capital inputs, total distribution lines (in kilometres) and transformer capacity (in mega volt ampere, MVA). An important decision in a benchmarking exercise is how to treat the capital inputs which can be considered endogenous or exogenous to the firm. The way these inputs are treated affects the model specification: an input distance function is the appropriate specification if capital inputs are endogenous; an input requirement function is preferable if capital inputs are exogenous and the only endogenous input is labour.

As noted by Neuberg (1977), Kumbakhar and Hjalmarsson (1998) and Hattori (2002), distributors have limited control over the length of distribution lines since the amount of capital in the form of network reflects geographical dispersion of customers rather than differences in productive efficiency. And this is also the case although perhaps to a lesser degree, for transformer capacity (in mega volt ampere, MVA). Therefore we treat distribution lines and transformer capacity as exogenous capital variables representing the characteristics of the network.[4] This leaves labour as the main variable input;[5] accordingly we focus on labour productivity.

Following the above considerations, we represent electricity distribution technology by means of a labour requirement function. The concept of efficiency used throughout the paper is labour use efficiency: a firm is inefficient if, given the capital inputs, it uses more labour to produce a given bundle of outputs than an otherwise efficient firm would.

4.   ECONOMETRIC MODEL

In order to estimate the parametric labour requirement function we use a translog functional form because it provides a good second order approximation to a broad class of functions and admits the Cobb-Douglas as a special case. A translog labour requirement model with three outputs and two exogenous capital inputs, for a panel of $i = 1,...,N$ firms producing in $c = 1,...,C$ countries and observed over $t = 1,...,T$ periods, may be specified as

$$l^{it} = \alpha + \alpha_c + \sum_{m=1}^{3} \varpi_m y_m^{it} + \frac{1}{2} \sum_{m=1}^{3} \sum_{n=1}^{3} \varpi_{mn} y_m^{it} y_n^{it} + \sum_{k=1}^{2} \beta_k x_k^{it} + \frac{1}{2} \sum_{k=1}^{2} \sum_{j=1}^{2} \beta_{kj} x_k^{it} x_j^{it} + \sum_{k=1}^{2} \sum_{m=1}^{3} \kappa_{km} x_k^{it} y_m^{it}$$

(3.1)

$$+ \theta_t t + \frac{1}{2} \theta_{tt} t^2 + \sum_{K=1}^{2} \varsigma_{kt} x_k^{it} t + \sum_{m=1}^{3} \varsigma_{mt} y_m^{it} t + \lambda \, Ln(GNP\,percapita^\alpha) + v^{it},$$

where l, y_1, y_2, y_3, x_1, and x_2 are the natural logarithms of labour, sales, customers, area, lines and transformer capacity and v is the random error term. GNP per capita varies over time and across countries and should control for productivity shocks at the national level. The country fixed effects (α_c) control for potential biases caused by any omitted variables that are country specific and time invariant.

The time trend variable appears in a second order polynomial in t and interacting with the outputs and the capital inputs. These terms introduce second order flexibility in the translog labour requirement function and will be used to identify technical change over time, which can vary from firm to firm and from one period to the next. In the model in equation 2.1, technical change is neutral with respect to the outputs and the capital input, and the environmental variables if, and only if, $H_0 : \varsigma_{kt} = \varsigma_{mt} = 0 \, \forall k, m$, and it is absent if, and only if, $H_0 : \theta_t = \theta_{tt} = \varsigma_{kt} = \varsigma_{mt} = 0 \, \forall k, m$.

In our model specification, the rate of technical change (ΔT) is obtained as the logarithmic derivative of the labour requirement function with respect to time:

$$\Delta T = \frac{\partial l}{\partial t} = \theta_t + \theta_{tt}t + \varsigma_{1t}x_1 + \varsigma_{2t}x_2 + \zeta_{3t}y_1 + \zeta_{2t}y_2 + \zeta_{3t}y_3 .$$

According to its effect on the relative input utilisation, the overall rate of technical change can further be decomposed into effects due to pure technical change $(\theta_t + 2\theta_{tt}t)$ and effects due to non neutral technical change $(\varsigma_{1t}x_1 + \varsigma_{2t}x_2 + \zeta_{3t}y_1 + \zeta_{2t}y_2 + \zeta_{3t}y_3)$.

5. EMPIRICAL RESULTS

Ordinary least squares (OLS) estimates of the labour requirement function model are reported in Table 3.3. As usual for translog function approximations the variables are expressed in deviations with respect to average values; therefore the first order output and capital input coefficients are elasticities evaluated at the sample mean.

Estimates regarding technological parameters are in line with the specialised literature on electricity distribution, yielding further confidence to the validity of our estimation strategy. The first order output coefficients have the expected signs regarding economic behavior – an increase in outputs is associated with an increase in the use of labour. We test the null hypothesis of a Cobb-Douglas specification against the more general translog using the likelihood ratio (LR) statistic[6] and we are able to reject the null at the 1 per cent level.

In Column (1) we present the model without technical change. In Column (2) we add a linear time trend to the model in (1). The coefficient on time is negative and significant at the 1 per cent level, and its value indicates an annual average increase in labour productivity at a rate about 6 per cent. In Column (3) we introduce the squared of the time trend to the model in (2). The coefficient on the squared time trend is not significant at the usual confidence levels. In Column (4) we present the general non-neutral specification corresponding to the equation (3.1). In this specification we reject the null hypothesis that there is no technical change, $H_0 : \theta_t = \theta_{tt} = \varsigma_{kt} = \zeta_{mt} = 0 \ \forall k,m$, at the 1 per cent level according to an LR test. The null hypothesis of neutral technical change, $H_0 : \varsigma_{kt} = \zeta_{mt} = 0 \ \forall k,m$, is also rejected at the 1 per cent level. Productivity change evaluated at the sample mean values, remains about 6 per cent per year.[7]

To check the robustness of the results we estimate an alternative specification including time fixed effects $(\psi_t; \ t = 1995,...,2001)$, instead of the polynomial on the time trend. Following Caves, Christensen and

Table 3.3　Ordinary least squares estimates

	Dependent variable: number of employees, in logs				
Variable	(1)	(2)	(3)	(4)	(5)
Ln (Sales)	0.407	0.489	0.489	0.437	0.490
	(4.69)	(5.76)	(5.77)	(5.51)	(5.74)
Ln (Customers)					
	0.194	0.074	0.072	0.142	0.071
	(1.48)	(0.60)	(0.58)	(1.22)	(0.57)
Ln (Service area)	0.149	0.144	0.145	0.157	0.144
	(6.72)	(6.93)	(7.00)	(7.70)	(6.92)
Ln (Distribution network)	-0.023	0.025	0.023	0.016	0.025
	(-0.29)	(0.33)	(0.31)	(0.21)	(0.33)
Ln (Transformer capacity)	0.169	0.160	0.161	0.146	0.161
	(2.77)	(3.00)	(3.03)	(2.64)	(3.01)
Ln (GNP per capita)	-0.614	-0.199	-0.215	-0.288	-0.255
	(-3.57)	(-1.17)	(-1.26)	(-1.66)	(-1.40)
Time		-0.061	-0.061	-0.059	
		(-6.06)	(-6.08)	(-6.19)	
$(Time)^2$			-0.004	-0.005	
			(-0.85)	(-1.27)	
Time*Ln (Sales)				0.076	
				(3.35)	
Time*Ln (Customers)				-0.135	
				(-4.59)	
Time*Ln (Service area)				-0.018	
				(-3.35)	
Time*Ln (Distribution network)				0.077	
				(3.96)	
Time*Ln (Transformer capacity)				-0.012	
				(-0.54)	
Dummy 1995					-0.034
					(-0.47)
Dummy 1996					-0.084
					(-1.18)
Dummy 1997					-0.110
					(-1.50)
Dummy 1998					-0.184
					(-2.46)
Dummy 1999					-0.300
					(-3.93)

Dummy 2000					-0.331
					(-4.17)
Dummy 2001					-0.408
					(-4.23)
Country dummies[b]	Yes	Yes	Yes	Yes	Yes
Log likelihood	-99.23	-78.06	-77.58	-63.68	-77.06
R-squared	0.94	0.95	0.95	0.95	0.95
Number of firms	80	80	80	80	80
Observations	352	352	352	352	352

Notes:
[a] t-ratios obtained by using heteroskedasticity-consistent standard errors are in parentheses. In all cases I am estimating a translog form. To save space, second order terms are not shown. In all models the Cobb-Douglas specification is rejected against a translog at the 1 per cent level.
[b] In all the country dummies are significant at the 1 per cent level.

Swanson (1981), neutral technical change can be calculated as the difference between the parameters of two time dummy variables. Thus the rate of technical change from t to $t+1$ is $\psi_{t+1} - \psi_t$ and the cumulated technical change at the end of the period is the coefficient of the dummy variable corresponding to the last period. The growth rate of technical change in the first period (from December 1994 to December 1995, since the data corresponds to December of each year) is equal to the coefficient of the first dummy variable (ψ_{1995}) because the model includes a constant. As shown in Column (5) the cumulative productivity change at the end of the sample period is about 41 per cent, implying an annual rate of about 6 per cent, which is similar to the ones found in previous specifications.

We also address some concerns related to the type of data we are using. First, surveys answered by firms may have selection bias – i.e. only the most efficient firms could be willing to answer the survey. To see how sensitive the results are to this potential bias we constructed a source dummy variable that takes the value of one when the observation comes from survey data and zero otherwise. The source dummy is not significant, indicating that there are no systematic differences in efficiency between the firms that answered the survey and the other firms in our sample.

Second, some firms in our sample are vertically integrated – i.e., they produce and transport electricity as well as distributing it. To explore the possibility that labour productivity might be correlated with different degrees of vertical integration, we added a dummy variable for vertically integrated firms. The vertically integrated firm dummy has a positive and significant coefficient, suggesting that vertically integrated firms are using more labour, *ceteris paribus*, than the other firms in our sample. The inclusion of the vertically integrated dummy, however, does not have any impact on the value or significance of other coefficients.[8] In particular the rate of productivity change remains about 5.5 per cent per year.

6. DISCUSSION

Apart from labour productivity or technical change in the sector as a whole, regulators might be interested in the impact of type of ownership and type of regulatory regime on labour productivity and labour productivity change. Estache and Rossi (2004a), using a similar database as the one used here, studied the impact of the reforms to the electricity sector in the region, documenting an increase in labour productivity in all the countries where restructuring and privatisation has taken place. According to their study privatised firms have higher labour productivity than their public counterparts (though not higher labour productivity change), results that are significant in economic terms – private firms use at least 20 per cent less labour to produce a given bundle of outputs than public firms - and relatively robust to controlling for the potential endogeneity of ownership that could arise if governments privatised those utilities with the highest labour productivity first (see also Rudnick, 1998; Fischer and Serra, 2000; and Rudnick and Zolezzi, 2001).

Privatisation, however, always involves changes in both ownership and regulation, since the alternative to state ownership is rarely purely private, unregulated firms. Estache and Rossi (2004b) separate ownership effects from type of regulation effects finding (i) that there is no significant difference in efficiency between public firms and private firms operating under a rate of return regime, (ii) that firms operating under a price cap regime are the most efficient – they use about 60 per cent fewer workers to produce a given bundle of outputs, and (iii) that firms operating under hybrid regimes lie somewhere in the middle – using about 20 per cent fewer workers, *ceteris paribus*.

In this chapter we estimated the labour productivity change in the electricity distribution sector in Latin America for the period 1994–2001 and we found an annual rate of labour productivity change of about 6 per cent. The current debate in the region is whether final consumers have benefited from this increase in labour productivity. As a first approach to address this issue, here we explore whether the increases in labour productivity have had an effect on lower prices for final consumers.

In Table 3.4 we list the average annual rate of change (over the period 1994–2001) in household and industrial electricity prices by country,[9] along with the average annual rate of labour productivity change. The countries' average rate of labour productivity change was obtained from Table 2 in Estache and Rossi (2004a). Table 3.4 shows that the coefficients on the countries' time trends are negative – i.e. an increase in labour productivity over time – for all countries but Venezuela.[10] A comparison of the changes in prices and labour productivity reveals that in most cases, final prices to customers did not fall to reflect the huge labour productivity gains that were achieved during the period under analysis.

Table 3.5 lists average household and industrial KWh electricity prices by country, both with taxes and without taxes, along with the share of private sector participation in the distribution activity and the type of regulatory regime under which firms' operate.

The simple correlations between the share of private sector participation in the distribution activity and household prices with taxes, industrial prices with taxes, household prices without taxes and industrial prices without taxes (all corresponding to the year 2001) are 0.07, 0.04, -0.23 and 0.36 respectively. This indicates that electricity prices at the household or industrial level, with taxes or without taxes, are not highly correlated with ownership.

It is premature to conclude, however, that the results presented above provide conclusive evidence that consumers have not benefited from the reform process in the region. As pointed out by Kridel, Sappington and Weisman (1996), low service rates are just one of many possible benefits from incentive regulation schemes. There is evidence, for instance, that quality of service has improved more in those countries where reform and privatisation have taken place (see Estache and Rossi 2004a). Besides that in most of the countries where privatisation has taken place, by 2001 no price reviews have taken place. This is important given that price-cap regulation – the main regulatory scheme adopted by reformist countries – is known to have an impact on prices only after at least one price review. Finally, the final price faced by households and industrial customers is influenced not only by the efficiency in the distribution activity but also by the generation and transmission stages. That is both further research and a longer time period after the reforms are needed before general conclusions can be drawn on whether final customers have benefited from the privatisation process in the electricity sector.

Table 3.4 Price changes vs labour productivity changes

Country	Number of observations in the sample					Annual rate of change				
	Total	Regulated by				Prices with taxes		Prices without taxes		LP
		Private	PC	HR	RoR	H	I	H	I	
Argentina	117	70	70	0	0	0.010	0.014	-0.02	0.01	-0.046 (-2.29)
Bolivia	12	7	0	7	0	-0.083	-0.091	-0.10	-0.11	-0.003 (-0.08)
Brazil	113	44	44	0	0	0.032	-0.010	0.04	0.01	-0.091 (-3.79)
Chile	14	14	0	14	0	-0.118	-0.102	-0.11	-0.10	-0.061 (-5.90)
Colombia	17	2	2	0	0	0.060	-0.088	-0.01	-0.04	-0.173 (-2.64)
Costa Rica	2	0	0	0	0	-0.025	-0.044			-0.062 (-1.24)
Ecuador	40	8	0	8	0	0.030	-0.075			-0.012 (-0.44)
El Salvador	12	12	0	12	0	0.137	0.116			-0.020 (-0.64)
Mexico	8	0	0	0	0	-0.030	-0.011			-0.035 (-4.40)
Paraguay	7	0	0	0	0	0.088	0.042	0.09	0.04	-0.043 (-3.76)
Peru	64	24	0	24	0	0.007	-0.001	0.04	-0.01	-0.151 (-6.05)
Uruguay	8	0	0	0	0	-0.037	-0.063	-0.05	-0.08	-0.081 (-9.53)
Venezuela	36	23	0	0	23	-0.029	-0.282		-0.33	0.036 (0.97)

Notes:

[a] t-ratios obtained from heteroskedasticity-consistent standard errors are in parentheses.

[b] PC = price cap; HR = hybrid regimes; RoR = rate of return; H = household prices; I = industrial prices; LP = labour productivity.

[c] Panama was excluded from the analysis since there is data for only one period.

[d] All KWh of electricity prices were converted into 2001 price levels using the US Consumer Price Index and expressed in terms of purchasing power parity.

Source: Estache and Rossi (2004a).

Table 3.5 Average electricity prices by country

| Country | Private sector participation in distribution (in %) | Regulatory regime | Prices corresponding to the year 2001 | | | |
| | | | With taxes | | Without taxes | |
			Household	Industrial	Household	Industrial
Argentina	70	Price cap	13.50	10.94	10.79	8.07
Bolivia	90	Hybrid	14.90	14.02	10.02	9.67
Brazil	60	Price cap	21.47	9.84	17.64	8.07
Chile	90	Hybrid	16.07	10.30	13.64	8.73
Colombia	50	Price cap	23.10	15.07	6.79	12.33
Costa Rica	10	Rate of return	15.04	17.75		
Ecuador	20	Hybrid	16.28	18.94		
El Salvador	40	Hybrid	33.84	38.75		
Mexico	10	Rate of return	11.12	7.71		
Panama	100	Price cap	20.16	16.52	20.16	16.52
Paraguay	0	Rate of return	24.13	13.80	22.02	12.62
Peru	60	Hybrid	22.58	12.87	22.56	12.93
Uruguay	0	Rate of return	18.81	9.58	15.32	7.52
Venezuela	20	Rate of return	6.46	3.29		2.06

Notes:
a   All prices are at the country level, and correspond to the year 2001, except for prices without taxes in Colombia, which correspond to the year 2000 and were converted into 2001 price levels by using the US Consumer Price Index.
b   Regulatory regimes and the share of private sector participation in the distribution activity for all countries but Panama, were obtained from Espinasa (2001). The share of private sector participation in the distribution activity for Panama was obtained from the regulator of the public services in Panama.
c   In order to harmonise electricity prices across countries, all prices are in 2001 US dollars per KWh of electricity and are expressed in terms of purchasing power parity.
Source: Estache and Rossi (2004a).

NOTES

1. For a theoretical discussion on how to set the *X* factor, see Bernstein and Sappington (1999, 2000 and 2001).
2. For a description of the reforms in the region, see Dussan (1996); Rudnick (1998); Fischer and Serra (2000); Espinasa (2001); Millan, Lora and Micco (2001); Rudnick and Zolezzi (2001).
3. Jamasb and Pollitt (2001) review the different input and output variables used in models of electricity distribution. They find that the most frequently used outputs are units of energy delivered, number of customers and the size of the service area, whereas the most widely used physical inputs are number of employees, transformer capacity and network length.
4. The Dutch regulator also specifies network length and transformer capacity as exogenous to the firm (DTe, 2000). The DTe argues that network length and transformer capacity can be seen as variables for customer dispersion.
5. Indeed while productivity in electricity generation is mainly determined by the technology, productivity in distribution is, to a large extent, driven by management and efficient labour use. Typically the labour cost share in generation amounts to less than 10 per cent while in distribution the figure is around 50 per cent.
6. The likelihood ratio (LR) statistic is defined by $LR = 2[L_U - L_R]$, where L_R is the log likelihood of the restricted model and L_U is the log likelihood of the unrestricted model. Under the null hypothesis, LR is asymptotically distributed as a chi-square with degrees of freedom equal to the number of restrictions involved.
7. In this specification, which is the preferred one according to LR tests, the coefficient on GNP per capita is significant at the 10 per cent level and it has the expected sign, in the sense that firms operating in countries with higher income use less labour, *ceteris paribus*.
8. All results reported but not presented are available from the author upon request.
9. Electricity prices were provided by OLADE (Organización Latinoamericana de Energía).
10. Venezuela is the only country where private firms operate under a rate of return scheme.

REFERENCES

Armstrong, M., S. Cowan and J. Vickers (1994), *Regulatory Reform. Economic Analysis and British Experience*, Cambridge, Massachusetts: The MIT Press.
Bernstein, J. and D. Sappington (1999), 'Setting the X Factor in Price-Cap Regulation Plans', *Journal of Regulatory Economics*, **16**, 5–25.
Bernstein, J. and D. Sappington (2000), 'How to Determine the X in RPI-X Regulation: A User's Guide', *Telecommunications Policy*, **24**, 63–68.
Bernstein, J. and D. Sappington (2001), 'Corrigendum. How to Determine the X in RPI-X Regulation: A User's Guide', *Telecommunications Policy*, **25**, 537.
Caves D., L. Christensen and J. Swanson (1981), 'Productivity Growth, Scale Economies and Capacity Utilization in U.S. Railroads 1955–74', *American Economic Review*, **71**, 994–1002.
Crew, M. and P. Kleindorfer (1986), *The Economics of Public Utility Regulation*, Cambridge: MIT Press.
Crew, M. and P. Kleindorfer (2002), 'Regulatory Economics: Twenty Years of Progress?', *Journal of Regulatory Economics*, **21** (January), 5–22.
DTe (2000), 'Choice of Model and Availability of Data for the Efficiency Analysis of Dutch Network and Supply Businesses in the Electricity Sector', Background Report, Netherlands Electricity Regulatory Service, February.
Dussan, M. (1996), 'Electric Power Sector Reform in Latin America and the Caribbean', Working Papers Series IFM-104.

Espinasa, R. (2001), 'Marco Institucional de los Sectores Electricidad y Telecomunicaciones en América Latina', Research Department, Inter-American Development Bank.

Estache, A. and M. Rossi (2004a), 'Who Gained from the Reforms in the Latin American Electricity Sector?', Mimeo, The World Bank.

Estache, A. and M. Rossi (2004b), 'Do Regulation and Ownership Drive the Efficiency of Electric Utilities? Evidence from Latin America', *Economics Letters*, **86** (2), 253–257.

Fischer, R. and P. Serra (2000), 'Regulating the Electricity Sector in Latin America', *Economia* (Fall), 155–218.

Førsund, F. and S. Kittelsen (1998), 'Productivity Development of Norwegian Electricity Distribution Utilities', *Resource and Energy Economics*, **20** (3), 207–224.

Hattori, T. (2002), 'Relative Performance of U.S. and Japanese Electricity Distribution: An Application of Stochastic Frontier Analysis', *Journal of Productivity Analysis*, **18**, 269–284.

Jamasb, T. and M. Pollitt (2001), 'Benchmarking and Regulation: International Electricity Experience', *Utilities Policy*, **9** (September), 107–130.

Kridel, D., D. Sappington and D. Weisman (1996), 'The Effects of Incentive Regulation in the Telecommunications Industry: A Survey', *Journal of Regulatory Economics*, **9** (3), 269–306.

Kumbhakar, S. and L. Hjalmarsson (1998), 'Relative Performance of Public and Private Ownership under Yardstick Competition: Electricity Retail Distribution', *European Economic Review*, **42** (1), 97–122.

Laffont, J.J. and J. Tirole (1993), *A Theory of Incentive in Procurement and Regulation*, Cambridge, Massachusetts: The MIT Press.

Millan, J., E. Lora and A. Micco (2001), 'Sustainability of the Electricity Sector Reforms in Latin America', Research Department, Inter-American Development Bank.

Neuberg, L. (1977), 'Two Issues in the Municipal Ownership of Electric Power Distribution Systems', *Bell Journal of Economics*, **8** (1), 303–323.

Rudnick, H. (1998), 'Restructuring in South America – Successes and Failures', *Power Economics Restructuring Review* (June), 37–39.

Rudnick, H. and J. Zolezzi (2001), 'Electric Sector Deregulation and Restructuring in Latin America: Lessons to be Learnt and Possible Ways Forward', *IEE Proceedings*, **148** (2), 180–184.

Sappington, D. (1994), 'Designing Incentive Regulation', *Review of Industrial Organization*, **9** (3), 245–272.

Vogelsang, I. (2002), 'Incentive Regulation and Competition in Public Utility Markets: A 20-year Perspective', *Journal of Regulatory Economics*, **22** (July), 5–27.

4. Monopoly regulation, Chilean style: The efficient firm standard in theory and practice
Alvaro Bustos and Alexander Galetovic

1. INTRODUCTION

The core of public utility regulation in Chile is the concept of the efficient firm – defined as a hypothetical firm that produces the quantity demanded at the lowest cost that is technically possible. Although efficient firm regulation has been used in Chile for nearly 20 years now, there is still considerable controversy surrounding its conceptual underpinnings. For example during the most recent price-setting processes for telecommunications and water and sanitation companies, bitter disputes arose between the regulator and the firms over the correct way to include depreciation in the price calculation. This chapter presents a simple model that makes it possible to consistently analyse the microeconomic foundations of efficient firm regulation; it compares this with the best known alternatives, namely regulation based on rate of return and the price-cap; and it analyses the extent to which the formulas used to set prices among water companies, electric power distributors and dominant phone companies correctly reflect the microeconomic principles that underpin them.[1] One of the chapter's contributions is to highlight the common structure and foundations underlying public utilities regulation in Chile.

The model starts from the sustainability condition that any regulation mechanism should respect, namely that the present value of cash flows generated by the assets invested by the regulated firm should cover the costs of the investment. The peculiarity of efficient firm regulation is that prices are directly based on this condition, which means pricing at the level of long run average cost, bearing in mind the intertemporal nature of the problem. As is well known this is optimal when the firm is required to be self financing. In addition, however, we show that this condition is very similar to the way prices are determined in competitive markets. The formula used to set prices in each of Chile's public services largely applies this condition, thereby providing a common structure to Chilean monopoly regulation that is based on sound basic microeconomic principles.

In contrast both rate of return and price-cap regulation (the best known alternative mechanisms) merely use the sustainability condition as a constraint. Extending the model developed by Newbery (1997) we show that there are multiple price paths that are sustainable, each of which is determined by the time path of accounting depreciation on the authorised assets. However only one of these paths is efficient. Conceptually this marks the main difference between efficient firm regulation and its alternatives. The model also shows that the sustainability condition requires assets to be valued on a historical cost basis, regardless of whether regulation is based on rate of return or a price-cap. Accordingly the incentive for overinvestment is very similar in both mechanisms.

Although we do not provide detail of the shortcomings of efficient firm regulation in this chapter, our analysis leads us to conclude that these are mainly practical rather than conceptual. They arise from the fact that the formulas and procedures used in setting prices assume that the regulator has sufficiently precise information to determine the costs of the hypothetically efficient firm, without the need for data from the real firm itself. Nonetheless modern regulatory theory and practice in Chile show that prices cannot be set without data from the real firm because information is asymmetric (Galetovic and Sanhueza, 2000). The model we develop allows us to analyse what would be gained by replacing efficient firm regulation with a price-cap. Our conclusion is that a price-cap also requires considerable information from the real firm and therefore we suggest that emphasis should be placed on improving regulatory procedures rather than replacing the mechanism itself. The burden of proof should fall on those who believe the correct course of action is to replace efficient firm regulation by a price-cap.

The remainder of this chapter is organised as follows. Section 2 briefly describes the origins of efficient firm regulation, in order to draw attention to the practical problems that were faced at the time by those who designed the regulations. Section 3 develops a simple model of efficient firm regulation. Section 4 applies the model to evaluate the price-setting formulas used in practice and Section 5 concludes by comparing the price-cap mechanism with efficient firm regulation.

2.   THE ORIGINS OF EFFICIENT FIRM REGULATION

Efficient firm regulation was conceived in the early 1980s, largely as a response to three problems faced by public utility firms at that time. Firstly, the electricity and telephone monopolies until then had been regulated on a rate of return basis; and the defects of this mechanism were already known, particularly the fact that it stimulated overinvestment and provided little or no incentive to control costs (indeed these shortcomings were mentioned in El Ladrillo, the economic plan of the 'Chicago Boys'). Secondly, governments in Chile had been setting populist prices since the 1930s at least, which had discouraged private enterprise participation in those sectors and had turned the public firms that took their place into frequent candidates for State subsidies, thereby further weakening any stimulus for efficiency and generating recurrent fiscal problems. Thirdly, the government did not have technical staff capable of regulating their own firms. State monopolies were simultaneously producers and regulators, a feature which implied a clear conflict of interest.

Several mechanisms were deployed to jointly address these problems. In order to force firms to be efficient and limit their market power, the regulator would set prices according to the costs of a 'model' or 'efficient' firm, designed from scratch and without considering the real firm. The latter would obtain a normal rate of return only if it was capable of emulating the hypothetically efficient firm; and thereafter the costs of any inefficiency would be borne by the owners of the firm rather than by users or taxpayers. Although the problem of regulatory discretion and politicisation remained, it was thought this could be overcome by drastically limiting the powers of the regulator through legislation, supported by detailed regulations indicating the methodology to be used to calculate prices, the frequency of the process and the procedure to be followed in each price-setting episode. At the same time this detailed legislation, based on a fictitious firm, would enable the government to regulate its own enterprises even if the technical staff involved did not wish to cooperate.

This latter point is worth stressing because Chilean regulatory laws were drafted when the immediate problem was that the owner of the firms did not know what the managers were doing, what economists call the 'principal agent problem'. Although this problem is very similar to regulating a private firm there are major differences. One is that the wealth effects of regulatory decisions, which are central when the firm is privately owned, are much less relevant in the case of state enterprises. The reason is that subject to well known provisos, private firms are profit maximisers; in the case of monopolies each additional peso on the price leads to higher profits. In contrast those forces controlling public enterprises such as executives, unions and political parties do not directly benefit from any profits made since they do not receive them as dividends. The major problem of public enterprises stems from the fact that their controllers obtain most of their benefits through inefficiencies that inflate real costs (overstaffing, above market wages for most workers and relaxed working conditions). Accordingly the incentive facing the controllers of a state enterprise is not to declare unrealistically high costs in order to inflate prices, but to incur higher than efficient costs and prevent the existence of an external benchmark that would make it possible to compare them with an efficient standard. In addition to this, historically the problem in Chile had been that prices were set below cost, so one can understand why the emphasis was not placed on reducing information asymmetry but on preventing prices and costs from being grossly inefficient.

Application of this model raised the technical standard of regulation to levels hitherto unknown in Chile and made it possible to privatise the electric power industry and telephone companies in the late 1980s. Nonetheless the passage of time has revealed that in practice the efficient firm cannot be modelled without data provided by the real firm. However it is the real firm that knows the costs, technology and demand that it faces, not the regulator (i.e. the problem of asymmetric information). Accordingly, although theoretically the benchmark for price-setting is a hypothetical model firm, in practice the benchmark is the real firm stripped of its most glaring inefficiencies. It should be noted that this is more or less appropriate when regulating public enterprises since, as mentioned above, the main problem in this case is gross inefficiency. Nonetheless the real firm minus gross inefficiency is not an appropriate criterion if the firm wishes to inflate its costs in order to achieve higher prices. As the regulatory frameworks introduced during the 1970s and 1980s were based on the premise that the regulator could calculate the relevant parameters of the efficient firm including demand, without major participation from the real firm, no procedures were established to force the firm to provide quality information.

In Sections 3 and 4 we show that the shortcomings of efficient firm regulation are not conceptual; in fact we argue that efficient firm regulation is 'optimal' and that the microeconomic concepts underpinning it are consistently applied by the laws governing each sector. Furthermore the model we develop shows that the price-cap mechanism shares some of the practical problems of regulation based on rate of return, which efficient firm regulation resolves. This will allow us, in Section 5, to put into perspective the suggestion that has insistently been made, that it would be better to replace efficient firm regulation by the price-cap.

3.   THE FUNDAMENTALS OF EFFICIENT FIRM REGULATION

The foundations of efficient firm regulation have seldom been set out formally. In this section we develop a simple model that summarises them and makes it possible to compare efficient firm regulation with the two most frequently used alternatives, namely rate of return regulation and the price-cap. The model is based on an extension of Newbery (1997). The section ends with three applications of the model.

3.1 A simple model

Suppose that production $q = Q(p)$ units demanded at a price p requires $K(q)$ units of capital and involves a constant variable cost of c pesos per unit. The useful life of the capital is T years, after which it becomes useless. If the cost of capital is r, then the net present value of profits generated by an industry that invests $K(q)$ in $t = 0$ is

$$NPV_0 \equiv \int_0^T (p_t - c)Q(p_t)e^{-rt}dt - K(q). \tag{4.1}$$

Expression (4.1) is simply an accounting identity that is independent of market structure. Nonetheless it can be turned into a theory if we also indicate how p_t is determined. A particularly relevant case is when $K(q)$ is equal to $k \cdot q$, with k fixed and there are constant returns to scale. In this case, the industry will be competitive and in equilibrium

$$NPV_0 = (p - c)\int_0^T e^{-rt}dt - k = 0; \tag{4.2}$$

or else, defining $R \equiv \int_0^T e^{-rt}dt$ and simplifying,

$$p = c + \frac{k}{R}.$$

In other words price is equal to the long run average cost, which coincides with the marginal cost. The reason for this result is well known, namely that a price set above $c + k/R$ stimulates entry into the industry whereas if the price falls lower, capital will move out as it comes to the end of its useful life.

The competitive equilibrium satisfies three properties. Firstly, the value of the marginal unit of consumption is equal to the long run marginal cost, which is known as allocative efficiency. Secondly, the good or service is produced at minimum cost since firms adopt the most efficient technology. This is productive efficiency. Thirdly, as can be deduced from condition (4.2), firms exactly cover their long run economic costs, so they are sustainable (i.e. long run average and marginal costs coincide). It is easy to show that this condition is satisfied for any project, regardless of when it enters the market (see Section 3.4).

The regulation of natural monopolies in Chile is based on 'emulating the competition', whose starting point is the condition

$$Q(p)(p - c)\int_0^T e^{-rt}dt - K(q) = 0; \tag{4.3}$$

In other words in the long run, the price should be such that the firm covers its economic costs, which is the analog of condition (4.2). Nonetheless there are three differences with regard to a competitive market. Firstly, if there are economies of scale ($K'q/K < 1$) and the price is equal to the long run marginal cost, then the firm will not cover its costs.[2] The solution in this case is to set p equal to the average cost,

$$p = c + \frac{K(q)}{Q(p) \cdot R},$$ (4.4)

which as will be seen later, is explicitly recognised by the respective sectoral laws. It can be shown that average cost pricing is optimal (in other words it is productively and allocatively efficient), subject to the constraint that the firm is self financing. This is also known as the Ramsey-Boiteaux solution.

The second difference with regard to a competitive market is that to set p, the regulator needs to estimate operating costs (c), rate of return (r) and the cost of capital and investments (K), since these are not market determined quantities. It is at this point that the drafters of the 1982 electric power and telecommunications laws introduced one of their key innovations. Prices should be fixed in order to cover the operating and investment costs of an 'efficient' or model firm rather than those of the real firm.

But what is an efficient firm? The most appropriate definition is given in the Telecommunications Act: an efficient firm is one which '[...] operates with the costs that are indispensable in providing the services [...] subject to price regulation, efficiently, and in accordance with available technology, and maintaining the quality established for the services in question'.[3]

The Electricity Act adds that the efficient firm '[...] operates in the country',[4] and the Sanitation Act requires account to be taken of '[...] the geographic, demographic and technological constraints under which it is required to operate'.[5] In other words the efficient firm operates at minimum cost with the best technology available at that time, maintaining the service quality standards required by law but adapting to the properties of geography and demand in each service area. Note that these conditions are precisely those of a competitive market: the agent that enters the market (and therefore determines the price) does so with the best available technology but is constrained by the objective properties of geography and demand.

The third characteristic of efficient firm regulation is that as in a competitive market, prices are deduced from a long run condition – condition (4.3) – which does not depend on the useful life remaining for existing assets at any point in time. Nonetheless in a competitive market this happens spontaneously because price is determined by the long run cost that would be incurred by an agent that had sufficient capacity to produce the marginal unit. In a regulated market on the other hand, this condition has to be imposed by the regulator.

3.2 Asymmetric information, rent extraction and incentives

Strictly speaking the regulator should design the efficient firm independently of the conditions facing the real firm. But this ignores a basic fact, namely that the firm knows cost and demand parameters more precisely than the regulator – in other words information is asymmetric. This means that in one way or another the regulator must ask the firm for information about the relevant parameters. There is a clear conflict of interest here, however, since the firm will not wish to admit that its costs are lower or demand is higher if this will result in lower prices being set. As can be seen from condition (4.4), the price that is set will be higher, the lower is projected demand, the larger the capital stock required by the efficient firm, the higher its operating costs and the shorter the useful life assumed for the assets. In all cases it is safe to assume that the firm has more precise information than the regulator. A fundamental result in regulatory theory due to Baron and Myerson (1982) states that it is impossible to completely limit the monopoly power of the firm when information on these parameters is asymmetric. Even if it is regulated optimally, the firm will obtain rents, and the price set will be above long run average cost.

Secondly, the firm's efficiency does not only depend on the 'technology' it uses but also on how it is run. Better management is more expensive and requires greater effort than bad management, so the level of efficiency will depend on the incentives facing the firm. Nonetheless if the firm knows that efficiency improvements will be fully passed on through lower prices, it will have no incentive to make an effort to act diligently. In principle this ought to be resolved if the regulator designs the efficient firm assuming that it is well managed, since the badly managed firm will lose money. But here again, the regulator depends on the firm for information on what constitutes good management since the regulator cannot observe effort and diligence, still less measure them. Laffont and Tirole (1993) have shown that in that case there is a trade-off between limiting the firm's rents (which is usually referred to as 'rent extraction') and stimulating it to be productively efficient. Only if the firm keeps a share of the higher profits resulting from better management will it have incentives to be efficient; but this means setting prices above long run average cost.

Chilean regulatory laws essentially turn a blind eye to the fact that it is impossible to ignore the real firm in practice. Possibly, with the exception of the legislation governing water companies, regulatory procedures are grossly inadequate and tend to exacerbate information asymmetries in terms of cost, capital and demand parameters that exist between the firm and the regulator. On the other hand the legislation is reasonably successful in resolving the problem of stimulating efficient management because prices are kept fixed for four or five years depending on the sector. Thus higher profits resulting from productivity improvements achieved during a given pricing period are pocketed by the firm, at least until the following price-setting procedure.

It is usually stated that in Chile incentives to promote efficiency stem from the fact that prices are set to cover the costs of an efficient firm; but this is only partially true. As condition (4.3) shows the efficient firm is mainly used to bring prices close to long run average cost and to extract monopoly rents – a task that is impossible to achieve in full when information is asymmetric. The stimulus to efficient management is provided mainly by the fixed and exogenous pricing period. Setting prices in order to finance an efficient firm stimulates efficiency only insofar as the real firm knows that inefficiencies will not be passed on through prices – which is not necessarily the case if the model firm ends up being assimilated to the real firm as a result of information asymmetries.

3.3   Efficient firm regulation compared

There are two alternatives to efficient firm regulation, namely rate of return and price-cap. In this section we briefly describe these alternatives and compare their strengths and weaknesses.

3.3.1   Rate of return regulation

Regulation by rate of return consists of setting prices to ensure the firm earns sufficient revenues to cover observed operating costs and depreciation and also obtains a return r on the assets invested. The rate of return is usually calculated by weighting the cost of capital and debt, and is set at a 'reasonable' level. Prices are typically determined in a two stage process. Firstly, the revenues needed to cover costs are calculated, which are estimated on the basis of historical information from a recent reference period. In this stage the regulator holds discussions with the firm to decide which costs are acceptable and how to measure the capital stock to be used as the basis for calculating return. This discussion tends to be highly controversial. In the second stage the pricing level is set consistently with the revenue needed to obtain the desired rate of return and relative prices between the different regulated services.

To compare this with efficient firm regulation, it is helpful to start by noting that to guarantee a given rate of return r on assets, the price needs to be set such that

$$p_t Q(p_t) = cQ(p_t) + D_t + rV_t, \tag{4.5}$$

in other words revenues must be sufficient to cover operating costs $(cQ,$

depreciation (D_t) and return on invested capital (V_t). As mentioned above c is obtained by observing the firm's recent costs. D_t is usually obtained from a depreciation rule established in the regulatory contract (e.g. linear depreciation) and V_t is usually obtained from the balance sheet after agreeing which assets are admissible. Accordingly rate of return regulation is based essentially on historical data. Once the values of c, D_t and V_t have been agreed, the price consistent with rate of return r is

$$p_t = c + \frac{D_t + rV_t}{Q(p_t)}. \tag{4.6}$$

What conditions need to be fulfilled for the firm to be sustainable? Sustainability depends firstly on the relation between D_t and V_t, and secondly on the acquisition cost of the assets, K. Three conditions must be simultaneously held for the firm's investments to generate a rate of return r throughout their useful life, and for the condition

$$\int_0^T (p_t - c)Q(p_t)e^{-rt}dt = K \tag{4.7}$$

to be fulfilled. (A rigorous proof of what follows is in Appendix A).

First, the initial value of the assets recognised for price-setting, V_0, should be equal to their acquisition cost, K; otherwise part of the invested capital will never earn a return. Also the algebraic sum of depreciation during the useful life of the assets should be equal to their acquisition cost, i.e. $\int_0^T D_t dt = K$. If at the end of their useful life the assets have not been fully depreciated by the firm, then the prices set according to (4.6) will not generate sufficient revenues to satisfy (4.7). Lastly, the value of the assets used to set the price in t, V_t, must be equal to

$$K - \int_0^T D_t dt,$$

i.e. the initial value of the assets minus the depreciation authorised up to that date.

It might seem that regulation based on rate of return is conceptually very similar to efficient firm regulation. After all both have to fulfill a very similar sustainability condition – (4.3) in efficient firm regulation and (4.7) in the rate of return case. Nonetheless there is a fundamental difference. Any depreciation path $(D_t)_0^T$ that satisfies the three conditions described above is consistent with satisfying the requirements that the firm's assets produce a rate of return equal to r. Once this is recognised, it is easy to see that there are multiple price paths p_t, some of which diverge sharply from long run average cost but are still consistent with the firm's assets yielding a return of r. In contrast efficient firm regulation bases pricing directly on condition (4.3), which forces them to be equal to long run average costs (naturally this assumes that the regulator correctly estimates the level of the relevant parameters).[6]

A different way to appreciate this point is by analysing the only case in which they are equivalent. If $D_t = (p - c)Q(p) - rV_t$, with $V_0 = K(q)$ and $V_T = 0$, then price would be equal to long run average cost $c + K(q)/(Q(p) \cdot R)$. It is easy to show that the firm is sustainable and that the assets yield a return of r throughout. Nonetheless note that as

$$V_t = (p-c)Q(p)\int_t^T e^{-r(s-t)}dt$$

$$= \frac{(p-c)Q(p)}{r}(e^{-rt} - e^{-rT}),$$

it follows that

$$D_t = (p-c)Q(p)(1+e^{-rT} - e^{-rt});$$

In other words the rate of depreciation rises over time. In contrast depreciation rules are usually linear or even accelerated. Accordingly under ideal information conditions it is unlikely that regulation based on rate of return will produce prices equal to long run average cost, which is required to achieve allocative efficiency.

The second discrepancy is that in rate of return regulation the stimulus to efficient management is also different. As discussed in the previous subsection the fixed and exogenous period between price-setting processes stimulates productive efficiency under efficient firm regulation because the firm appropriates the higher profits, at least until the next price review. In contrast the spirit of rate of return regulation is that condition (4.5) is satisfied at all times. Accordingly the pricing period is neither fixed nor exogenous and the firm can request a price review whenever it deems costs to have risen. This together with constraints imposed by asymmetric information suggests that the stimulus to efficient management is weak because cost increases (and reductions) are passed on to prices relatively quickly. Accordingly rate of return regulation does not stimulate productive efficiency.

The best known inefficiency caused by rate of return regulation is the incentive to overinvest in capital, which is known as the 'Averch-Johnson effect' (Averch and Johnson, 1962). We know from Baron and Myerson (1982) that the cost of capital rate set by the regulator will tend to be higher than the true rate, in which case it suits the firm to raise its capital above the optimal level. Although efficient firm regulation solves this problem in principle, information is asymmetric in practice. Accordingly the cost of capital set by the regulator will be higher than the true rate and the design of the efficient firm also depends partly on what is revealed by the real firm. Once again how serious this problem is in practice depends on the appropriateness of the regulator's data collection procedures.

The third difference between the two mechanisms concerns procedures. In Chile the methodology for calculating rate of return and prices is established by law, whereas in the United States the regulator sets a 'reasonable' rate of return. In principle this gives regulators more discretion but their power is limited because the rate of return usually forms part of the regulatory contract and in the end prices have to be consistent with constitutional guarantees that protect against expropriation without due cause.

3.3.2 The price-cap

The term price-cap or price-ceiling was introduced when British Telecom was privatised in 1984 and a decision was made to impose an explicit limit on telephone service prices (Green and Pardina, 1999). The origins of the price-cap are best understood by seeing it as a substitute for rate of return regulation. Its designers were aware that the latter system failed to stimulate productive efficiency. As we have seen part of the reason for this was that the period between price-setting processes is not fixed, and cost changes are passed on to prices rather easily. To correct this, the price-cap mechanism was designed with the intention that the period between price-setting processes would be fixed and exogenous (although in practice in the UK regulators can bring forward the price-setting process if they consider that there is justification).[7]

The second difference from rate of return regulation is that in principle prices would not be set so as to cover operating costs observed in the recent past. Instead they would generate sufficient revenues to cover projected costs during the pricing period, assuming that the firm is managed efficiently, in addition to generating a given rate of return presumably based on the firm's cost of capital. Delinking prices from effective costs together with the fixed and exogenous period between price-setting processes, would improve incentives for productive efficiency.

Both the emphasis placed on delinking prices from the costs of the real firm and setting them with reference to an efficient standard, and the fixed and exogenous period between price-setting episodes, makes the price-cap similar to efficient firm regulation. Nonetheless prices also clearly have to generate a return on capital invested. In this dimension the price-cap mechanism is very similar to regulation by rate of return because, once r, D_t and V_t are determined, prices are calculated on the basis of a formula such as (4.6). In other words

$$p_t = c + \frac{D_t + rV_t}{Q(p_t)}.$$

Many analysts thought that, as in the case of costs, assets should be valued with reference to their market price and that this would provide corrective incentives to invest efficiently. Nonetheless Newbery (1997) showed that it is impossible to base the price-setting formula on the market value of assets since ultimately this obviously depends on the price-setting formula decided by the regulator. At one extreme if the market anticipates that the regulator will set low prices, then the firm's assets will be worth little, thereby justifying the low price set by the regulator. And at the other extreme if the market anticipates that the regulator will set high prices, then the assets will be worth a lot, which also justifies the high prices needed to generate an adequate return on those assets. As Newbery (1997) shows the only way of ensuring sustainability and rent extraction is for the price-setting formula to respect (4.7) and the three conditions indicated above, which is exactly the same as regulating by rate of return.

Once this has been recognised it is easy to see that the prices set using the price-cap mechanism will most likely diverge from long run average cost. As we saw in the previous section long run average cost pricing requires depreciation to be rising over time, which contradicts the standard rules of depreciation. Furthermore such rules tend to produce high prices when investments have recently been made and low prices when they are approaching the end of their useful life. Nonetheless as Newbery (1997) argues, the intensity with which indivisible investments are actually used is precisely the opposite – low (in relation to capacity) just after new investments have been made but high when the time for reinvesting is approaching, because demand growth requires this. Accordingly in practice there is a bias towards charging high prices when infrastructure is underused, which is precisely the opposite of what allocative efficiency requires.

Against this downside, price-cap regulation simplifies in principle the calculation of the asset base used to set prices. Recall that sustainability requires that $V_t = K - \int_0^t D_s ds$, which means that

$$V_t = V_{t-1} - \int_{t-1}^t D_s ds$$

Accordingly once the depreciation rule is known, it is sufficient to deduct the depreciation authorised during the current pricing period from the assets' accounting value in the previous price-setting process (if there is investment between consecutive pricing rounds, the value of those investments is added to the asset value at the time of the investment, and then depreciation is applied according to the authorised rule). Furthermore, provided the depreciation rules satisfy the three conditions that guarantee sustainability, the real firm can even be allowed to decide its own depreciation scheme. In contrast efficient firm regulation requires the value of the assets that the model firm would install to be recalculated each time, which seems more complex.

Nonetheless the similarity between the price-cap mechanism and regulation by rate of return suggests that the mechanism cannot be that automatic after all. Bearing in mind the Baron and Myerson (1982) result, the rate of return *r* used to set prices will also tend to be higher than the true price under the price-cap mechanism. So the regulator must guard against overinvestment, which makes it inevitable that the procedure must evaluate which assets are necessary and which are not.

The foregoing discussion relates to how the level of prices is set. The price-cap introduced three additional innovations in the price-setting process. The first of these – obvious in Chile since the 1970s but a novelty in developed countries – consisted of authorising the firm to index fixed nominal prices to variations in the consumer price index CPI (or the retail price index, RPI, in the UK). The second consisted of recognising that part of the productivity increases achieved in regulated firms corresponds to improvements that do not depend on the firm's own efforts but are exogenous. For example data processing costs depend on the rate of technological progress in the computer industry, which has little or nothing to do with what the regulated firm does. Retaining larger profits by definition does not stimulate productive efficiency, so prices could be reduced immediately. In this way prices would vary exogenously by (ΔCPI -x)/100 every period, where x is the estimated exogenous rate of productivity growth. This innovation speeds up rent extraction and is soundly based on the theory of regulation by incentives. On the other hand it raises the problem of how to calculate the x factor, which has caused several controversies.

The third innovation consisted of imposing a limit on an index of the cost of a basket of services rather than on each service individually. The firm is allowed to set the price of each service provided the overall index does not exceed the limit, thereby relieving the regulator of the complicated task of setting relative prices and allowing the firm to adjust these to changing demand conditions. In this way the limit behaves according to

$$\sum_{i=1}^{n} \lambda_i p_{it} = \left[1 + \frac{\Delta CPI_{t-1} - x}{100}\right] \cdot \sum_{i=1}^{n} \lambda_i p_{it-1}, \qquad (4.8)$$

where λ_i is the share of each service in the basket comprising the index (with $\Sigma_i\lambda_i=1$), and p_{it} is the price of service i set by the firm in period t.

The main advantage of setting limits on a basket rather than on each individual price is that the regulator does not have to worry about estimating correct relative prices. In addition the firm is given flexibility to adapt relative prices between price-setting rounds, which is beneficial since demand conditions usually alter in the interim. The downside is that the firm could take strategic advantage of errors made by the regulator in setting the λ_i. For example if the real share of a given service is much less than that set by the regulator, the firm could lower its price and raise that of other services, thereby raising the price of the effective basket above the level intended by the regulator.

3.4   Applications

The model we have developed makes it possible to study several issues that frequently give rise to dispute. Here we use it to discuss the treatment of obsolescence and depreciation and to show that the economic profitability of assets regulated on an efficient firm basis is always r, regardless of the frequency of price-setting processes.

3.4.1   Obsolescence

A particularly important topic in regulation is the treatment of asset obsolescence (i.e. stranded assets). In Chile the three laws that mention the efficient firm state that it incorporates the best current technology. This means that the risk of obsolescence must be borne by the regulated firm, just as it would be in a competitive market with free entry. Nonetheless we shall see below that sustainability requires this risk transfer to be compensated by a higher discount rate, as also happens in a competitive market.

To model this problem, suppose that in t the density function of the date of the asset's economic (but not physical) obsolescence is $f\ (s - t)$. Then $F(s-t) = \int_{t}^{s} f(u-t)du$ is the probability that the asset becomes technically obsolete in at least $s-t$ years. Note that we assume the process has no memory; for example the likelihood of the asset becoming obsolete during the next four years is independent of t. In addition, and solely for the purpose of simplifying the exposition, we also assume that once obsolete, the best policy is to offload the asset immediately and replace it with the most efficient substitute.

The expected present value of our asset when prices are set in $t = 0$ is now

$$NPV_0 = \int_0^T f(t)\int_0^t (p_s - c)Q(p_s)e^{-rs}\,ds\,dt + [1 - F(T)]\int_0^T (p_t - c)Q(p_t)e^{-rt}\,dt.$$

Note that $f(t)$ is the probability that the asset becomes obsolete in t, in which case the present value of the flows delivered by the asset will be

$$\int_0^t (p_s - c)Q(p_s)e^{-rs}\,ds$$

On the other hand $1-F(T)$ is the probability that the asset does not become obsolete before completing its physical life; in which case flows would be equal to

$$\int_0^T (p_t - c)Q(p_t)e^{-rt}dt$$

as in the case where there is no risk of obsolescence. Sustainability now requires setting prices such that

$$(p-c)Q(p)\left\{\int_0^T f(t)\int_0^t e^{-rs}dsdt + [1-F(T)]\int_0^T e^{-rt}dt\right\} = K.$$

Noting that

$$\int_0^T f(t)\int_0^t e^{-rs}dsdt = \int_0^T e^{-rt}\int_t^T f(s)dsdt,$$

and after a little algebra, this condition can be rewritten as

$$(p-c)Q(p)\int_0^T [1-F(t)]e^{-rt}dt = K. \tag{4.9}$$

Condition (4.9) is very similar to (4.3), except that the term $F(t)$ increases the discount and consequently the equivalent rate. The discount rises with T because the asset is more likely to become obsolete in five rather than three years. This means that moving the risk onto the firm requires it to be compensated through higher prices until the asset becomes obsolete.[8] Nonetheless this is not easy to do with precision, as $F(t)$ requires estimating.

A graphic case is when the asset becomes obsolete according to an exponential process with a density function $f(t) = \pi e^{-\pi t}$. In that case $1 - F(t) = e^{-\pi t}$ and (4.9) can be rewritten as

$$(p-c)Q(p)\int_0^T e^{-(r+\pi)t}dt = K,$$

where π represents the risk premium.

Efficient firm regulation differs from regulation by rate of return in the way it treats obsolescence. For example in the United States, the regulatory contract and constitutional guarantees that protect against expropriation without fair compensation shift the risk of obsolescence on to consumers. In that case the correct condition for calculating prices remains (4.7).

3.4.2 Depreciation

So far we have ignored depreciation and taxes. Depreciation is important because it affects the firm's post tax profitability. Similarly the fact that firms can deduct interest paid on debt as an expense, but not the return required by capital, means that post tax profit will depend on the firm's debt equity gearing.

To analyse the consequences of depreciation we assume the firm is financed entirely with equity (i.e. there is no interest deduction). If the authorised tax depreciation is $(D_t^I)_{t=0}^T$ (the superscript I denotes 'taxes'), then the present value of our asset is

$$\int_0^T \left\{ (1-\tau)\left[Q(p)(p-c) - D_t^I\right] + D_t^I \right\} e^{-r(1-\tau)t} dt - K, \tag{4.10}$$

where τ is the tax on profits. Obviously taxes reduce the firm's net cash flow but the magnitude of this effect depends on the depreciation allowed by the tax law, since tax depreciation which is not a cash flow is accepted as an expense and therefore reduces the tax liability. In addition taxes also require adjustment of the rate of return used to discount the flows: the after tax rate of return should be used since this is the opportunity cost of investing one peso in the regulated sector.

Defining $r' \equiv r(1-\tau)$ the after tax rate of return, expression (4.10) can be rewritten as

$$(1-\tau)Q(p)(p-c)R(r') + \tau \int_0^T D_t^I e^{-r't} dt - K.$$

To extract all the monopoly rents we require that

$$pQ(p)R(r') = \frac{K}{(1-\tau)} + cQ(p)R(r') - \frac{\tau}{(1-\tau)} \int_0^T D_t^I e^{-r't} dt. \tag{4.11}$$

As we shall see below this formula is actually used to set prices in the drinking water and telecom sectors, although to be consistent, the after tax rate of return $r(1-\tau)$ should be used.

Expression (4.11) highlights the importance of distinguishing between the useful life of the asset *(T)* and the depreciation rule used, $(D_t^I)_{t=0}^T$. An asset's useful life determines the period in which it generates cash flows, in contrast its useful tax life depends on the depreciation rule $(D_t^I)_{t=0}^T$ used which does not necessarily coincide with its economically useful life and obviously does not determine the period in which the asset generates cash flows. Accordingly price-setting should always use the economically useful life; the term

$$\int_0^T D_t^I e^{-r't} dt$$

fully incorporates the effect of tax depreciation on cash flows.

It could be argued that by considering taxes and including tax depreciation, one is abandoning optimal pricing – after all the social opportunity cost of the capital in the example is r and not $r(1-\tau)$; and tax depreciation does not represent a resource sacrifice. But here one needs to remember that average cost pricing is optimal subject to the firm's self financing constraint. Condition (4.11) only extends that constraint to the case where the firm pays taxes, recognising that the tax and depreciation regime is an additional constraint in the regulatory process.[9]

3.4.3   The useful life of assets and the duration of pricing periods

One of the key features of efficient firm regulation is that it provides an economic rate of return of r to the firm's assets at all times, regardless of the frequency or timeliness of price-setting. To appreciate this, note that by definition the economic rate of return of a regulated asset in t is

$$\frac{(p-c)Q(p)-D_t^e}{V_t^e},\tag{4.12}$$

where D_t^e is the economic depreciation of the asset in t and V_t^e is its economic value. If regulation is based on the efficient firm, the value in t of an asset whose useful life is T years and was invested in $t = 0$ is

$$V_t^e = (p-c)Q(p)\int_0^T e^{-(s-t)}ds,$$

where p is such that $V_0^e = K$. Differentiating V_t^e with respect to t gives

$$\frac{\partial V_t^e}{\partial t} = -D_t^e = -(p-c)Q(p)+rV_t^e$$

Substituting in (4.12) we have

$$\frac{(p-c)Q(p)-D_t^e}{V_t^e} = \frac{rV_t^e}{V_t^e} = r,\tag{4.13}$$

which is independent of t, and of the useful life remaining to the asset $(T - t$ in this example), and also of the time at which p is set. Note too that the benchmark for calculating prices is K; at no time is it necessary to determine the economic value of the existing assets.

4.   EFFICIENT FIRM REGULATION IN PRACTICE

In this section we review the formulas used to set prices in each of the three regulated sectors. As shown in the previous section, efficient firm regulation is based on sound microeconomic principles. Accordingly in each sector we need to determine the extent to which specific price-setting rules put these principles into practice.

The prices charged by each of the three monopolies are established in price-setting rounds. These are governed by laws and their respective regulations, but in each case technical economic ground rules are prepared which indicate how to apply the law to the circumstances of each price-setting process. What follows is based on the ground rules for price-setting in the phone company CTC (between 1999–2004); the potable water company EMOS (for the period 2000–2005); and electric power distributors (for the period 2000–2004).

4.1   General considerations

4.1.1   Concept

Prices are calculated in two stages. The outcome of the first stage yields efficient prices. In telecom and water companies these are calculated to ensure that expansion projects are self financing and yield a net present value (NPV) equal to zero. Formally the price is such that

$$(p^e - c)\Delta Q \int_0^T e^{-rt} dt - \Delta K = 0, \qquad (4.14)$$

where ΔQ is the estimated variation in demand, and ΔK is the investment needed to satisfy this (of course, we are ignoring taxes here to simplify the exposition).

Nonetheless if there are economies of scale, these prices would not be sufficient to self finance the whole firm, in other words, what is desirable is that

$$(p^e - c)\Delta Q \int_0^T e^{-rt} dt - (K_0 + \Delta K) < 0$$

(Q_0 is the initial level of demand and K_0 is the capital stock of an efficient firm designed to satisfy demand at the level Q_0). If this occurs efficient prices are corrected in the second stage, in principle in the least distorting way possible, to enable the efficient firm to be completely self financing. In other words

$$(p^d - c)(Q_0 + \Delta Q) \int_0^T e^{-rt} dt - (K_0 + \Delta K) = 0 \qquad (4.15)$$

and p^d is referred to as the definitive price.

Note that efficient prices correspond to the average but incremental cost. If the expansion alone had to be priced, these would be efficient prices subject to the firm's self financing constraint. Efficient prices are corrected in the second stage only if they are insufficient to self finance the efficient firm, which means that allocative efficiency is prioritised ahead of rent extraction.

4.1.2 The pricing area

Once the rationale and concepts underlying Chilean monopoly regulation are understood it is easy to grasp the difference between efficient and definitive prices. Nonetheless these concepts have no content until their variables and parameters are measured when setting prices. Equations 4.14 and 4.15 are also useful for describing what the regulators need to specify to give content to the technical economic ground rules. These specifications can be grouped into three categories:

(a) the production technology with which the efficient firm will produce the regulated services (what economists refer to as the 'production function');
(b) the price of inputs and the cost of the assets needed to construct the efficient firm; and
(c) the estimated demand for the regulated services.

Given the cost minimisation assumption, the first two categories determine the cost function of the efficient firm; in our equations these are represented by the function K and the parameters T and c. Knowledge of demand is needed because efficient average costs depend on the scale of production (K is a function of q).

Obviously to determine conditions (a), (b) and (c) one needs to know what services need to be regulated; but this becomes known when the ground rules are drawn up. The key aspect of the ground rules is that they define the pricing areas (or typical areas) that each efficient firm is required to serve. The service has by definition the same price throughout a given pricing area. But in practice, uniform prices should be a consequence of the fact that areas are defined so that the average cost of providing the service is the same throughout the area. Accordingly although the criterion for defining the area may be geological, technical or demographic, the idea is that it should be defined by the main determinants of the cost of providing the service. Differences in these key determinants define different areas.

For example the most important variable in electric power distribution is the number of customers per km^2, or density. A given concession holder serving a continuous area (e.g. Chilectra) might have different pricing areas if density is much greater in some geographic zones than in others; and two distribution firms can have the same pricing areas if they have similar densities. By contrast in the case of water companies, the basic concept is that of the 'system', as defined in the corresponding law '[...] installations, sources or receptor bodies and other elements, feasible of interacting, associated with the various stages of the water/sanitation service, *which should be considered as a whole*, in order to minimize the long-run costs of providing the water/sanitation service.' [emphasis added]

In that case the criterion is geological, and each real firm tends to be different (unless they share the same system).

4.2   Sectoral regulations

4.2.1   Telecommunications

Prices are set for 29 telephone services, 23 of which are classified explicitly by the Antitrust Resolutory Commission, and six by law.[10] In the most recent price-setting round four pricing areas were defined.

The pricing study is conducted by the regulated firm and then the regulator makes observations on it (for further details see Tabja, 1997 and Galetovic and Sanhueza, 2002). The starting point involves projecting the demand for each of the regulated services in each pricing area over the next five years; once demand has been projected an efficient firm is designed which incurs the costs that are essential in providing the regulated services alone.

If there is an expansion project its incremental cost is calculated, together with the revenues needed for the project's NPV to be equal to zero – given investment and operating costs, the useful life of the assets associated with the expansion, the tax rate on profits and the cost of capital. Formally,

$$\frac{1}{1-\tau}\left[\sum_{t=1}^{5}\frac{I_t}{(1+r)^t}+\sum_{t=1}^{5}\frac{(1-\tau)\Delta C_t-\tau D_t}{(1+r)^t}-\frac{(\text{residual value})_{t=5}}{(1+r)^5}\right], \qquad (4.16)$$

where I_t is the investment in t and ΔC_t is the increase in total costs in t associated with the expansion project. The efficient price for the respective service is obtained from the equation

$$p^e\cdot\sum_{t=1}^{5}\frac{\Delta q_t}{(1+r)^t}=\frac{1}{1-\tau}\left[\sum_{t=1}^{5}\frac{I_t}{(1+r)^t}+\sum_{t=1}^{5}\frac{(1-\tau)\Delta C_t-\tau D_t}{(1+r)^t}-\frac{(\text{residual value})_{t=5}}{(1+r)^5}\right],$$

where Δq denotes the change in demand for the service that satisfies the expansion project.

Definitive prices are determined with an expression analogous to (4.16). The scale of the efficient firm is designed to optimally satisfy total average demand projected during the pricing period (the next five years), which is known as 'equivalent demand' and denoted by q^*. If efficient prices cover these costs then they are definitive. Otherwise the prices of each service must be adjusted until total projected revenues coincide with the total cost of the efficient firm designed to serve q^*. The law is silent on how the adjustment between the different services should be shared out, apart from stating that 'any inefficiencies introduced should be kept to a minimum'.

Expression (4.16) is formally very similar to the right hand side of (4.11) which we repeat here for convenience with a number of minor modifications,

$$\frac{\Delta K}{(1-\tau)} + \int_0^T c\Delta Q e^{-rt}\,dt - \frac{\tau}{(1-\tau)}\int_0^T D_t\,e^{-rt}\,dt,$$

except that in practice time is discrete. Expression (4.11) can be rewritten as

$$\frac{1}{1-\tau}\left\{\frac{\Delta K}{(1-\tau)} + \int_0^5 \left[(1-\tau)c\Delta Q - \tau D_t\right]e^{-rt}\,dt + e^{-r5}\,(\text{residual value})_{t=5}\right\}, \qquad (4.17)$$

where $(\text{residual value})_{t=5} \equiv c\Delta Q \int_5^T e^{-r(t-5)}\,dt - \tau\int_5^T D_t e^{-r(t-5)}\,dt$, and clearly

$$\Delta K \equiv \sum_{t=1}^5 \frac{I_t}{(1+r)^t}.$$

Accordingly price-setting for telephone services correctly applies the principles of efficient firm regulation, since r is the after tax rate of return, depreciation corresponds to tax depreciation and the residual value of the assets is correctly calculated, which requires appropriate estimation of its useful economic and physical life.

The cost of capital rate used in practice is obtained from the expression

$$r = r_f + \beta \cdot (\text{market risk premium})$$

where r_f is equal to the rate paid on a savings account with deferred withdrawals at the Banco del Estado de Chile[11] and β is the covariance of the return earned by the firm relative to the market portfolio. In any event, r cannot fall below 7 per cent.

Needless to say, the calculation of beta and the risk premium have led to major disputes in price-setting processes (see for example Ahumada, 2000). Here we will only mention that this criterion for determining the cost of capital rate is largely circular because much of the firm's specific risk depends on the rule used in setting its prices. In this regard using international betas is not the most appropriate policy, since they are obtained from industries that are regulated with different rules. Nonetheless it is clear that in principle the cost of capital of the efficient firm should be equal to the market rate.

4.2.2 Drinking water supply

Each stage of the water and sanitation service is priced: i.e. captation of untreated water, production of potable water and its distribution, collection of wastewater and disposal thereof.[12,13] Price-setting is done per firm and each pricing area corresponds to a system.[14] The aim of defining a system is to arrange the installations of the efficient firm in order to satisfy projected demand at minimum cost.

Unlike the telephone case, both the firm and regulator conduct a pricing study with discrepancies being resolved by binding arbitration (for further details see Medina, 2000 or Galetovic and Sanhueza, 2002). The study starts with a demand projection for the next 15 years (after the 15th year it is assumed that demand grows no further). This distinguishes between periods of peak consumption (which typically coincide with the summer months), and periods of lower 'off peak' consumption. An efficient firm is then designed. As in the telephone case the incremental costs of any expansion project are calculated. The formal expression in this case is

$$\frac{1}{1-\tau}\left[\sum_{t=1}^{35}\frac{I_t}{(1+r)^t}+\sum_{t=1}^{35}\frac{(1-\tau)\Delta C_t-\tau D_t}{(1+r)^t}-\frac{(\text{residual value})_{t=35}}{(1+r)^{35}}\right]. \quad (4.18)$$

Note that unlike the telephone sector, the evaluation horizon, 35 years, does not coincide with the duration of the pricing period (five years in the case of water companies). Furthermore although we do not go into details here, investment earns a return only from the fees paid by users that consume water during the peak period. The pricing structure is described in Appendix B. Nonetheless, a reasoning similar to the telephone case indicates that expression (4.18) is formally equivalent to the right hand side of (4.11), thereby revealing the common structure of regulation in both sectors.

The sustainability check is very similar to that in the telephone sector. The scale of the efficient firm is designed to optimally satisfy equivalent demand. This is equal to

$$q^* = r\frac{(1+r)^5}{(1+r)^5-1}\cdot\sum_{t=1}^{5}\frac{q_t}{(1+r)^t}.$$

Once this firm has been designed, the long run total costs of satisfying projected demand are calculated in setting efficient prices. If efficient prices cover these costs then they are definitive. Otherwise each charge is adjusted proportionately until projected revenues coincide with the total cost of the efficient firm designed to satisfy q^*.

Unlike the telecommunications case, here the law does indicate how to adjust efficient prices. Note that the uniform adjustment required means going against Ramsey pricing, which recommends charging the difference by making adjustments in amounts inversely proportional to the elasticity of demand – which in this case probably would mean raising fixed charges relatively more (see Appendix B).

4.2.3 Electric power distribution

The regulation of distribution charges in the electric power sector displays significant differences in comparison to the telephone and water cases (Rudnick and Raineri, 1997; Molina, 1998; Bernstein, 2000; Briant, 2000; Rudnick and Donoso, 2000). The most important of these is that regulation applies to the entire set of distributors, since the key determinant of costs is customer density in the service area and not the scale of production.[15] The basic premise is that two distributors that serve areas of similar density should have similar costs even though the sizes of their firms may be very different. In other words once adjusted for density, returns to scale in electric power distribution should be constant.

In this way pricing areas (which in this case are referred to as 'typical areas') are defined by their density. For each typical area a geographic zone is selected from one of the real firms that represent it. For that geographic zone, an efficient firm is designed according to demand. The results are then applied to the geographic zones of other firms with similar densities.[16] The regulator (in this case the National Energy Commission) and the firms make separate pricing studies from consultants and a weighted average of the results is calculated, in which the study commissioned by the regulator has a two thirds weighting.

Distribution prices, also known as value added in distribution (VAD) transfer three types of cost to users: fixed costs, mainly covering administration of the distribution firms; the cost of losses of energy and power transmitted by the lines, including theft; and the cost of investment, operation and maintenance of the infrastructure needed to distribute the electricity. In each case a distinction is made between high voltage users (connected at over 23 KV) and low voltage consumers. In this section we are particularly interested in the third item, namely the calculation of infrastructure costs.

As mentioned above, infrastructure corresponds to that of an efficient firm adapted to demand in the geographic zone of the real firm used to define the typical area, assuming that installations have a 30 year useful life. The formula in this case is

$$\frac{1}{KW} \cdot \left[K_0 + \sum_{t=1}^{30} \frac{(\text{operation and maintenance costs})_t}{(1+0.1)^t} \right], \qquad (4.19)$$

where KW is the maximum demand faced by the real firm and K_0 is the value of the infrastructure of the efficient firm designed to satisfy demand in the base year, valued at the cost that the firm would have to pay to acquire it outright. Clearly this expression is very similar to those used to set efficient prices in the telephone and water sectors, but it differs by not calculating the cost of an expansion project. Instead, it directly calculates the average costs of the efficient firm. This simplification is consistent with the premise that returns to scale in distribution are constant once adjustment has been made for density. In this case marginal and average costs coincide and there is no need to calculate efficient prices.

The second difference is that the profitability of the efficient firm is not calculated, since the law sets this at 10 per cent, which could lead to gross overestimates of the cost of capital should the long term interest rate in Chile fall. It is preferable for the discount rate to be tied to the risk free interest rate, in order to reflect variations over time. Lastly the formula does not consider tax depreciation. Although this is consistent with calculating pre tax profitability, the discussion in Section 3.4 shows that the tax saving arising from depreciation reduces the revenues needed to enable the firm to self finance.

The result of these calculations provides the so-called basic prices for each typical area, which should cover fixed costs, energy and power losses and the costs of construction, operation and maintenance of infrastructure (Molina, 1998). Once calculated, a profitability check is carried out. Unlike price-setting in the drinking water and telephone sectors, sustainability is not measured in relation to the efficient firm (this was done in the previous stage when calculating long run average cost) but with respect to the set of real firms.

Before designing the efficient firm, real firms value their installations at their new replacement value (NRV), in other words the cost of replacing existing installations (definitive values are established after the Superintendency of Electricity and Fuels has reviewed the amounts declared by each firm and any discrepancies are resolved through arbitration). In addition firms report their operating costs. These NRVs and costs are then used to calculate the profitability which the set of firms would have obtained had the energy and power consumed during the year preceding the price-setting round been sold at basic prices for 30 years. Formally if firm i declared NRV_i, and operating costs are denoted by c_i, its sales are q_i and the corresponding basic price is p_i, then the profitability of the set of firms is

$$r = \frac{\sum_i p_i q_i - c_i}{\sum_i NRV_i} = \sum_i \alpha_i r_i,$$

where

$$\alpha_i = NRV_i \Big/ \sum_j NRV_j$$

(all of this is measured before tax). If r is between 6 per cent and 14 per cent then the basic prices are definitive. If profitability falls outside this range however, prices are adjusted proportionately until they reach the nearest limit.[17]

It has been argued that the profitability check to some extent obliges firms to compete on the basis of comparison (i.e. yardstick competition) (Rudnick and Raineri, 1997; Rudnick and Donoso, 2000). For example if the r_i of a small firm was considerably lower than the average, this would not have much effect on prices and the firm would have to assume the costs of its inefficiency. Nonetheless in principle basic prices are fixed according to the costs of an efficient firm, so the second stage does not add much. Another shortcoming of the second stage is that the outcome of the exercise depends heavily on the results of Chilectra, whose NRV accounts for over 45 per cent of the total.

5. CONCLUSION: PRICE-CAP OR EFFICIENT FIRM REGULATION?

It is a cliché that there is no perfect regulation mechanism; nonetheless some mechanisms are better than others. Efficient firm regulation has significant virtues: it is optimal subject to the firm's self financing constraint – a property that is not true of the main alternatives, namely regulation based on rate of return and the price-cap. Furthermore fixed pricing periods stimulate efficient management in a similar way to price-cap regulation which, in turn, is clearly superior in this regard to rate of return regulation. Thirdly it gives clear guidelines, although only in principle, on how to determine which assets should be remunerated by the regulated prices and which not, which is not true of price-cap or rate of return regulation. Lastly the conceptual clarity of efficient firm regulation allows a lot to be expressed in writing, in laws and regulations. As price-cap and rate of return regulation have both been developed in countries with legal systems that are much more effective than Chile's in terms of legally restricting the undesirable consequences of regulatory discretion, they would seem less appropriate for Chile than a legalistic approach to regulation.

Nonetheless several studies suggest that efficient firm regulation has not been sufficiently effective in extracting rents from regulated firms once they have been privatised (Serra, 2000). We suggest this is because the procedures used are unsuitable for extracting reliable information on technology, costs and demand from the regulated firms: there are no systematic and continuous data collection mechanisms and each price-setting round starts by redesigning the efficient firm from scratch, without making much use of lessons learned from previous price-setting processes. Although it is well known that asymmetric information results in prices being set above long run average cost, in Chile the difference is likely to be larger than justifiable.

It has also been argued that the intensity of the asymmetry could be moderated by replacing efficient firm regulation by a price-cap, where it would not be necessary to redesign the efficient firm every time prices were set. Nonetheless we have shown in this chapter that the price-cap mechanism requires assets to be valued at historic cost, which stimulates overinvestment and cost activation just as in the case of regulation by rate of return. Accordingly the price-cap mechanism cannot be applied without giving the regulator the power to veto 'unnecessary' investments and expenses. The purpose of efficient firm regulation is precisely to determine which assets and expenses are necessary (or efficient). The advantages over the price-cap are that the conceptual criterion for carrying out this exercise is very clear and is now institutionalised in Chile. Its disadvantage is that regulation on an efficient firm basis requires each price-setting round to decide upon the admissible value of the assets of the firm as a whole and not just the new investments.

Clearly the arguments of the previous paragraph are not sufficient to rule out the price-cap alternative; but nor do we think it is clearly advisable to abandon efficient firm regulation. To decide on a reasoned basis whether it is advisable to adopt the price-cap, it would firstly be necessary to perform a detailed study of the extent to which it would reduce the need to obtain information from the true firm; and secondly to design suitable procedures and rules to determine which expenses and investments are admissible, while at the same time respecting the constraints imposed by Chile's institutions and legal system. If changing the regulation mechanism made it possible to significantly reduce information asymmetries and improve the possibilities for rent extraction, then the price-cap should be considered as an alternative to efficient firm regulation, despite this meaning the abandonment of (efficient) pricing at long run average cost. Nonetheless the price-cap mechanism would also clearly require substantial improvements in procedures because it cannot be applied without information from the real firm. Given that a change of regulatory mechanism would also face a series of legal obstacles – among other things because it would require changes to existing contracts – in our opinion the emphasis during the next few years should be placed on significantly improving procedures for data collection and fine tuning price-setting formulas, rather than replacing efficient firm regulation as a whole. The burden of proof should fall on those who believe that price-setting rules ought to be changed.

NOTES

1. Hereinafter the term 'water company' will be used to encompass both drinking water supply and sewerage services.
2. The total cost of producing q units during T years is $qcR + K(q)$. The marginal cost of an additional unit is therefore,

$$\frac{1}{R}\frac{\partial C}{\partial q} = c + \frac{K'(q)}{R} < c + \frac{K(q)}{qR}$$

   if $\frac{K'}{K}q < 1$.

3. Article 30 A and C, Title V, Law 18.168 of 1982.
4. Articles 294 through 296 of DFL No. 1 of 1982.
5. Article 27 of DFL No. 70 of 1988.
6. A somewhat surprising implication of this observation is that, once the arbitrary depreciation path has been decided upon, this coincides with economic depreciation. The reason is that prices are set to ensure that the rate of return on assets will always be equal to r , given the arbitrary depreciation rule.
7. For example in 1995, the British electric power regulator unilaterally lowered the price of electric energy distributed by between 11 per cent and 17 per cent, and then again by a further 10–13 per cent in 1996. See Westlake and Beckett (1995).
8. It is important to note that if it remains worthwhile to continue using technically obsolete assets until the end of their useful physical life, then expression (4.9) exaggerates the premium, because flows generated between the moment of technical obsolescence and the end of their physical useful life will not be zero.
9. The reader will surely note that the firm's shareholders pay taxes. In Bustos, Engel and Galetovic (2000) we showed that characteristics of the Chilean tax system mean that the tax rate that should be corrected to take account of this is Primera Categoría (first category) tax, paid by firms.
10. The most important of these are local calls between users of the same company (the local metered service – LMS); access charges paid to use the local network in long distance calls, or calls to a mobile phone; and the access charge paid when a subscriber from another company calls a subscriber of the regulated company.
11. Or, if this type of savings account disappears, the rate payable on the replacement instrument indicated by the Superintendency of Banks and Financial Institutions.
12. The Ministry of Economic Affairs also establishes what can be charged for other services such as disconnection and reconnection of users in arrears, maintenance of public and private standpipes, direct control of liquid industrial waste (LIW) and a review of engineering projects for LIW treatment systems.
13. For further details on regulation of the sector see the collection of articles edited by Oxman and Oxer (2000). Gómez-Lobo and Vargas (2001) make a detailed analysis of recent EMOS price-setting processes and also explain the rationale behind regulation of the sector.
14. A 'system' consists of installations in the different stages of the sanitation service that can physically interact, and which should be jointly optimised to minimise the long run costs of providing the service. Note that to apply this definition, one needs to know the distribution of consumption.
15. The most commonly used measurements of density (or density parameters) are the ratios between (i) peak demand in the system and the number of kilometres in the distribution network; (ii) the number of clients connected to the network and the number of kilometres in the distribution network; (iii) the number of urban homes in relation to the total surface area served by the distributor; and (iv) electric energy sold to regulated customers in relation to the number of inhabitants. See Bernstein (2000).
16. This criterion was altered in the 2000 price-setting round. Six standard areas were defined, and each real firm was assigned to one of these.
17. In addition, the profitability of the set of firms in each year subsequent to the price-setting round should be between 5 per cent and 15 per cent. The Electricity Regulation of

September 1998 allows the NEC to cancel prices in advance, and start a new pricing period, if measured profitability falls outside the band.

REFERENCES

Ahumada, G. (2000), 'Análisis de la Política y Gestión Tarifaria y de Subsidios en Servicios de Utilidad Pública', Ministerio de Economía, *Experiencias Regulatorias de una Década*. Santiago: LOM Ediciones.

Averch, H. and L. Johnson (1962), 'Behavior of the Firm Under Regulatory Constraint', *American Economic Review*, **52**, 1053–1069.

Baron D., and Myerson (1982), 'Regulating a Monopolist with Unknown Cost', *Econometrica*, **50**, 911–930.

Bernstein, S. (2000), 'Regulación en el sector de distribución eléctrica', thesis for industrial civil engineering degree, Santiago: P. Universidad Católica.

Briant, M. (2000), 'Análisis y Evaluación de las Experiencias Tarifarias en el Sector de Distribución Eléctrica', Ministerio de Economía, *Experiencias regulatorias de una Década*, Santiago: LOM Ediciones.

Bustos, A., E. Engel and A. Galetovic, (2004), 'Could Higher Taxes Increase the Demand for Capital? Theory and Evidence from Chile', *Journal of Development Economics*, **73**, 675–697.

Galetovic, A. and R. Sanhueza (2000), 'Regulación de Servicios Públicos, ¿Hacia Dónde Debemos Ir?', *Estudios Públicos*, **85**, 101–137.

Gómez-Lobo A. and M. Vargas (2001), 'La Regulación de Empresas Sanitarias en Chile: Una Revisión del Caso Emos y una Propuesta de Reforma Regulatoria', *Working Paper* No.177, Economics Department, University of Chile.

Green, R. and M. Pardina (1999), *Resetting Price Controls for Privatized Utilities: A Manual for Regulators*, Washington: World Bank.

Laffont, J. and J. Tirole (1993), *A Theory of Incentives in Procurement and Regulation*, Cambridge: MIT Press.

Medina, A. (2000), 'Legislación Tarifaria en el Sector Sanitario', Ministerio de Economía, *Experiencias Regulatorias de una Década*, Santiago: LOM Ediciones.

Molina, P. (1998), 'Tarificación Eléctrica Chilena a Nivel de Empresas de Distribución', thesis for degree of Master of Science in Engineering, Santiago: P. Universidad Católica de Chile.

Newbery, D. (1997), 'Determining the Regulatory Asset Base for Utility Price Regulation', *Utilities Policy*, **6**, 1–8.

Oxman, S. and P. Oxer (2000), *Privatización del Sector Sanitario Chileno: Análisis de un Proceso Inconcluso*, Santiago: Ediciones 2000 CESOC.

Rudnick, H. and R. Raineri (1997), 'Chilean Distribution Tariffs: Incentive Regulation', F. Morandé and R. Raineri (eds), *(De)regulation and Competition: The Electric Industry in Chile*, Santiago: Ilades/Georgetown University.

Rudnick, H. and J. Donoso (2000), 'Integration of Price-cap and Yardstick Competition Schemes in Electrical Distribution Generation', *IEES PES Transactions on Power Systems*, **15**, 1428–1433.

Serra P. (2000), 'Evaluación de los Servicios Públicos Privatizados en Chile', Mimeo, Center for Applied Economics.

Tabja, R. (1997), 'Análisis de la Tarificación para la Telefonía Pública Local en Chile', thesis for masters degree in Engineering Sciences, Santiago: University of Chile.

Westlake B. and R. Beckett. (1995), 'The OFFER Electricity Distribution Review and its Aftermath', *Utilities Policy*, **5**, 207–218.

APPENDIX A

Rate of return regulation and sustainability

The text states that the following conditions must be satisfied simultaneously to ensure that the assets of a firm regulated on a rate of return basis according to

$$p_i Q(p_t) = cQ(p_t) + D_t + rV_t \qquad (3A.1)$$

yield r: (i) $V_0 = K$; (ii) $\int_0^T D_t dt = V_0$; (iii) $V_t = K - \int_0^t D_s ds$. We show this below.

Consider any path $(V_t, D_t)_0^T$ for depreciation that satisfies (A.1) and condition (iii). In that case, the present value of the asset in $t = 0$ is

$$\int_0^T (p_t - c)Q(p_t)e^{-rt} dt = \int_0^T \left[D_t + r\left(V_0 - \int_0^t D_s ds \right) \right] e^{-rt} dt.$$

The right hand side of this equality can be rewritten as

$$rV_0 \int_0^T e^{-rt} dt + \int_0^T D_t \left[e^{-rt} - r\int_t^T e^{-rs} ds \right] dt$$

$$= V_0 (1 - e^{-rT}) + \int_0^T D_t \left[e^{-rt} + e^{-rT} - e^{rt} \right] dt$$

$$= V_0 (1 - e^{-rT}) + e^{-rT} \int_0^T D_t dt.$$

If condition (ii) is fulfilled, then $\int_0^T D_t dt = V_0$ and

$$\int_0^T (p_t - c)Q(p_t)e^{-rt} = V_0 = K,$$

where the latter equality follows from condition (i).

APPENDIX B

Drinking water charges

This appendix illustrates calculation of the pricing structure for drinking water. The aim is to give a clear idea of the concept underlying the pricing structure, without going into the details that distinguish each type of user.

Potable water charges distinguish between fixed and variable costs, which in turn distinguish between consumption in peak and off peak periods. The monthly fixed charge, FC, is obtained from the expression

$$FC \cdot \sum_{t=1}^{35} \frac{\text{clients}_t - \text{clients}_0}{(1+r)^t} = \sum_{t=1}^{35} \frac{(\text{fixed costs})_t - (\text{fixed costs})_0}{(1+r)^t}.$$

In other words, the fixed charge distributes fixed costs that do not depend on the number of users, among all customers projected for the next 35 years (this projection is obtained from the pricing study). Expenses of this type mainly include administration and sales.

Variable charges distinguish between peak and off peak periods. Consumption in the off peak period only pays operating and maintenance costs (or variable expenses). The price per m^3 in the off peak period, OC^n (the superscript n denotes off peak), is obtained from the expression

$$OC^n \cdot \sum_{t=1}^{35} \frac{(\text{consumption})_t^n - (\text{consumption})_0^n}{(1+r)^t} =$$

$$\sum_{t=1}^{35} \frac{(\text{variable expenses})_t^n - (\text{variable expenses})_0^n}{(1+r)^t}$$

where $(\text{consumption})_t^n$ is monthly average consumption in the off peak months of year t, and $(\text{variable expenses})_t^n$ represent average variable expenses in the off peak months of that year.

Peak period consumption must cover capacity costs in addition to variable costs. The operating cost charge in the peak period, OC^p, is obtained, mutatis mutandis, from an expression analogous to that of OC^n. The capacity cost is assumed to be variable (in other words, for pricing purposes it is assumed that investment costs rise with the number of m^3 served). This gives the expression

$$CC \cdot (\# \text{peak months}) \cdot \sum_{t=1}^{35} \frac{(1-\tau)\left[(\text{consumption})_0^p - (\text{consumption})_0^p\right]}{(1+r)^t} =$$

$$\Delta K - \sum_{t=1}^{35} \frac{\tau D_t}{(1+r)^t} - \frac{(\text{residual value})_{t=35}}{(1+r)^{35}}$$

where CC is the capacity charge per m^3, the superscript p denotes 'peak' period, $(\text{consumption})_t^p$ is average monthly consumption during the peak period of year t, and ΔK is the updated investment of the expansion plan for the service.

CC, OC^n and OC^p are used to construct the price per m^3, distinguishing between peak and off peak periods as follows. During the peak period, a customer's total consumption is divided between normal and over consumption. Normal consumption consists of cubic meters that do not exceed the average amount consumed during the off peak months. Over consumption is the amount that exceeds the off peak average. The price per normal m³ is

$$OC^p + \frac{\#\,\text{peak months}}{12} \cdot CC.$$

The price per m³ of over consumption is

$$OC^p + CC.$$

Lastly, the price per m³ in the off peak period is

$$OC^n + \frac{\#\,\text{peak months}}{12} \cdot CC.$$

The formulas described above imply that all capacity is paid for exclusively by those who consume during the peak period, despite the charge of (# peak months)/12· CC. which appears in the account during the off peak period. To understand this point, note that the total annual account of a user that consumes q_n on average in each off peak month, and q_p in each peak month (with $q_n < q_p$) is

$$\text{Total expenditure} = (12 - m)(OC^n + \frac{m}{12}CC)q_n +$$

$$m\left[(OC^p + \frac{m}{12}CC)q_n + (OC^p + CC)(q_p - q_n).\right]$$

$$= (OC^n + \frac{m}{12}CC)Q_n + \left[(OC^p + \frac{m}{12}CC)\frac{m}{12-m}Q_n + (OC^p + CC)(Q_p - \frac{m}{12-m}Q_n)\right]$$

where m is the number of peak months and Q is the total consumption during the period. Note that the increase in the customer's bill as result of consuming an additional m³ in the off peak period is

$$\frac{\partial \text{Total expenditure}}{\partial Q_n}$$

$$= (OC^n + \frac{m}{12}CC) + \left[(OC^p + \frac{m}{12}CC)\frac{m}{12-m} - (OC^p + CC)\frac{m}{12-m}\right] = OC^n.$$

When an additional m³ is consumed during the off peak period, the direct cost is $OC^n + m/12 \cdot CC$. Nonetheless, this additional m³ raises the limit from which over consumption is charged during the peak period, thereby reducing the customer's bill by

$$\left(OC^P + m/12 \cdot CC\right)m/(12-m) - \left(OC^P + CC\right)m/(12-m) = \frac{m}{12}CC$$

during the peak period, by shifting the over consumption limit. On the other hand, the direct cost of consuming an additional m^3 in the peak period is

$$\frac{\partial \text{Total expenditure}}{\partial Q_p} = OC^P + CC.$$

In other words all capacity is charged to those who exceed their over consumption limit during the peak period.

5. Estimation of productive efficiency based on non parametric techniques: The case of electricity distribution in Argentina[1]

Paula Margaretic and Carlos A. Romero

1. INTRODUCTION

During the last decade Argentina has faced an extended process of privatisation of utilities, in particular in the electricity sector. One of the main objectives of privatisation was to increase the efficiency in the supply of these services through the transfer from public to private ownership and through the adoption of more powerful incentive schemes, such as price-cap regimes.

The evaluation of the results of this process requires the development of objective measures of the functioning and the operation of the different natural monopolies through time, in order to promote competition, give incentives to cost minimisation and ensure that users benefit from these cost reductions. Additionally an assessment of efficiency is useful for price reviews and the regulatory challenge. If the efficiency gain used to fix the new price-cap is specific to firm and is based on past gains, the firm would not have incentives to reduce its costs in the future. However when it is possible to introduce some kind of yardstick competition (Schleifer, 1985), if the expected efficiency gains for the next period are based on the aggregate development of the industry, the firm would have incentives to be more efficient and to produce at a lower level of costs than the average of the industry.

One of the main instruments to measure the efficiency of utilities is the efficiency frontier.[2] Efficiency gains from a firm can come from two main sources: shifts in the frontier reflecting efficiency gains at the sectoral level and efficiency gains at the firm level, reflecting a catching up effect. The latter are the gains to be made by firms not yet on the frontier. These firms should be able to achieve not only the industry gain but also specific gains offsetting firm specific inefficiencies.

Baldwin and Cave (1999) identify a number of conditions for a successful implementation of a benchmarking methodology: a considerable number of comparable firms, a common regulator and enough data for all the firms. **I** this chapter we use a set of 17 regional firms specialising in the electricit distribution in Argentina for the period 1993–2001. Even though there is nc a common regulator for all of them, local legislation does not var significantly to make comparability a problem. In the case of a federa country such as Argentina, a substitute for a common regulator may be National Office such as Competition Commission. In any case, using benchmarking analysis incorporating different jurisdictions compensates fc the absence of a common regulator and reduces the asymmetry c information between the firms and regulators (Bondorevsky et al., 2002).

Therefore in this chapter we address these issues and concentrate on th applied aspects of the efficiency measurement in a regulatory context. W estimate the efficiency of firms based on a cost function. To measure th efficiency of utilities we apply the Data Envelopment Analysis (DEA methodology. In the first place we assume that the level of efficiency of eacl firm is constant through the period of reference. We obtain efficienc measures for each of the firms of the set under different assumption regarding the type of technology and the environment of operation. W consider constant, variable and non-increasing returns to scale.[3] In addtio we aim to capture the role of the environment in the development of eacl firm and therefore in the level of efficiency at which they operate. I particular we analyse the role of type of ownership in the level of efficiency.

2. EMPIRICAL ANALYSIS OF DATA

2.1 Description of variables and sources

The data covering the period 1993 to 2001 consists of an unbalanced panel The data was collected from ADEERA (Argentine Distribution of Electricit Association) and firms' financial statements. Data for costs was extracte from each firm's financial statements. We consider both operating and tota costs. Total costs include operating, administrative and marketing expenses as well as energy purchases. Operating costs includes both generation an distribution expenditures. Even though all the firms belong to the distributio sector, the difficulty of disaggregating them makes it necessary to includ both. Wages include salary and social payments. Information on outsourcin, was not available. The variable energy sales appear in physical units (MWh) Information related to employment was extracted from the financia statements of annual reports and include both permanent and temporar employees. Area refers to the area of operation assigned to each company i square kilometres. Density was calculated as the ratio of the number o customers for each area. Market structure was constructed as the proportio of residential sales to total sales. The information on electricity lines includes low, medium and high-tension lines. Finally customers include the total number of customers.

2.1.1   Data analysis

In the context of DEA with panel data, several options are available. One is to construct a frontier for each year and estimate the relative efficiency of each firm for the annual frontier. Another possibility is to treat each observation in the panel as independent and construct a single frontier for the whole period. The relative efficiency of each firm is measured in terms of this single frontier. In both cases it is possible to obtain an average of the measures. This last option was the one chosen in this chapter for our analysis.

Electricity distribution in Argentina includes small, medium and large firms operating in areas with significantly different density rates. Table 5.1 presents the descriptive statistics of each of the variables for the estimation.

Table 5.1   Argentina, electricity distribution 1993–2002

Variable	Mean	Std Dev	Min	Max
Sales (MWh/year)	2 267 329	3 471 627	123 914	13 715 117
Clients (number)	452 390	634 099	31 415	2 264 307
Employment (number)	1119	1268	60	5051
Area (km2)	78 244	55 768	3309	203 013
Lines (km)	12 985	10 554	2576	46 865
Structure of demand*	0.40	0.11	0.11	0.60
Density (clients/area)	71.41	178.82	0.33	637.42
Total wage ($/year)	31 684	12 840	13 348	98 260
Total costs (million $)	172 036	240 248	19 977	1 013 406

Notes:
(*) residential sales / total sales.

Source: Own calculation.

The main conclusion that can be extracted from Table 5.1 is that the s
includes a considerable variety of firms that differ not only in size but also i
the environment within which they operate. The majority of firms have le:
than 100 000 customers, except for two firms, which have over two millio
These two firms were different from the rest: both the number of clients an
total sales exceeded the mean of the group. Additionally the areas they serve
were highly populated. The differences between these firms and the rest (
the group make the analysis of the environmental variables quite sensiti
and require the proper control of the environmental issues in the estimation.

3. MODEL ESTIMATION

Econometric techniques have been used in order to reach a robu
specification for the model.[4] We started by estimating different models und
the assumption of constant returns to scale (CRS). The basic line:
(envelopment) programme was solved for the estimation of the efficie
frontiers as follows:

$$\min_{\theta} \theta$$
$$\text{subject to:}_{\theta, \lambda} \quad y_j \le \lambda Y$$
$$\lambda X \le \theta x_j$$
$$\lambda Z = z_j$$
$$\lambda \in R_+^J$$

where Y is a N×r matrix of outputs (N: number of firms; r: number (
outputs); X stands for a N×m matrix of inputs (m: number of inputs);
represents a N×s matrix with information about s environmental variables;
is a scalar and λ is a Nx1 vector of constants. The value of θ obtained will b
the efficiency score for the ith DMU (Decision Making Unit). It will satisfy
< 1, with a value of 1 indicating a point on the frontier and hence
technically efficient DMU, according to the Farrell (1957) definition. Th
linear programming problem must be solved N times, once for each DMU i
the sample. A value of θ is then obtained for each DMU (see Coelli et a
1998).

The CRS assumption is only appropriate when all DMUs are operating ;
an optimal scale. Imperfect competition or constraints on finance, amon
others, may cause a DMU not to operate optimally. Banker et al. (1984) ha
suggested an extension of the CRS DEA model to account for variab
returns to scale (VRS). The use of the CRS specification, when not all DML
are operating at the optimal scale, will result in measures of total efficienc
(TE). The measure of scale efficiencies (SE) can be obtained by calculatin
the ratio of CRS TE to VRS TE for each firm. This information will also b
included in the estimations. The CRS linear programming problem can b

easily modified to account for VRS by adding the convexity constraint: $\Sigma_j \lambda_j = 1$ to the previous problem. One shortcoming of this measure of efficiency is that the value does not indicate whether the DMU is operating in an area of increasing or decreasing returns to scale. This may be determined by running an additional DEA problem with a non-increasing returns to scale (NIRS) assumption. This can be done by altering the VRS model by substituting the $\Sigma_j \lambda_j = 1$ restriction with $\Sigma_j \lambda_j \leq 1$. The nature of the scale inefficiencies (i.e. due to increasing or decreasing returns to scale) for a particular DMU can be determined by whether or not the NIRS TE score is equal to the VRS TE score. If they are unequal, increasing returns to scale exist for that DMU. If they are equal, decreasing returns to scale apply.

The first model estimated (CRS M1) assumes CRS and includes the number of clients as output, total costs as inputs and two environmental variables: density and structure of demand. In this case the average of the efficiency measures is relatively high (0.81). The standard deviation is 0.17 (see Table 5.2).

Several alternative specifications were calculated. First, we did not include any environmental variable (CRS M1A). The average of measures is relatively low (0.62) and only one firm appears to be 100 per cent efficient. In this case, the omission of any variable that might capture the effect of the environment makes the firms in the set appear as relatively inefficient. It penalises the relative efficiency measurement for the majority of firms.

Second, we included the environmental variables one by one. The impact of each variable on the efficiency measures is considerable but the result depends on the firm's environment. For example, if a firm operates in a highly populated area, not considering the density of demand as an environmental variable distorts its measurement compared with the model that only considers the structure of demand. In contrast the measures obtained in the model that only include the density rate for firms, which operate in an area with smaller density rate, does not differ significantly from the original model. Comparing the model that only includes structure of demand (CRS M1R) to one that includes only the density rate (CRS M1D), shows that major increases in the efficiency measures belong to firms that operate in areas that are not highly populated, but with a demand concentrated on residential sales. Therefore this sensitivity analysis justifies the inclusion of both variables in order to capture the environment in which the firms operate. Table 5.2 shows the average efficiency for each of the models considered.[5]

A third set of models estimated include output measured by sales (CRS M2) and clients and sales (CRS M3) respectively. Both models include the two environmental variables. The first thing to notice is the tendency of

Table 5.2   Argentina, electricity distribution. Average efficiency for different models [*]

Full Sample	Mean	Std. Dev	Min
CRS 1	0.808	0.173	0.259
CRS M1A	0.620	0.143	0.203
CRS M1R	0.705	0.166	0.205
CRS M1D	0.731	0.177	0.232
CRS M2	0.869	0.133	0.356
CRS M3	0.885	0.130	0.477
CRS M4	0.828	0.174	0.259
CRS M5	0.851	0.174	0.259
VRS M1	0.887	0.125	0.338
SE M1	0.912	0.142	0.264
NIRS M1	0.827	0.174	0.259

Notes:
(*) CRS M1: output equals the number of clients, inputs are total costs as inputs and two environmental variables: density and structure of demand. CRS M1A: CRS M1 without environmental variables. CRS M1R: CRS M1 with only structure of demand as an environmental variable. CRS M1D: CRS M1 with only density as an environmental variable. CRS M2: sales as output, the rest equal to CRS M1. CRS M3: output equals the number of clients and sales, the rest equal to CRS M1. CRS M4 (Non-oriented Lines): output equals the number of clients and lines, the rest equal to CRS M1. CRS M5 (Non-oriented Employment): inputs are total costs and Employment, rest equal to CRS M1. VRS M1, SE M1, NIRS M1: stand for CRS M1, with different assumptions regarding returns to scale, scale effects and non-increasing returns to scale respectively.

Source: Own calculation.

the mean of the measures to increase through the above specifications. The standard deviation tends to reduce. However one can make a point concerning the adequacy of this specification, in particular, the inclusion of the sales variable. On the one hand, energy sold is not necessarily important for a distributor in the presence of cost pass through. Having reached a particular customer, the amount of energy a customer consumes is not as relevant as a cost driver. This variable does not fully capture maximising behaviour and is why, in empirical applications, sales are replaced with other variables to measure output. On the other hand the influence of the structure of demand (a different proportion of residential sales), which in fact might be influencing the relative performance of firms, is already being captured by the environmental variable structure of demand. For the above reasons the models that incorporated sales as a measure of output were considered less relevant than models that include clients as a measure of output.

A point can also be made concerning the orientation of the model. Electricity distributors are obliged to satisfy demand and that is why in public sector utilities, outputs are at least predetermined. This explains why an input orientation was selected. However we also included additional variables of control such as lines and employment. In many applications these variables are considered as inputs in a production function; however, lines might also be labelled as an output.

In any case the consideration of these two variables made it necessary to alter the orientation of the model. To be more precise, it required defining a non-orientated model.[6] We began by specifying a model in which lines were treated as an output that the firm controlled to some extent (CRS M4). Next we considered employment as an input (CRS M5). The mean of the efficiency measures in each case were 0.83 and 0.85 respectively and their standard deviation was similar.

We found that the efficiency measures predicted by both models were consistent and fulfilled some desirable properties, such as stability. Additionally considering the data concerning the evolution of lines and employment, one can argue that these variables have acted as control variables for the firms during the period. The number of employees has significantly changed through time. These issues can be related to the economic reforms in the sector that have had an impact in productivity and can be used to justify, in theoretical terms, the adequacy of these specifications for the estimation of relative efficiency in the electricity distribution sector. We can also highlight the similarities between the two non-oriented models and CRS M1. The mean of the measures are similar, although those corresponding to the non-oriented models are higher. The standard deviation and minimum values are also similar. Finally there is a high correlation in the measures between CRS M1, CRS M4 and CRS M5.

Further insights can be gained by altering the assumption for returns to scale. First, we consider the original model CRS M1, but assume that the returns are variable (VRS M1). Using models CRS M1 and VRS M1, we calculate scale efficiencies (SE M1). Second, we considered an additional DEA problem with non-increasing returns to scale (NIRS M1) which provides information on whether the DMU is operating in an area of increasing or decreasing returns to scale. We also compared the results obtained by each of the models in terms of their efficiency scores and we included some general information concerning the relationship between efficiency, area of returns to scale at which each firm is operating and scale.[7]

To do this we considered the capacity that each of the preceding models ha to identify the same firms as the best and worst performers in the set. We constructed quartiles with the efficiency scores, dividing the firms in the se into four quartiles, where the first quartile corresponds to the 25 per cent o the least efficient firms. We repeated this for each of the models under consideration: CRS M1, VRS M1 and NIRS M1. Table 5.3 presents the comparative results.

The upper left side of Table 5.3 shows the number of firms both models have identified as relatively least efficient, while the lower right side shows those that are relatively efficient. The models tend to identify reasonably well the same firms as relatively more and less efficient.

We also construct quartiles for the variables total cost and number of clients in order to distinguish the relationship, if any, between scale and the efficiency scores. We do not find a defined relationship between efficiency and size, when measured in terms of clients. To some extent, the analysis of partial productivity indexes is consistent with this result.[8] Additionally we analysed the relationship between the kind of returns to scale exhibited by the firms and efficiency scores. In general we conclude that the most efficient firms are those that exhibit decreasing returns to scale.

4.   THE ROLE OF OWNERSHIP IN RELATIVE EFFICIENCY

At the beginning of the period many firms were publicly owned and were privatised during the 1990s. It is interesting to analyse whether this process has had any effect on the relative efficiency. Table 5.4 can be used as a preliminary check on whether or not there are substantial differences between private or publicly owned firms. For the comparison we select three models: the original model CRS M1 and the non-oriented models CRS M4 and CRS M5. Table 5.4 shows average efficiency and some descriptive statistics for the sample that includes all the firms and two sub-samples of private and public firms.

Compared with the full sample the mean of the measures for the private firm group were on average 5 per cent above the mean, while with the public firm subset they were on average 16 per cent below the mean. The standard deviation for the sub-sample of private firms had measures that were relatively less dispersed and their minimum values were higher. Therefore from the values for the mean and standard deviation it is possible to argue that private firms tend to have a better performance on average than their publicly owned counterparts. This justifies a positive analysis of the privatisation with respect to relative efficiency measurement, which motivates the next section.

Table 5.3   *Argentina, electricity distribution – consistency between models*

		Quartiles VRS M1				
		Q1	Q2	Q3	Q4	Total
Quartiles CRS M1	Q1	18	4	2	1	25
		72%	17%	8%	4%	100%
	Q2	7	10	4	3	24
		28%	42%	17%	13%	100%
	Q3		10	10	4	24
			42%	42%	17%	100%
	Q4			8	16	24
				33%	67%	100%
	Total	25	24	24	24	97
		100%	100%	100%	100%	100%
		Quartiles NIRS M1				
		Q1	Q2	Q3	Q4	Total
Quartiles CRS M1	Q1	23	2			25
		92%	8%			100%
	Q2	2	21	1		24
		8%	88%	4%		100%
	Q3		1	18	5	24
			4%	75%	21%	100%
	Q4			5	19	24
				21%	79%	100%
	Total	25	24	24	24	97
		100%	100%	100%	100%	100%

Source: Own calculation.

Table 5.4   Argentina, electricity distribution – average efficiency of private and publicly owned firms

		Mean	Std. Dev	Min	Max
CRS 1		0.808	0.173	0.259	1
CRS M4	All firms	0.828	0.174	0.259	1
CRS M5		0.851	0.174	0.259	1
CRS 1		0.846	0.130	0.530	1
CRS M4	Private ownership	0.864	0.128	0.530	1
CRS M5		0.900	0.113	0.537	1
CRS 1		0.670	0.229	0.259	1
CRS M4	Public ownership	0.696	0.242	0.259	1
CRS M5		0.671	0.229	0.259	1

Source: Own calculation.

In most DEA applications, even those where the DMUs exhibit a large degree of homogeneity, it is possible to find ways to group them by exogenous (e.g. geography, demographics) or operational (e.g. labour shifts, management) characteristics. Therefore programme evaluation, the identification of inherent efficiency differences across such groups, separately from the potential inefficiency of individual DMUs, becomes an important element in the evaluation of the relative efficiency of firms.[9] In this context we analyse the role of ownership as a potential attribute to identify programmes.[10] From the information presented above ownership appears to be relevant.

To isolate the programmatic evaluation objective from other dimensions that might have influenced the analysis, we conduct the following experiment. We focus on the attribute type of ownership. We divide the set of firms into private and publicly owned firms and generate two programmes. We adjust for differences in managerial efficiency while evaluating the programme and apply DEA techniques. The procedure can be summarised as follows:

1.   Divide the group of all DMUs (j=1,...,n) into two programmes consisting of n1 and n2 DMUs (n1 + n2 = n). Run DEA separately for the two groups. We consider the model named as CRS M1. The proportions of efficient DMUs in the two groups are compared (using a t-test). Additionally we compare the mean efficiency scores and the

entire distributions.

2. In each of the two groups separately, adjust inefficient DMUs to their 'level if efficient' value by projecting each DMU onto the efficiency frontier of its group.

3. Run a pooled (or 'inter-envelop') DEA with all the n DMUs at their adjusted efficiency levels.

4. Apply a statistical test to the results of Step 3 to determine if the two groups have the same distribution of efficiency values within the pooled DEA set.

In Step 3, the original data for DMUs that were identified as inefficient within their programme have been replaced with the corresponding adjusted-to-efficiency values. If the hypothesis that the two programmes were drawn from the same distribution (same efficiency frontier for the two programmes) were true, then running DEA separately for each group in Step 1, ought to reveal the same frontier for both groups. Further, after the adjustment in Step 2, we ought to expect to see all (or most) of the DMUs rated as efficient in Step 3. This situation corresponds to a null that the two programmes share the same frontier. If, on the other hand, one programme is superior to the other, even after adjusting the values of inefficient DMUs in the two programmes, then we shall still witness an efficiency gap for the DMUs in the inferior programme when the two are evaluated simultaneously.

To execute Step 4, a suitable statistic is needed to measure the distance between the distribution of efficiency ratings determined in Step 3 for each group and a distribution in which all the ratings are equal to unity (i.e. all the DMUs are efficient). We use the Mann Withney rank test.

We tested some hypotheses in order to compare the efficiency scores and rankings of the two sets. First, we compare the mean of the rankings and measures. We used two-sample t tests of the hypothesis that the mean of private firms' rankings equals the mean of public firms' rankings. We consider both cases: that the two-sample data are assumed to have equal variances and not. In both cases we rejected the null that the mean of the efficiency scores are equal independently of ownership. Second, we compared the entire distributions. To do this we considered a Kruskal-Wallis equality of populations rank test, which tests the hypothesis that several samples are from the same population. Again the evidence allows us to reject the null that both subsets were from the same population.[11]

These tests, however, were of limited value. Therefore to measure the distance between the distribution of efficiency ratings determined in Step 3 for each group and a distribution in which all ratings are equal to unity (are all efficient), we used a Mann-Withney rank test. The number of observations for the two subsets were $n1=76$ and $n2=21$. When we conducted the test, we found that the null hypothesis cannot be rejected (U=2227; Z=12.52). However when we tested the differences in means or the distributions of efficiency ratings we concluded that the means were different and the scores belonged to different distributions. This apparent puzzle can be rationalised in terms of one programme outperforming the other up to a certain point (input resource level) and then the frontier intersects and the other programme becomes the more efficient. A way around this problem is to repeat Step 4 for the subsets of the two programmes grouped by a magnitude of input. The idea is to identify some indicator, such as size, that could capture the intersection point between the two frontiers. Econometric techniques can be used to find this indicator. Then it is necessary to test the null only for the DMUs, whose size is smaller than or equal to the intersection point and if the characterisation is correct, the test ought to reveal the superiority of the corresponding programme in that region.

5. CONCLUSIONS

In this chapter we applied the DEA methodology to measure efficiency. From the results obtained, it appears that DEA is appropriate for the estimation of relative efficiency and, at the same time, provides more information.

We used assumptions regarding the returns to scale and found that the estimation of relative efficiency among different models was consistent. We therefore consider the CRS assumption to be a robust specification. With respect to the role of ownership, we found that on average private firms tend to be relatively more efficient than publicly owned firms.

NOTES

1. We would like to thank Mr Mariano Alvarez for extremely competent research assistance.
2. The frontier can be specified either as a production function, or a cost function. The production function allows for the estimation of technical efficiency, while the cost function gives a measure of productive efficiency.
3. The objective here is to determine if there is any evidence that the level and scale of production condition the relative efficiency of firms in electricity distribution.
4. To do this, we tried a number of alternative variables for output, inputs and costs. The aim was to obtain a model whose variables would significantly explain the variability of total cost. The criteria for the final selection was to have reasonable values for the estimated coefficients and the level of significance. We used panel data estimation; in particular, we considered generalised least squares (random effect) and maximum likelihood estimators. We constructed stochastic frontier models (see Kumbhakar and Lovell, 2000).
5. This approach forms a convex hull of intersecting planes which envelope the data points more tightly than the CRS conical hull and thus provides technical efficiency scores which are greater than or equal to those obtained using the CRS model. The VRS specification has been the most commonly used specification in the 1990s.
6. In terms of model specification, we define two kinds of output variables, a non-oriented variable (with the same interpretation as the other models) and an oriented variable, which

captures the idea that firms can control the length of lines or the use of labour.
7. See the consistency conditions applied to utilities introduced by Rossi and Ruzzier (2000) based on Bauer et. al (1998).
8. Furthermore, if we replace the variable clients with total costs, as a proxy for scale, we arrive at similar conclusions, indicating that there is a lack of correlation.
9. See Banker (1993) and especially Brockett and Golany (1996) for a detailed description of programme evaluation.
10. A programme is a grouping of DMUs who share certain characteristics. Under these circumstances, it is often desirable to evaluate aggregate performance at the programme level and compare it with other programmes.
11. The statistic value is 34.56 which is to be compared with a Chi-square distribution with one degree of freedom.

REFERENCES

Baldwin, R. and M. Cave (1999), *Understanding Regulation. Theory, Strategy and Practice*, New York: Oxford University Press.
Banker, R. (1993), 'Maximum Likelihood, Consistency and Data Envelopment Analysis: A Statistical Foundation', *Management Science*, **39** (10), 1265–1274.
Banker, R., A. Charnes and W. Cooper (1984), 'Some Models for Estimating Technical and Scale Inefficiencies in Data Envelopment Analysis', *Management Science*, **30** (9), 1078–1092.
Bauer, P., A. Berger, G. Ferrier and D. Humphrey (1998), 'Consistency Conditions for Regulatory Analysis of Financial Institutions: A Comparison of Frontier Efficiency Methods', *Journal of Economics and Business*, **50**, 85–114.
Brockett, P. and B. Golany (1996), 'Using Rank Statistics for Determining Programmatic Efficiency Differences in Data Envelopment Analysis', *Management Science*, **42**, 466–472.
Bondorevsky, D., D. Petrecolla, C. Romero and C. Ruzzier (2001), 'Competencia por Comparación en el Sector de Distribución Eléctrica: El Papel de Defensa de la Competencia', XXXVI Reunión Anual de la Asociación Argentina de Economía Política, November, Buenos Aires.
Coelli, T., D. Prasada Rao and G. Battese (1998), *An Introduction to Efficiency and Productivity Analysis*, Norwell, Kluwer Academic Publishers.
Farell, M. (1957), 'The Measurement of Productive Efficiency', *Journal of the Royal Statistical Society*, **A** (120), 253–281.
Kumbhakar, S. and C. Lovell (2000), *Stochastic Frontier Analysis*, Cambridge, Cambridge University Press.
Rossi, M. and C. Ruzzier (2000), 'On the Regulatory Application of Efficiency Measures', *Utilities Policy*, **9**, 81–92.
Schleifer, A. (1985), 'A Theory of Yardstick Competition', *Rand Journal of Economics*, **16** (3), 319–327.

6. Evolution of Mexico's port efficiency in a multiproduct context: A distance function approach

Lourdes Trujillo and Maria Manuela González

1. INTRODUCTION

The 1990s reform of public service sectors has tended to emphasise the search for competition in and for markets, to stimulate efficiency and to transform the role and size of the public sector in the economy. This is why the private sector has become an increasingly important actor in the delivery of many services traditionally managed by the public sector such as telecoms, energy and water. In a number of activities, however, the public sector is likely to continue to be a major actor simply because the economic characteristics of the sector limit competition (e.g. natural monopolies or oligopolies) or simply because the size and nature of the market limits the interest of potential private sector providers.

When competition is limited, economic theory has long ago shown that economic regulation becomes a necessary to provide incentives equivalent to those the market would have generated not only in terms of output levels but also quality and efficiency. In this context, it is indeed quite important to monitor the evolution of these variables.

The main focus of this chapter is the evolution of the efficiency of the Mexican port sector in the years that followed its reform. Its main contribution to the economic literature is to complement the earlier assessments (Estache et al., 2002 and Estache et al., 2004) by addressing explicitly the multi-output nature of port activity with a parametric approach, as opposed to a mono-production assumption being used. The parametric approach allows a separation of the effect caused by random exogenous factors from technical efficiency and therefore differs from the traditional Data Envelopment Analysis (DEA). To be able to do this, we also need to rely on a distance function. Our analysis represents the first use of a distance function in a multi-output port context applied to a developing country. Indeed, despite the fact that the multi-output nature of port industry has been addressed in studies applying DEA, there are only three multi-output parametric distance functions applications in the port sector (González, 2004; Gonzalez and Trujillo, 2005; Rodriguez-Alvarez et al., 2004). The chapter has three main objectives. First, to quantify the technical efficiency of port infrastructure in the most important Port Administration (Administraciones Portuarias Integrales, APIs) system in Mexico. Second, to analyse the impact of port reforms on the level of efficiency. Third, to analyse whether or not there are other factors that influence the efficiency of the port system.

The chapter is organised as follows. Section 2 presents a brief survey on port efficiency. Section 3 describes the theoretical aspects of a distance function. Section 4 applies an econometric model to examine port efficiency and reports the main results. The final section draws conclusions.

2. PORT EFFICIENCY

The studies analysing ports from an economic point of view date from the 1960s and focus on aspects such as pricing port facilities, port capacity and investment policies (Goss, 1967; Heggie, 1974). During the following decades, the first manuals on port economics appeared (Peston and Rees, 1971; Bennathan and Walters, 1979; Jansson and Shneerson, 1982). At the same time the literature on ports broadened and began to deal with different aspects of the port industry including infrastructure, productivity, investment and planning, costs and economies of scale, port privatisation and the promotion of port competition.

Considering the profusion of studies, the literature on port efficiency is relatively new and modest, particularly when compared to studies carried out for other public services such as electricity, water, banking, health and education.

It is mainly from the 1990s that we have witnessed an important growth in the studies on efficiency and productivity in the port sector. In recent years maritime transport has undergone an important transformation with the increase in ship size and the development of containerised cargo transport, which make the sector a particularly interesting one to study. These changes have forced ports to grow to be able to handle the larger number of containers. However, not all ports have been able to increase their mooring and storage capacity and therefore, a substantial improvement in operational efficiency has been required.

The first attempts to assess port efficiency and productivity applied partial indicators of productivity. Talley (1994) and Tongzon (1995a and 1995b) used them to compare the productivity of different ports. Numerous organisations have also employed them as instruments for the promotion of competition among ports. However, the main drawback of partial indicators is that they fail to consider the contribution of all inputs to production or give an acceptable treatment to multi-output processes. This problem becomes particularly relevant in the port sector since port products are very diverse and a wide range of inputs are involved in their production. To overcome these limitations, a new generation of studies, based on formal efficiency measures, has developed. The study by Chang (1978) can be considered as the starting point by estimating a port production function, which has led to the estimation of production frontiers.

The methodologies used in the assessment of port efficiency consist of stochastic frontiers and DEA (Roll and Hayuth, 1993; Martínez et al., 1999; Tongzon, 2001; Martín, 2002). Their use is evenly distributed and is evidence of the lack of a consensus on which approach best captures the complexity of measuring efficiency in the port sector.

From all the studies using stochastic frontiers, three estimate a production frontier to calculate technical efficiency (Liu, 1995; Estache et al., 2002; Cullinane et al., 2002), of which two (Coto et al., 2000; Baños et al., 1999) quantify economic efficiency through a cost frontier. The latter also estimates a distance function, such as Gonzalez (2004) for port authorities and Rodriguez-Alvarez el al. (2004) for port handling.

Other studies are varied and have analysed the relation between the type of ownership and port efficiency (Cullinane et al., 2002; Liu, 1995), and the effects of port reforms (Estache et al., 2002; Estache et al., 2004; Martín, 2002; González, 2004 and Gonzalez and Trujillo, 2005). The additional international benchmarking of ports has also been studied (Tongzon, 2001).

The heterogeneity of port activities (which include not only complex activities such as loading and unloading the cargo but also simpler activities such as mooring of ships) makes it difficult to estimate cost and production functions for the port sector as a whole. Even when focusing on a specific activity, there is still diversity. A port not only renders services to vessels but also to passengers and cargo. Moreover, cargo cannot be considered as a homogenous good, since each type of commodity calls for very specific loading and unloading devices. Containers also use specialised cranes and bulks employ pipe systems. However, even though the multi-output nature is captured in the studies applying DEA, all the parametric applications use a simple measure of output, except González (2004) and González and Trujillo (2005).

From the point of view of economic and business policies, it is useful to analyse the environment within which firms develop, such as institutional factors and market characteristics that can affect their efficiency. Liu (1995) relies on four variables: ownership, port size, localisation and capital intensity and Coto et al. (2000) use two: a dummy that captures the influence of the type of organisation and port size. In both studies, the authors estimate efficiency ratios as a first stage and regress these on the environmental variables in the next stage.

While intuitively quite attractive, the idea of using environmental variables to explain efficiency has been much criticised. This criticism is based on the inconsistency between the assumptions made at each stage of the analysis. The different solutions proposed (Kumbhakar et al., 1991; Reifschneider and Stevenson, 1991; Battese and Coelli, 1995) consist of specifications where the effects of technical inefficiency are defined as a function of specific firm factors influencing efficiency, so the estimation of all parameters is performed in a single stage through a maximum likelihood method.

As for the analysis of the relevance of environmental variables, the paper by González (2004) highlights their importance for the ranking of performance. In this paper, the fact that ports are serving an island or are continental proves to be relevant. It is thus quite important to include these dimensions in the assessment to ensure that the efficiency measures are not 'contaminated' by these variables.

Considering all the different approaches applied to the port sector, this study shows the following advantages: it is a parametric approach whose main feature –as compared to the DEA – is that it allows separation of the effect caused by random exogenous factors of technical efficiency. Among the different variations of this methodology, we have selected the distance function for many reasons. In the first place, because it is not necessary to establish assumptions on the economic behaviour of port authorities; second, because it easily admits the multi-output nature of port activities; and, third, because it does not require the prices of productive factors. It represents a novel technique for the analysis of the port industry which is combined with the model suggested by Battese and Coelli (1992) for the analysis of time varying efficiency.

3.   THE REFORM OF THE MEXICAN PORTS[1]

The reform of the Mexican port system started in 1993 and followed a pattern similar to that of many other reforming countries. In Mexico, as in most countries, the port system was until then managed centrally by a network of public firms. This section describes the Mexican port system and its reform, emphasising the institutional framework with which changes have taken place and the factors that have affected performance.

Mexico is supported by a large port system composed of 108 ports and terminals distributed along the 11500 km coastline of the country, with a total berth length of 110 kilometres. Half of these facilities are located on the Pacific coast, and the other half on the Mexican Gulf and the Caribbean.

There are 39 ports dedicated to commercial activities, and a similar number are fishing ports; 22 ports specialise in tourist traffic, and eight in oil traffic. The port system handles 85 percent of total international trade, and more than seven million passengers.

Modernisation and reform of Mexican ports started in 1993. To facilitate reform an adequate legal framework was needed to allow private firms to enter the port industry as operators. This was built in the new Ports Law passed in 1993. Reform also required the dismantling of the public agency Puertos Mexicanos (PUMEX), responsible up to 1993 for the ports network and the only agency in the country authorised to build port infrastructure and provide port services. Overall the reform rested on the three key instruments of decentralisation, privatisation and the introduction of competition.

Decentralisation implies that each port must have an autonomous, self-financing Port Administration, so that the government will have only a supervisory role over the system. This was pursued by creating an independent Port Administration (Administraciones Portuarias Integrales, APIs) at each port or group of small ports. These are publicly owned companies responsible for the administration of ports. Privatisation implies that the port industry must be open to the participation of private investors, both nationals and foreign, for the operation of terminals and other facilities, and eventually even port administration. Liberalisation and competition between ports and between operators within ports, resulted from some restriction in the auctions for concessions and required liberalisation of tariffs and the elimination of cross-subsidies and barriers to entry.

Overall the most relevant fact emerging from this brief overview is that competition between ports is required to improve competitiveness. To achieve this goal and to make the most of the regulatory tools the reform has granted to its regulator, Mexico needs to be able to measure the improvements in efficiency in each port in absolute and relative terms. It requires an absolute measure because the limits to the regulated tariff will have to reflect every five years the average efficiency gains achieved. It needs a relative measure because the spirit of the reform requires competition to be sustained as a matter of process and that this, in turn, requires a regular assessment of the relative performance of the main ports, therefore creating the basis of a system of yardstick competition. After ten years since the reforms began there is enough data to make a fair assessment of the absolute and relative efficiency improvements in the main Mexican ports.

4.   METHODOLOGY: THE INPUT DISTANCE FUNCTION

The distance function, introduced by Shephard (1953, 1970), allows for the estimation of the relative efficiency of firms in relation to the technological frontier, with fewer restrictions than other methods of frontier estimation. The main advantages can be summarised as follows:

- It allows multi-output processes to be captured which cannot be achieved with a production frontier. The alternative use of a cost frontier would make it necessary to assume cost minimisation and to know input prices.
- It does not require the use of optimising assumptions. The validity of the assumption of cost minimisation has been challenged in the context of public or regulated firms. This is reaffirmed in the port sector by Coto et al. (2000).
- It only uses physical data and, therefore, it is not necessary to have information on outputs or factors prices. As in other regulated sectors, the literature on ports recognises the difficulty of getting reliable prices (for example, on the effects of subsidies on inputs prices).
- Distance functions can be input-oriented or output-oriented. An input-oriented distance function features technology through the minimum equiproportional reduction of the input vector, given an output vector. An output-oriented distance function features technology through the maximum equiproportional expansion of the output vector, given an input vector.

An input-oriented distance function is defined as the largest scalar by which all output factors can be proportionally divided and still the same amount of output can be obtained. Mathematically, it is expressed as follows:

$$D_I(y,x) = \max_{\delta} \{\delta : x/\delta \in L(y)\} \qquad (6.1)$$

where y is the output vector, x represents the vector of factors and $L(y)$ the input set, which define the group of all inputs x that can be used to obtain the output vector y. A value of D_I equal to one reveals that production is efficiently carried out, whereas a value of D_I greater than one will indicate the degree of technical efficiency achieved.

An output-oriented distance function is defined as the smallest scalar by which all outputs can be proportionally divided, using the same level of productive factors. Formally, it is defined as follows:

$$D_O(y,x) = \min_{\mu} \{\mu : y/\mu \in P(x)\} \qquad (6.2)$$

where $P(x)$ is the output set, which represents all output vectors y that can be obtained using the input vector x. If the value of D_O equals unity, it is evidence of technical efficiency, while a value smaller than one shows the degree of technical efficiency achieved.

While they are quite flexible, distance functions are required to meet the properties which need to be tested. These properties are summarised in Table 6.1 (for more details see Färe and Primont, 1995).

Table 6.1 Properties of distance functions

Input-oriented	Output-oriented
Homogeneous of degree 1 in input Non-increasing in output Quasi-convex in output Non-decreasing in input Concave in input Dual of cost function $D_I(y,x) \geq 1$, if $x \in L(y)$ $D_I(y,x)=1$, if x is on the frontier of $L(y)$	Homogeneous of degree 1 in output Non-increasing in input Quasi-concave in input Non-decreasing in output Convex in output Dual of income function $D_O(x,y) \leq 1$, if $y \in P(x)$ $D_O(x,y)=1$, if y is on the frontier of $P(x)$

The analysis of the conditions under which port authorities develop their activities led us to the estimation of an output-oriented distance function. This is because in the provision of infrastructure services, port authorities have some power to decide on the production level through the use of two mechanisms: commercial policies and concessions. The port authorities also market their services and attract new traffic. Furthermore, as long as port authorities decide on the type of firm that can operate at the different ports, they are also deciding on the ships and goods that will be handled. For instance, a port intended to attract fish processing needs freezing companies to be established.

Considering this capacity to influence output, port authorities encounter difficulties in adjusting the productive factors used in the provision of infrastructure services, particularly in relation to berths, area and labour. The first two are quasi-fixed factors that, due to their indivisible nature, find it difficult to adapt to the changes in production, especially if the change is downwards. Because the labour factor generally implies personnel, the difficulty is in making adjustments, particularly when the number of personnel needs to be reduced.

4.1 The functional form

The empirical application of a distance function calls for the definition of an appropriate functional form. It is desirable that the functional form has the following advantages: it must be flexible, it must be easy to calculate and, lastly, it must allow for the imposition of the homogeneity condition. The translogarithmic functional form (hereinafter translog) meets these conditions and this is the reason why, at present, most authors use it in all research fields. It consists of a flexible functional form that provides a local second-order approximation to an unknown functional form. In other words, no a priori restrictions about production technology are assumed and, thus, the criticisms associated with some restrictive properties of the Cobb-Douglas production function are overcome.

For all these reasons, we estimate a translog distance function that, when output-oriented, can be expressed as follows:

$$
\ln D_O = \alpha_0 + \sum_{m=1}^{M} \alpha_m \ln y_{mit} + 1/2 \sum_{m=1}^{M} \sum_{n=1}^{M} \alpha_{mn} \ln y_{mit} \ln y_{nit} +
$$
$$
\sum_{k=1}^{K} \beta_k \ln x_{kit} + 1/2 \sum_{k=1}^{K} \sum_{l=1}^{K} \beta_{kl} \ln x_{kit} \ln x_{lit} + \sum_{k=1}^{K} \sum_{m=1}^{M} \delta_{km} \ln x_{kit} \ln y_{mit} +
$$
$$
\sum_{h=1}^{H} \psi_h d_h + \psi_0 t + 1/2 \psi_{00} t^2 + \sum_{k=1}^{K} \xi_{kt} t \ln x_{kit} + \sum_{m=1}^{M} \tau_{jt} t \ln y_{mit} + \varepsilon_{it}
$$

(6.3)

where y is a vector of M outputs, x is a vector of K factors, i relates to the i-th firm, t relates to the time trend, h refers to the environmental variables, Ψ_t is the coefficient of the environmental dummy variables d, γ_t is the coefficient for the time trend variable T and ε_{it} is an error term which is discussed later. Variables are expressed in relation to their deviation from the geometric mean; therefore, the estimated coefficients can be construed as elasticities at the sample mean.

4.2 Homogeneity of degree 1 in outputs

In order to determine the frontier, D_O needs to be equal to unity and, in that case, the term on the left of the equation, according to the neperian logarithm, will equal zero. Consequently, it is necessary that outputs meet the homogeneity condition of degree 1 in order that the following restrictions are verified:

$$
\sum_{m=1}^{M} \alpha_m = 1; \quad \sum_{m=1}^{M} \alpha_{mn} = 0; \quad \sum_{k=1}^{K} \delta_{km} = 0
$$
(6.4)

The symmetry conditions requires: $\alpha_{mn} = \alpha_{nm}$, $\beta_{kl} = \beta_{lk}$ y $\delta_{kl} = \delta_{lk}$
Following Lovell et al. (1994),[2] this condition has been imposed by normalising the distance function with one of the outputs. This starts from the assumption that homogeneity implies that:

$$
D_O(x, wy) = w D_O(x, y)
$$
(6.5)

for any $w > 0$. The output chosen does not influence the results (Cuesta and Orea, 2002).

If in a translog distance function (with M outputs and K inputs) any output is chosen, say y_M, so that $w = 1/y_M$, the following expression results:

$$\ln\left(D_0/y_M\right) = \alpha_0 + \sum_{m=1}^{M-1} \alpha_m \ln y^*_{mit} + 1/2 \sum_{m=1}^{M-1}\sum_{n=1}^{M-1} \alpha_{mn} \ln y^*_{mit} \ln y^*_{nit} +$$
$$\sum_{k=1}^{K} \beta_k \ln x_{kit} + 1/2 \sum_{k=1}^{K}\sum_{l=1}^{K} \beta_{kl} \ln x_{kit} \ln x_{lit} + \sum_{k=1}^{K}\sum_{m=1}^{M-1} \delta_{km} \ln x_{kit} \ln y^*_{mit}$$

$$(6.6)$$

where $y^*_{mit} = y_{mit}/y_{Mit}$. Note that when $y_{mi} = y_{Mi}$, the ratio y^*_{mi} is equal to 1 so that its logarithm is equal to zero. This is why the sum where they intervene always has one less term (M-1).

Equation (6.6) can thus be rewritten as:

$$\ln\left(D_O/y_M\right) = TL\left(x_{it,}\ y_{it}/y_{Mit},\alpha,\beta,\delta\right) \qquad (6.7)$$

yielding the final expression:

$$-\ln\left(y_{Mit}\right) = TL\left(x_{it,}\ y_{it}/y_{Mit},\alpha,\beta,\delta\right) - \ln\left(D_O\right) \qquad (6.8)$$

In equation (6.8), the $-ln(D_O)$ term can be interpreted as an error term which captures technical inefficiency.

4.3 Structure of the error terms

The distance function estimated is stochastic. For the purpose of estimating Equation 6.8, it is necessary to determine the random disturbance term. We applied the methodology developed by Battese and Coelli (1992) for panel data and apply an additive term, as suggested by Cuesta and Orea (2002), to account for the fact that we are estimating an output-oriented distance function. The error term thus has the following form:

$$v_{it} + u_{it} \qquad (6.9)$$

where, v_{it} is a symmetrical error term, independent and identically distributed with a zero average (which represents the random variables uncontrollable by the operator) and u_i is a one-sided negative error term (which measures the technical inefficiency of each operator that is constant over time) and is distributed independently of v_{it}. The inefficiency term is specified as an exponential function of the time:

$$u_{it} = \{\exp[-\eta(t-T)]\}u_i \qquad (6.10)$$

Applied to the distance function, this yields

$$-\ln\left(y_{Mit}\right) = TL\left(x_{it},\, y_{it}/y_{Mit},\alpha,\beta,\delta\right) + v_{it} + u_{it} \qquad (6.11)$$

This equation can be estimated by the maximum likelihood method which requires some distributional assumptions on the random shock. This assumes that v_{it} follows a $N(0,\ \sigma_v^2)$ distribution and u_{it} follows a $\lvert N(0,\ \sigma_u^2)\rvert$ distribution (Ritter and Simar, 1997).

5. THE ESTIMATION

5.1 The data[3]

The heterogeneity of activities and the diversity of commodities handled by ports suggests narrowing the study to a limited number of ports and a specific type of cargo. Following the foregoing recommendation, this study concentrates on the main APIs (Port Authorities) in Mexico.

Statistical information has been gathered from data published annually by the APIs in their Annual Reports. We sought additional clarifications about the data from people responsible for various functions in the ports.

While the reform was decided in 1993 and the bulk of its implementation took place in 1994, the new autonomous APIs needed a further couple of years to put together a reasonable monitoring system demanded by the Transport Subsecretariat. The data available is annual and spans four years starting in 1996 and ending in 1999. It only covers 13 APIs but these represent the main ones. This provides a panel of data of 52 observations which is large enough to rely on parametric methods and, in particular, on a production frontier. The limited coverage is good enough to allow a fair assessment of the continued progress and efforts made by the APIs to meet the mandate assigned by the reformers. It is also good enough to allow an assessment of the evolution of the relative performance of the main APIs.

The APIs covered by the study are: Ensenada, Guaymas, Topolobampo, Mazatlán, Manzanillo, Lázaro Cárdenas and Salina Cruz, on the Pacific coast of Mexico and Altamira, Tampico, Tuxpan, Veracruz, Coatzacoalcos and Progreso, on the Atlantic coast. Excluding oil and its derivatives, these APIs handle 70 per cent of the traffic going through the Mexican port system. This is significant. Among the largest ports, the main ports missing are Puerto Madero, Puerto Vallarta and Acapulco. We lacked comparable data for these ports. Puerto Madero was closed for a number of years while under repair. Puerto Vallarta is mostly a tourist port and has very little cargo. Acapulco is mainly a passenger-oriented port and has the only privatised API so far (since 1997). Since Mexican law prevents the regulator from requesting any cost information, which could also be used by the fiscal authorities, no data is available for Acapulco. The rest of the ports are generally too small to allocate major resources to meet detailed regulatory informational requirements.

Since the ports are subject to a price cap and their interactions are designed to be competitive, it would make sense to construct both cost and production efficiency measures to identify possible rents from a revision of tariffs. The econometric techniques available, however, do not allow much to be inferred from a comparison of the level of efficiency estimated from cost and production functions.[4] While an estimation of both the production and cost frontier through stochastic models should, in principle, allow for calculation of technical and allocative efficiency from different but related information bases, the reality is that such comparisons are still almost impossible to conduct in any robust way.

In view of the data restriction on the cost side, the analysis of the efficiency effect of the reforms is based on an output distance function. An output distance function assumes output maximisation instead of a cost minimisation effort.[5] This may be a reasonable assumption when focusing on the promotion of competition, but may not be the most desirable one in view of the fact that the regulated tariffs are under a price-cap regime with the explicit purpose of promoting cost reductions. The fact that market shares are a clear concern for API´s managers, and that most of the initial investment decisions were taken for them as part of the restructuring process, suggests that the production orientation is overall a reasonable one. Indeed, the efficiency measures generated from the output distance function in a sector with scale economies provide information on the opportunities for expansion of outputs for a given quantity of inputs, for a given level of costs.[6]

The production variable reflecting the output of the infrastructure has been approximated by the volume of general merchandise and bulk cargo[7] (both in tons) handled in each API, to address the multi-product nature of the API´s activities through a disaggregation of the various types of cargoes handled. General cargo includes containerised merchandise and bulk cargo includes solid and liquid bulk.

Although APIs also provide other services such as equipment rental, commercial building and space rental and water services to the ships, and these activities confirm the multi-product nature of the API´s activities, the data on these other activities is unfortunately not available for each port for the period covered.

In order to perform their function as infrastructure service providers, the APIs use three productive factors (see Table 6.2 for a quantitative summary).

First, they employ the labour, approximated by the mean number of employees in each API,[8] where administrative and more specialised technical employees are included.

The capital input is approximated by the surface concessioned by the government to the API and by the length of docks. Table 6.2 summarises the mean values of the variables and illustrates the diversity of Mexican ports.

Table 6.2   Output and input means per port authority, 1996–1999

API's	General cargo (tonnes)	Bulk cargo (tonnes)	Berths (meters)	Surface (meters^2)	Labour (employees)
Ensenada	186 638	817 926	5549	102 130	39
Guaymas	83 539	4 835 578	7295	175 374	51
Topolobampo	712 984	2 704 656	2074	137 700	18
Mazatlán	521 849	1 549 919	4991	84 897	33
Manzanillo	2 605 470	7 046 884	1626	7,398	93
Lázaro Cárdenas	2 675 141	11 550 626	3782	241 331	50
Salina Cruz	202 699	16 352 572	2693	101 414	43
Altamira	1 678 677	197 295	1435	351 273	81
Tampico	1 809 865	6 608 156	10 453	145 668	97
Tuxpan	232 405	8 421 491	2743	334 176	28
Veracruz	4 240 970	6 662 859	7410	271 494	225
Coatzacoalcos	308 229	2 240 509	2214	122 846	62
Progreso	215 472	2 468 197	1040	26 973	40

Occasionally, specific factors may influence production without any possible interference from the port authorities. These factors include geographical location, the degree of competition in the sector and the type of ownership. The main factor accounting for differences in the port environment in Mexico is geographic location. Some ports are located on the Pacific coast of Mexico and other ports are located on the Atlantic coast.

5.2   The results

Table 6.3 shows the main results obtained from the distance function output oriented that was estimated by maximum likelihood. The output distance function is well behaved. It can be noted that the first-order parameters present the expected signs and, in addition, they are significant (except the labour variable coefficient). In other words, the parameters of the output variables are positive and, thus, indicate that the distance from the frontier increases when production grows (remember that the output-oriented distance function takes a value between zero and one). On the contrary, input parameters are negative, suggesting that if inputs increase, for a given output level, the distance will be reduced.

The coefficients for the time trend show results for technological change. This coefficient is not significant. The regression results also show that the geographic location matters. It has a negative and statistically significant coefficient. This means that ports on the Pacific Coast benefit from an outward shift of the frontier more than the others (*ceteris paribus*).

With the statistical results settled, we can now assess the technical efficiency of each port in each year based on the translog production function specified earlier. The annual estimates and their average for each port and for the system as a whole are reported in Table 6.4. The average technical efficiency of the Mexican ports for the period is 55.25. This is within the order of magnitude of other estimates in the sector (Estache et al., 2002 find the average technical efficiency to be 58.8). During the period, the annual average technical efficiency increased from 54.7 percent in 1996 to 55.8 per cent in 1999.[9] The variance across ports is however generally quite high. It varies from 4.3 per cent in Ensenada in 1996 to 93.7 per cent in Salina Cruz. From an overall policy viewpoint, the results confirm that the expected gains from reform are becoming a reality.

Table 6.4 also shows the changes in efficiency over the period. The average annual growth rate in efficiency is 1.9 per cent with spread varying from 16.4 per cent and 0.3 per cent. The APIs with the highest growth rates are those which started at the lowest efficiency levels. The ports with high initial efficiency levels have maintained their performance. This implies that reforms may have been effective at stimulating a catching-up among the poor performers.

6.   CONCLUDING COMMENTS

This chapter has shown that it is relatively straightforward to address the multiproduct nature of the port sector with a parametric distance function in a sector with little data on prices. Indeed, the chapter shows that, compared to

Table 6.3   Parameters estimated

Variable	Coefficient	t-test
Constant	-0.241	-0.747
L(general cargo)	0.366	6.136
L(bulk cargo)	0.634	10.644
L(berth)	-0.541	-2.087
L(surface)	-0.309	-1.762
L(labour)	-0.164	-1.064
L(general cargo).L(general cargo)	0.057	1.468
L(bulk cargo).L(bulk cargo)	0.057	1.468
L(berth).L(berth)	-1.354	2.459
L(surface).L(surface)	-0.204	1.215
L(labour).L(labour)	-0.543	1.243
L(general cargo).L(berth)	-0.150	-1.527
L(general cargo).L(surface)	0.243	2.663
L(general cargo).L(labour)	0.295	5.316
L(bulk cargo).L(berth)	0.150	1.527
L(bulk cargo).L(surface)	-0.243	-2.663
L(bulk cargo).L(labour)	-0.295	-5.316
L(berth).L(surface)	0.165	1.082
L(berth).L(labour)	0.255	0.654
L(surface).L(labour)	-0.152	-0.785
T	-0.044	-1.716
TT	0.097	2.831
T.L(general cargo)	-0.045	-2.884
T.L(bulk cargo)	0.045	2.884
T.L(berth	0.074	2.288
T.L(surface)	-0.039	-1.716
T.L(labour)	0.041	0.964
Localisation	-0.868	-2.445
σ^2*	1.758	2.301
$\gamma*$	0.995	428.3

Notes:
* $\sigma^2 = \sigma^2_v + \sigma^2_u$; $\gamma = \sigma^2_u/(\sigma^2_v + \sigma^2_u)$ (Battese and Corra, 1977).

the traditional reliance on cost functions, distance functions have the advantage of not requiring price information and do not require cost minimisation behaviour. These features are relevant for the study of the port sector where data is scarce and where the optimising behaviour seems to often go well beyond a concern for the costs of the port activity. When compared to approaches that use production functions to estimate productivity, our analysis has permitted an explicit consideration of the multiproduct dimension of the sector. Moreover, the stochastic dimension offers the advantage over the DEA models of allowing an explicit separation of efficiency and the random factors that affect performance.

Table 6.4   Evolution of efficiency per port authority (per cent)

APIs	1996	1997	1998	1999	Mean	Average Growth Rate 96–99
Ensenada	4.32	4.55	4.78	5.03	4.67	16.35
Guaymas	8.60	8.95	9.31	9.68	9.14	12.59
Topolobampo	26.52	27.10	27.68	28.27	27.39	6.61
Mazatlán	9.85	10.23	10.62	11.02	10.43	11.82
Manzanillo	88.86	89.04	89.21	89.37	89.12	0.58
Lázaro Cárdenas	89.32	89.49	89.65	89.81	89.57	0.55
Salina Cruz	93.39	93.50	93.60	93.71	93.55	0.33
Altamira	88.81	88.98	89.15	89.32	89.07	0.58
Tampico	35.82	36.42	37.03	37.64	36.73	5.08
Tuxpan	65.10	65.56	66.02	66.47	65.79	2.09
Veracruz	90.85	90.99	91.14	91.28	91.06	0.47
Coatzacoalcos	45.97	46.56	47.15	47.73	46.85	3.82
Progreso	64.24	64.71	65.17	65.63	64.94	2.16
Mean	54.74	55.08	55.42	55.76	55.25	1.87

NOTES

1. For a more in-depth explanation of Mexican port reform see Estache et al. (2002).
2. This methodology has been applied in some empirical papers (Coelli and Perelman, 1999, 2000; Morrison et al. 2000; Orea, 2002; González and Trujillo, 2005, among others).
3. For more details about the data and variables see Estache et al. (2002).
4. See Coelli et al. (2003)

5.   In Mexico, the lack of a tradition of regulatory accounting is also a source of concern for the confidence that can be attached to cost data and the estimation of a cost function.

6.   Under constant returns to scale, the results are quite different: instead of increasing production x per cent, the firm could get the same output by cutting inputs by 1/x per cent and the corresponding change in costs can be calculated immediately when factor prices are known.

7.   Operating revenue mostly arise from the services provided to ships and merchandise. The cargo arrives at ports in vessels and, therefore, these two elements are correlated. Actually, they constitute two alternative ways of measuring the same output.

8.   This number excludes all workers allocated only to loading and unloading of ships, since that activity is not being measured in this production function.

9.   It is interesting to note that the ranking based on an explicit modelling of the multi-output nature of the Mexican APIS proposed here does not alter significantly the ranking according to technical efficiency identified in Estache et al. (2002). However, as expected since efficiency is a relative measure, because new ports have been added to that original study, the specific technical efficiency measures have changed.

REFERENCES

Baños Pino, J., P. Coto Millán and A. Rodríguez Álvarez (1999), 'Allocative Efficiency and Over-capitalization: an Application', *International Journal of Transport Economics, XXVI* (2), 181–199.

Battese, G.E. and Corra (1977), 'Estimation of a Production Frontier Model: with Application to the Pastoral Zone of Eastern Australia', *Australian Journal of Agricultural Economics*, 21, 169–179.

Battese, G.E. and T.J. Coelli (1992), 'Frontier Production Functions Technical Efficiency and Panel Data: With Applications to Paddy Farmers in India', *Journal of Productivity Analysis*, 3, 153–169.

Battese, G.E. and T.J. Coelli (1995), 'A Model for Technical Inefficiency Effects in a Stochastic Frontier Production for Panel Data', *Empirical Economics*, 20, 325–333.

Battese, G.E. and Corra, G. S. (1977), ' Estimation of a Production Frontier Model: with Application to the Pastoral Zone of Eastern Australia', *Australian Journal of Agricultural Economics*, 21, 169-179

Bennathan, E. and A.A. Walters (1979), *Port Pricing and Investment Policy for Developing Countries*, Oxford, Oxford University Press.

Chang, S. (1978), 'Production Function and Capacity Utilization of the Port of Mobile', *Maritime Policy and Management*, 5, 297–305.

Coelli, T. and S. Perelman (1999), 'A Comparison of Parametric and Non-Parametric Distance Functions: with Application to European Railways', *European Journal of Operational Research*, 117, 326–339.

Coelli, T. and S. Perelman (2000), 'Technical Efficiency of European Railways: a Distance Function Approach', *Applied Economics*, 32, 1967–1976.

Coelli, T., A. Estache, S. Perelman and L. Trujillo (2003), A *Primer on Efficiency Measurement for Utilities and Transport Regulators*, World Bank Institute Publications, Studies in Development Series.

Coto Millán, P., J. Baños Pino and A. Rodríguez Álvarez (2000), 'Economic Efficiency in Spanish Ports: some Empirical Evidence', *Maritime Policy and Management*, 27 (2), 169–174.

Cuesta, R.A. and L. Orea, (2002) 'Mergers and Technical Efficiency in Spanish Saving Banks: a Stochastic Distance Function Approach', *Journal of Banking and*

Finance, **26**, 2231–2247.

Cullinane, K., D.W. Song and R. Gray (2002), 'A Stochastic Frontier Model of the Efficiency of Major Container Terminals in Asia: Assessing the Influence of Administrative and Ownership Structures', *Transportation Research*, Part A, **36**, 743–762.

Estache, A., M. González and L. Trujillo (2002), 'Efficiency Gains from Port Reform and the Potential for Yardstick Competition: Lessons from Mexico', *World Development*, **30** (4), 545–560.

Estache, A., B. Tovar de la Fe and L. Trujillo (2004), 'Sources of Efficiency Gains in Port Reform: A DEA Decomposition of a Malmquist TFP Index for Mexico', *Utilities Policy*, **12** (4), 231–230.

Färe, R. and D. Primont (1995), *Multi-Output Production and Duality: Theory and Applications* Norwell, Massachusetts: Kluwer Academic Publishers.

González, M. (2004), 'Eficiencia en la provisión de servicios de infraestructura portuaria: una aplicación al tráfico de contenedores en España', Thesis, Universidad de Las Palmas de Gran Canaria.

González, M. and Trujillo, L. (2005), 'Reforms and Infrastructure Efficiency in Spain's Container Ports', *Policy Research Working Paper 3515, The World Bank*

Goss, R. (1967), 'Towards an Economic Appraisal of Port Investment', *Journal of Transport Economics and Policy*, **1** (3), 249–272.

Heggie, I. (1974), 'Charging for Port Facilities', *Journal of Transport Economic and Policy*, **8** (1), 3–25.

Jansson, J.O. and D. Shneerson (1982), *Port Economics* Massachusetts: The MIT Press.

Kumbhakar, S.C., S. Ghosh and J.T. McGuckin (1991), 'A Generalized Production Frontier Approach for Estimating Determinants of Inefficiency in U.S. Dairy Farms' *Journal of Business and Economic Statistics*, **9**, 279–286.

Liu, Z. (1995), 'The Comparative Performance of Public and Private Enterprise. The Case of British Ports', *Journal of Transport Economics and Policy*, **29** (3), 263–274.

Lovell, C.A.K., S. Richardson, P. Travers and L. Wood (1994), 'Resources and Functionings: a New View of Inequality in Australia' in Eichhorn, W. (ed.), *Models and Measurement of Welfare and Inequality* Berlin: Springer-Verlag.

Martín, M. (2002), 'El Sistema Portuario Español: Regulación, Entorno Competitivo y Resultados. Una Aplicación del Análisis Envolvente de Datos', Doctoral Thesis, Universitat Rovira I Virgili.

Martínez Budría, E., R. Díaz Armas, M. Navarro Ibáñez and T. Ravelo Mesa (1999), 'A Study of the Efficiency of Spanish Port Authorities Using Data Envelopment Analysis', *International Journal of Transport Economics*, **XXVI** (2), 237–253.

Morrison, C.J., W.E. Johnston and G.A.G. Frengley (2000), 'Efficiency in New Zealand Sheep and Beef Farming: the Impacts of Regulation Reform', *Review of Economics and Statistics*, **82** (2), 325–337.

Orea, L. (2002), 'Parametric Decomposition of a Generalized Malmquist Productivity Index', *Journal of Productivity Analysis*, **18**, 5–22.

Peston, M.H. and R. Rees (1971), *Port Costs and the Demand for Port Facilities* London: National Ports Council.

Puertos del Estado (various years), *Anuario estadístico del sistema portuario de titularidad estatal*.

Reifschneider, D. and R. Stevenson (1991), 'Systematic Departures from the Frontier: a Framework for the Analysis of Firm Inefficiency', *International Economic Review*, **32** (3), 715–723.

Ritter, C. and L. Simar (1997), 'Pitfalls of Normal Gamma Stochastic Frontie Models', *Journal of Productivity Analysis*, **8** (2), 121–129.
Rodríguez-Álvarez, A., Tovar, de la Fé, B. and Trujillo, L. (2005), 'Firm and Time Varying Technical and Allocative Efficiency: An Application for Port Carge Handling Firms. *Fundación de las Cajas de Ahorro*. Documento de trabajo número 201/2005
Roll, Y. and Y. Hayuth (1993), 'Port Performance Comparison Applying Data Envelopment Analysis (DEA)', *Maritime Policy and Management*, **20** (2), 153–161.
Shephard, R.W. (1953), *Cost and Production Functions* Princeton: Princeton University Press.
Shephard, R.W. (1970), *Theory of Cost and Production Functions* Princeton: Princeton University Press.
Talley, W.K. (1994), 'Performance Indicators and Port Performance Evaluation'. *Logistics and Transportation Review*, **30** (14), 339–352.
Tongzon, J.L. (1995a), 'Systematizing International Benchmarking for Ports', *Maritime Policy and Management*, **22** (12), 171–177.
Tongzon, J.L. (1995b), 'Determinants of Port Performance and Efficiency', *Transportation Research*, Part A, **29** (3), 245–252.
Tongzon, J.L. (2001), 'Efficiency Measurement of Selected Australian and Other International Ports Using Data Envelopment Analysis', *Transportation Research*, Part A, **35**, 113–128.

7. Lessons from computable general equilibrium models applied to regulatory economics
Omar O. Chisari, Antonio Estache and Carlos Romero

1. INTRODUCTION

Most approaches to regulatory economics are presented in partial equilibrium environments. Simplified representations and partial equilibrium models are the adequate setting to discuss most issues of industrial organisation and the trade-offs imposed by asymmetries of information. However, the introduction of the general equilibrium perspective contributes to the enrichment of the analysis especially when regulated sectors represent a high proportion of GDP and investments of the whole economy and when they are crucial for the determination of relative prices. But very rarely studies address the interaction between regulated sectors and the rest of the economy and between regulated sectors themselves (of course, several exceptions can be quoted).

When the dimension and the influence of regulated sectors are not negligible, microeconomic strategies could have significant macroeconomic consequences, including on income distribution, unemployment and trade. And wider perspectives are needed for a correct cost-benefit appraisal of regulatory interventions (e.g. pricing policies); that is why CGE models can help.

This issue is particularly relevant for economies under development, which are relatively more sensitive and fragile with respect to regulations and microeconomic polices and where regulated sectors (like electricity, telecommunications and transport) represent a high proportion of value added and investments, and enter as key determinant of costs in most sectors of the economy.

This chapter summarises the results we obtained in our work with the Computable General Equilibrium model applied to regulatory economics. The following are some of the lessons we learned from our models and simulations:

1. *The design of good regulatory rules should take into account how regulated sectors are linked through the input-output matrix and thei substitutability or complementarity at the consumption level.* Gas ane electricity are clear examples of this kind of deep relation; ou simulations show that a cost-plus regulation in gas combined with price-cap regulation in electricity could create excessive profits and undesirable transfers of rents.

2. *Effectiveness of regulatory rules and agencies is an important elemen for income distribution.* Transfers of rents must be anticipated an minimised by regulatory authorities. Effective regulatory action ca reduce transfer of rents and this is important for the poor who receiv most of the benefits of progress in the form of lower prices rather thai higher factor prices.

3. *The public sector is an implicit 'shareholder' of regulated sector through the tax system.* Infrastructure sectors contribute a significan proportion of total revenue in less developed countries. Thei contribution can be channelled mainly through profits tax – as ii Argentina – or be collected directly from the prices of services paid fo by customers – as in Uruguay. Both cases illustrate the temptation o governments to persue collection objectives rather than welfar maximising strategies when choosing regulations and pricing regimes This is also important for income distribution when prices are used to finance the public sector (as is the case of Uruguay).

4. *Macroeconomic shocks might jeopardise the gains in efficiency ane productivity obtained from successful macroeconomic reforms.* Despite the relevance of regulated sectors for the whole economy macroeconomic shocks due to changes in interest rate or commoditie prices could reduce or even reverse the efficiency and productivity gain obtained from privatisations and good regulation in fragile economies as in the Latin American case. This is important when results o privatisations are evaluated.

5. *Price-cap and cost-plus regimes might have differential effects o trade balance. This implies that microeconomic reforms are relevant fo macroeconomic performance.* Price cap is the much praised regime used to minimise rent transfers due to asymmetries of information, while cost-plus reduces the cost of capital due to risk premia charged by operators. Our simulations show that the gains and losses of each regime must be balanced taking into account their effects on capital flows ane the implicit stress on the objective of equilibrating trade balance. This i important for less developed countries that face recurrent trade accoun crisis and where infrastructure sectors are a high proportion of GDP and

transfers of their profits abroad represent an important burden on total trade surplus.

6. *The X-factor used to capture technological change in the RPI-X is exogenous to the firm, but when all utilities are taken together their efficiency gains could influence technological gains of the economy to a significant degree.* When several infrastructure sectors introduce changes simultaneously, individual sectors can experience gains that they could have contributed to create.

In the following section we present the basic elements of the analytical structure of our CGE models and elaborate on the methods we used to adapt the general equilibrium framework to include sector under regulatory scrutiny. The analytical structure itself is included in an Appendix. Section 3 is devoted to the discussion of results obtained with applications to the case of Argentina; we estimate the order of magnitude of welfare gains obtained after the privatisation of state owned enterprises, and we discuss how that welfare would be distributed depending on the efficiency of the regulatory process. Then we consider how macroeconomic shocks could put in danger or offset the gains of reforms in a country with high financial fragility (Section 4). In Section 5 we study the influence of pricing regimes on the trade account. Section 6 addresses the case of potential reforms of public utilities in Uruguay. Argentina and Uruguay provide interesting cases of study for several reasons. First, Argentina's privatisation has been wide and deep, and privatised sectors have a significant role in determining relative prices. Second, Uruguay, however, is on the verge of adopting reforms that would increase efficiency and productivity and change the pricing rules, by consenting to more private participation and by upgrading the quality of the public sector. Third, the data are readily available for all regulated utilities. The last section summarises the main results.

REGULATORY REGIMES AND CGE MODELS: ELEMENTS OF THE ANALYTIC FRAMEWORK

Our analytical framework is provided by a computable general equilibrium model. This approach is particularly useful for the study of the impact of privatisations and regulations for the following reasons.

First, most reforms of public utilities and infrastructure services are developed in a context of structural adjustment. The methodology of computable economics allows a careful calibration of the key technological parameters based on information requirements and it is less demanding than those of econometric models. However, the data required exceeds many times what is publicly available and requires a consistent effort of adaptation to be used in the simulations; for example, efficiency gains must be define measured and adapted to be introduced in the CGE treatment of productic functions. This necessitates not only sensible decisions regarding relevanc and adaptation, but also surveys and direct enquiries to operators in regulate sectors about the characteristics and meaning of their information, includin both information from their balance sheets as well as direct communicatic of operational parameters.

Second, comparative static simulations of the impact of changes within th sector or across the economy can be performed one at the time (simultaneously. Often changes occur simultaneously and it is necessary t examine their interaction. If we take changes one by one, then it is possible t follow direct and indirect impacts of all the changes. The direct effect focuse on the impact of these changes through the direct consumption of th privatised goods. Indirect impact accounts for importance of reforms on th capital and labour markets, and through the consumption of other goods an services.

One main concern is that comparative static effects can easily becom poorly determined when accounting for too many factors under the standar assumptions of the model, and especially under structural change. I particular, since regulatory regimes follow prices under special rules (adjustment, it is difficult to determine qualitatively the net effect. We thu suggest it should be assessed by adding up numerical (non-linear) impac using a CGE model.

Third, CGE models are useful tools under structural uncertainty on relativ prices. Most probably, public sector reforms and private sector participatic change relative prices and factors rewards. The net impact on househol welfare, real wages and government budget will be uncertain and it is natur to face some social concern on the reforms under risk aversion. A CGE ca give illustrations of final impacts on welfare and income distribution, help t estimate direct and indirect effects in their just proportion and give warning on non desired effects.

An additional advantage of the tool is the possibility of using the design (the model's closure rules of the model to assess the importance of th effectiveness of the regulator in determining the interpersonal an intersectoral distribution of gains and losses from utilities' privatisations. I the quality of regulation important for the poor? Our results show it is.

Fourth, CGE modellisation allows an assessment of the interactior between privatisation and other significant macroeconomic change Modifications in the international cost of funds and shocks in commoditie prices can be studied to understand how they will influence regulated sector indicators; but the reverse is also possible, since to what extent, and hov what happens in the regulated sectors will impact on the macroeconomi performance, can also be explored. Is the rule chosen to regulate prices for the macroeconomy neutral? Our results show it is not.

The analysis is based on a general equilibrium model as it is the sensible way to analyse explicitly and quantitatively the interactions between the regulated sector and the rest of the economy. The model needs to reflect the fact that regulation influences prices and that factor mobility assumptions would influence these price changes and interact with the regulator's job. Since this factor mobility is highly specific to the regulated industries, we need to model this specificity explicitly (a Ricardo-Viner framework allows us to do this, especially for trade). This general equilibrium model which recognises the specificity of production factors provides the analytical framework needed to assess the impact of changes in the regulated industries on the rest of the economy and vice versa.

The standard CGE model needs to be adapted to represent the workings of regulatory regimes. First of all, and to make the model as realistic as possible, it is important to take into account the fact that contracts with private operators generally specify explicit large service obligations because the services they deliver are often perceived as essential to the wellbeing of the poorest. In our model, service obligation is interpreted as the passive adjustment of service supply to demand in the regulated sector. This assumption prevents the need to rely on rationing, which is quite realistic in the context of modern infrastructure reforms.[1]

Most regulatory regimes establish explicitly this obligation in the contract, and its violation has not only direct economic costs but also impacts on the reputation of the firm. Service obligation increases costs to the firm (real and expected) and is compensated for by the tariff and, very often, by the commitment of the regulator to protect incumbents by legally blocking the entry of new competitors. A temporary 'no entry' condition is a second, important characteristic of modern infrastructure reforms, which guarantees a return on assets, when perceived commercial risk levels could be aggravated by the concern for entry and become a participation constraint for the private sector.

If the Service Obligation hypothesis is accepted, there will be two possible cases to address it:

.   *Mark-Up Method (MUM).* In the first case, there is enough installed capacity to cover the necessities of clients and the main issue is for the firm to obtain a subsidy to cover the difference between marginal cost and regulated price. We assume that the subsidy is paid by the shareholders of the firm in the case of the price-cap regime. With this strategy, existence of equilibrium can be shown using the proof already available for the standard general equilibrium models with taxes. The price cap or the rate-of-return regulation can be interpreted as special mark-up rules that are in fact taxes for which the revenue accrues to (o is extracted from) the owners of the firms.

2. *Additional Investment Solution (AIS).* In the second case, capacity i insufficient and additional investment is needed. This second optio (with constant marginal costs) is used exceptionally when deman becomes too high.

To simplify the presentation of both cases, it may be useful to complemen the discussion with a graphic beginning with the model of alternativ technology. Figure 7.1 shows the case of an alternative technology whe demand (Da) is low enough as to have excess of installed capacity. P_R and q denote the tariff in terms of the numeraire and the production level in th regulated sector, respectively. MC represents the marginal cost of the existin technology (the increasing segment) and an alternative technology (th constant marginal cost section of the curve), and $1/\mu$ stands for th benchmark regulated price.

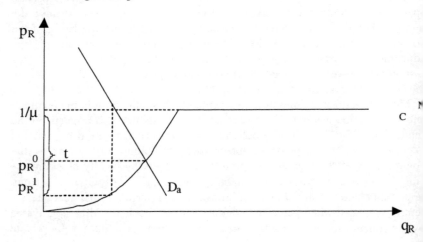

Figure 7.1   Non-operative price cap

Given D_a, p_R should fall to p_R^0. However, a tax t is imposed (mark-up) t compensate owners of capital so that $p_R^1(1+t) = p_R^* = 1/\mu$.

'Tax' revenue is transferred from customers to shareholders of th regulated firm. This t could be negative as it is shown in Figure 7.2, that it i a subsidy s. If an alternative technology does not exist, the firm will continu operating if the additional units (A) marginal costs are covered (triangle S) Since the obligation of service was established in the original contrac between the regulators and shareholders, we assume that the shareholder cover the excess of costs – implicitly in the form of a subsidy to the operativ management of the firm. This internal subsidy *s* is depicted in the figure below; in this case *s* is computed so that net price to customers equals the price cap settled at level p_R.

In summary, Figure 7.2 shows the case of an internal subsidy, funded by a tax on the shareholders of the regulated firm that managers take as an incentive for production. We will see later that when shareholders are located abroad, this subsidy will be accompanied by an inflow of capital that reduces the need for trade surplus.

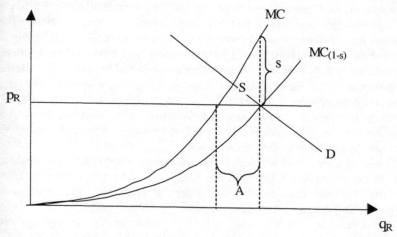

Figure 7.2   Subsidy and alternative technology

So far, we have discussed the MUM approach. Figure 7.2 also illustrates a case where the firm has the alternative of importing international capital; this is the case of AIS. The incremental cost of the new technology is given by w^*A/μ, where w^* is the foreign factor reward and μ its average productivity; now the firm will compare this cost with S, to choose the method for servicing the market. Less domestic resources will be needed and marginal costs will not rise for the firm. However, this will have consequences on the current account; if the firm covers the deficit with the existing technology there will be an inflow of capital (though temporary); instead, if the alternative technology is employed, the additional reward of foreign factors will impose a burden upon the economy.

3. EFFICIENCY, WELFARE GAINS AND INCOME DISTRIBUTION – A MODEL FOR ARGENTINA[2]

In 1989, Argentina initiated a process of privatisation of its infrastructur
services that was at the forefront of the international experience. The breadt
of the sectoral changes and their quick implementation did not initially reflec
a dramatic concern for efficiency in the delivery of basic public services
They were driven instead by the need to alleviate the fiscal burden impose
by public utilities and the need to get the private sector involved in financin
the increasingly pressing expansion requirements of these sectors. Th
concern for efficiency was a byproduct of the need to regulate the sector t
avoid abuse by the private providers of activities with monopolistic features
But efficiency improvements are now becoming one of the expected benefit
of the changes as more is known about the regulatory options availabl
throughout the country.

When the model was constructed, Argentina's reforms were not ye
concluded as many provincial water and electricity distribution companie
were still in the hands of the public sector.

The main purpose of this section is to summarise the results we obtaine
in a previous papers; the intention of which was to assess both the efficiency
and distributional impacts of privatisation in electricity, gas, water an
sanitation, and telecommunications services.[3]

The electricity sector was vertically disintegrated in generation
transmission and distribution. Generation was open to competition, whil
transmission and distribution were concessioned and put under regulatory
scrutiny. The regulatory mechanism adopted was essentially an RPI-x
productivity gains x were meant to be adjusted after five years: gas is th
major input for the privatised companies and sales were meant to be
concluded at an unregulated price. However, since the other activities were
controlled by local monopolies, as in electricity, a good regulation of tarif
and quality was needed and was introduced with the reform. The regulatory
mechanism was also an RPI-x with productivity gains adjusted after five
years. The largest and the best documented was the privatisation tha
transferred the responsibility for water and sanitation service in the Buenos
Aires Metropolitan Area to Aguas Argentina in May 1993. Competition wa
achieved through a bidding process and the resulting concession contract ha
become the main regulatory instrument available to the regulators. I
stipulates service obligation, investment requirements and quality standards
monitored by the national sector regulator. The tariff adjustments are based
on a cost plus rule. The transfer of the telecoms company to private operators
was concluded in November 1990. In fact it was the first infrastructure
service concessioned. The service is now provided by two companies,
regionally separated. Their tariffs are regulated and service and quality

obligations detailed in their concession contracts. The regulatory mechanism is essentially an RPI-x where the productivity gains x will be adjusted after five years. Contracts are under discussion at present due to the 2001 crisis.

Basic structure of the model

The social accounting matrix (SAM) of the model was constructed in 1993.[4] It was consistent with national accounts for 1993, which is also the first year in which all national utilities were formally managed by private operators. Its basic structure is shown in Table 7.1. The figures in parenthesis provide the value (in billion US$) at current prices. As can be seen, spending has to equate to revenue for each aggregate account. The model identifies 21 domestic production sectors, 10 for goods and 11 for services. In addition to the usual activities under services, the SAM identifies electricity generation, electricity distribution, gas, water and communications as separate sectors. Three factors of production are accounted for: labour, physical capital and financial capital. Labour and financial capital are mobile across sectors while physical capital is sector specific. Domestic consumer groups are divided into five income classes and there is only one foreign consumer and one foreign producer. The small open economy assumption is relied on, implying that Argentina is a price taker in the international markets.[5]

The base year was 1993, the first year in which private operators were in charge in each one of the sectors previously under national government management. It was also the first year for which detailed data were available for private operators in all sectors through their annual report and balances. It is important to remember that these indicators do not measure the changes that occurred with the change in ownership but rather the changes that occurred in a two year period under private sector management. Table 7.2 shows the changes in labour productivity observed just before the private operators actually took over.

The largest increases in relative terms occurred in the first year of operation of each firm. None of the available quality indicators can easily be modelled so only simulations on the yields from gains in this area for three sectors could be completed, excluding water. Finally, average tariffs continued to fall in electricity and gas. After a reduction in tariff at the time of the privatisation in water, the average tariff had begun to increase even when the legal tariff was still below what it was under public management. Our best estimates of some of these indicators are shown in Table 7.3.

We considered the total operational gains achieved in each utilities' sub-sector to be the sum of the effects of four specific changes:

1. *Efficiency*: changes in input per unit of output modelled as a reduction in input coefficient. Efficiency gains are taken as reductions in the quantity

of input used by the privatised sector to obtain one unit of output (i.e. a a cut in the same proportion of the input-output coefficients of the column corresponding to the specific sector); the gains ar unincorporated and generate an increase in capacity of the economy t generate a surplus.

2. *Productivity*: changes in labour productivity modelled as a reduction i the relevant coefficient of labour intensiveness. Productivity gains ar computed as efficiency gains in work so that less units of labour ar needed to obtain a given level of service.

3. *Quality*: computed as a reduction in the coefficient of the quantity of th privatised inputs needed to produce one unit of output in the othe sectors.

4. *Tariffs*: modelled as the actual utilities price changes observed.

There are two benchmarks for the closure rules:

1. *Flexible price*: under this closure rule, all domestic prices – includin those under regulation – adjust to clear the markets, except salarie which are fixed in nominal terms; recall that Argentina was under Currency Board and the peso was pegged to the dollar in a one-to-on relation. Prices of tradeable goods are fixed in foreign currency sinc Argentina was assumed to be a price taker in international markets.

2. *Fixed price*: under this rule, the prices of privatised services are give in dollar terms, but the rule for the determination of tradeable an non-tradeable prices and the rules for the labour market are no altered.

To solve the model we used the AIS method, described above. The strateg seemed correct given that at the time Argentina was open to internationa trade and under a regime of currency board. However, effects on trad balance accounts were expected, those observed for the model were tiny Total effects can be separated into two main types: macroeconomic an income distributional. Table 7.4 presents a summary of a general equilibriun calculation of the levels and distribution of gains across income classes fron the efficiency and quality improvements due to the reform and those tha could be achieved from effective regulation. To give some perspective on th relative importance of the gains achieved, these gains are also expressed i terms of the annual expenditures of each income class on utilities in 1993.

his was the key table of the paper and it showed that:

- Operational gains clearly benefit strongly all income groups: on average these gains represent the equivalent of 41 per cent of the amount that households tend to spend on utilities services even when the regulator allows the new owner of the sector to keep as much as possible of these gains as a quasi-rent; these gains also represent about US$2.3 billion or 0.9 per cent of Argentina's GDP.
- The gains from effective regulation add up to 16 per cent on average when the regulator is as effective as it should be and the quasi-rents generated by improvements in efficiency, productivity, quality and tariffs are distributed throughout the economy; these gains also represent a gain of almost US$1 billion or 0.35 per cent of GDP which can be seen as an approximation of the shadow price of effective regulation; it also shows why private operators have a very strong incentive to contest any decision by regulators that forces them to share the quasi-rent with the rest of the economy.
- The direct gains are relatively significantly increased for the higher income classes (59 per cent as compared to 29 per cent for the poorest) and this is explained by the fact that when regulation is not effective, the gains from privatisation are turned into a quasi-rent captured by the richest who are the largest domestic owners of capital in the infrastructure services; part of these gains are also captured by foreign consumers and by the government since they own a large share of the 'privatised' assets.
- The indirect gains through effective regulation, in contrast, tend to favour the poorest income classes relatively more even if it is clear that all tend to gain from efficient regulation, even the richest.

Table 7.1 *Argentina: summary SAM and economic features of the model for 1993 (in billion US$; 1993 GDP: US$256.329 billion)*

		Expenditures			
		Domestic prod. sectors	Private consumption	Government consumption	Investment	External sector
Revenues	Domestic production sectors (21 sectors, including separated infrastructure services)	Domestic Purchases: *CES value added for private firms *Leontief value added for privatised firms *non-tradeable prices are market clearing for given levels of rationing in factor markets *combination with other goods and services in fixed proportions (132.370)	Spending on domestic goods: * Cobb-Douglas utility in goods * fixed proportion with goods for retail trade * separate quantity, price and quality for each privatised service * rationing possible (175.082)	Spending on goods and services: * Cobb-Douglas social welfare function in purchases of goods and service, bonds, retirees services and investment; * purchases of goods and services are in fixed proportions (6.085)	Final demand for investment goods (42.816)	Exports: * the foreign consumer has a Cobb-Douglas utility in exports and imports * he can issue bonds to pay for net imports *Argentina is a price taker in exports and imports * whatever Argentina can't consume is sold abroad at given price (16.237)
	External Sector	Imports fixed proportion with value added (8.182) Trade tax revenue (1.282)	Spending on imports: * imperfect substitution with domestic substitutes (8.727) Trade tax revenue (1.133)		Imports of capital goods: * fixed proportion with value added (4.150)	

Government	Direct taxes paid by firms (22.461)	Direct taxes paid by households (4.519)		
	Indirect taxes (25.283)			
Families (5 income classes)	Labour income net of taxes: * initial unemployment (60.786)		Salaries and Public Sector Transfers (43645)	
	Capital income net of taxes: * can be domestic or foreign (122.266)			
Investment		Private savings (37.196)	Public savings (4.948)	Foreign savings (4.822)

Source: Chisari, Estache and Romero (1999).

Table 7.2   Argentina: public services – changes in performance between 1993 and 1995

	Electricity generation	Electricity distribution	Gas distribution	Water distribution	Telecoms
First year of private operation	1992	1992	1992	1993	1990
Efficiency gains (measured as reduction in intermediate inputs purchases as a share of total sales value)	19.51%	6.26%	8.84%	4.86%	11.28%
Labour productivity gains (measured as GWh/staff for electricity, 000m3/staff for gas, population served/staff for water, lines in service/staff for phones)	23.1%	17.59%	4.79%	-27.58%	21.25%
Increases in investment (as in concession contracts for gas and actual investments for the other sectors)	8.65%	n.a.	4.56%	75.97%	28.1%

Improvements in quality
(measured as reductions in losses (net of consumption by transmission)/ production for electricity and gas, water unaccounted for/production for water, lines in repair/lines in service for phones)

n.a.	10%	27.8%	6.12%	4.56%

Changes in legal average tariffs
(defined as legal tariffs defalcted by retail price index)

n.a.	-9.5%	-0.5%	5.5%	-4.9%

Notes:
The table reflects the changes achieved under private management of the services. Indeed, 1993 data reflects the first year in which all sectors had benefited from some initial adjustment by the private operator. 1995 is the last year for which data is available at the time of writing.

Source: Chisari, Estache and Romero (1999).

Table 7.3   Argentina: changes in performance at the time of privatisation

	Electricity generation	Electricity distribution	Gas distribution	Water distribution	Telecoms
Efficiency gains (measured as reduction in intermediate inputs purchases as % of total sales value)	43.4%	21.3%	1.3%	n.a.	n.a.
Labour productivity gains (measured as GWh/staff for electricity, 000m3/staff for gas, population served/staff for water, lines in service/staff for phones)	95.1%	80.3%	35.6%	75.2%	37.8%
Changes in real average tariffs (defined as total sales value by a physical indicator of production)	n.a.	4%	n.a.	-1.92%	n.a.

Source: Chisari, Estache and Romero (1999).

Table 7.4   Argentina: gains from private operation of public utilities

Income class	Savings from operational gains (A) (in millions of 1993 US$)	Savings from effective regulation (B) (in millions of 1993 US$)	(A)/income class expenditure on utilities	(B)/income class expenditure on utilities
1 (poorest)	197	138	29%	20%
2	259	142	31%	17%
3	373	121	37%	12%
4	403	214	32%	17%
5 (richest)	1047	302	59%	17%
Total	2279	915	41%	16%

Notes:
These figures represent annual gains. (A) is the equivalent variation computed in terms of the $ revenue of each income class. It is calculated by applying the total gains in the fixed price simulation to the income in the base year. (B) is computed by applying the differences in gains between the fixed price and the flexible price simulations. In net present value and over a period of 10 years, the (A) gains represent a total varying between US$8.2 billion and US$14.4 billion with discount rates varying between 12 per cent and 18 per cent and amortisation rates between 0 per cent and 10 per cent. The gains from efficient regulation under similar assumptions vary between US$3.3 billion and US$5.8.

Source: Chisari, Estache and Romero (1999).

All sectors did not contribute equally to these changes. Table 7.5 summarises an estimate of the relative contribution of each sector to initial changes and to the general equilibrium effects of the reforms. It demonstrates that the main initial shock came from electricity distribution (33 per cent) while water had the smallest initial impact (0.2 per cent). The largest general equilibrium gains came from gas which is a key input not only for various industries but also for heating and cooking in many of the poorest households. Note also that the gains from reform in electricity only increased modestly after the initial shock. This is because all the gains were achieved through the creation of a competitive market that remains competitive in the longer runs and that only benefits from marginal improvements from privatisation in some of its own infrastructure inputs. Note finally that the general equilibrium gains in the water sector are much larger than the initial shock, reflecting the employment increases needed to ensure the expansion of the network and from increased access by the poor to the service.

Table 7.5   Argentina: relative sectoral contribution to changes (as a percentage of total changes)

	Participation in initial change	Participation in general equilibrium welfare gains	
		Fixed price	Flexible price
Electricity generation	13.2	14.4	15.8
Electricity distribution	33.0	22.3	19.5
Gas	26.0	44.9	41.4
Water	0.2	5.5	2.4
Telecoms	27.0	12.9	20.9

Notes:
The contribution to changes is calculated with respect to changes in the value added and is computed as a percentage of the total value in US$. The general equilibrium effects are based on the sum of the sector specific simulations for all changes.

Source: Own calculation.

The following section provides details as to how these estimates were calculated and how these conclusions were reached.

4. REGULATORY REGIMES AND INCOME DISTRIBUTION

There are many ways of looking at the distributional implications of the reforms. One is to compare factor incomes. The standard way is to compute the Gini coefficient. A more revealing indicator however is to compute the impact on the income level of families in terms of some form of welfare indicator. In this chapter, it is computed in terms of equivalent variation adapted to compute the effect of changes in prices as well as in quality.

In general terms, to identify the sources in the welfare changes for each income class, the following facts need to be recognised: (i) the relative importance of the cost of services provided by privatised sectors in the household budget; and (ii) the distribution of factor ownership across income classes.

As discussed in more detail below, the effects of technological improvements and efficiency gains have substantial impact on the interpersonal distribution of income through the effects of changes in the unemployment rate and through government transfers.

The poorest tend to depend much more than the richest on the state of the labour market and this is turn is directly and indirectly influenced by the privatisation of utilities. The impact of privatisation is indeed not only through labour productivity gains in utilities and through reduction in the costs of sectors using utilities services as an input, but also through reductions in input requirements of the production of utilities services. For instance, the privatised utilities bought intermediate inputs from the manufacturing sectors for an equivalent of 23 per cent of their value added, services for 19 per cent and primary inputs for 12 per cent. The interaction between utilities is quite significant as well: the water sector is the largest client of the electricity sector for instance.

Better results of privatised companies reduce the need for subsidies and increase revenue due to taxes on profits. In its turn, this higher revenue is used to increase transfers to income brackets, and the poor receive indirect benefits from those sources.

Table 7.6 shows that the relative importance of the utilities services was higher for the poorest income classes in the subsectors of gas and electricity. For water the opposite is true, and telecom services were relatively more important to the middle class than to any other class.

Table 7.6   Argentina: composition of household expenditures per income class (as a percentage of total expenditures)

	Income classes				
	1 (poorest)	2	3	4	5 (richest)
Agricultural goods	6.06	4.22	3.33	2.73	1.76
Industrial goods	45.74	42.69	40.66	38.64	34.05
Non-utilities services	43.73	49.45	42.78	55.65	61.46
Utilities (total)	4.47	3.65	3.23	2.98	2.72
Electricity	2.19	1.51	1.20	0.99	0.69
Gas	1.05	0.73	0.58	0.48	0.33
Water	0.33	0.34	0.36	0.41	0.66
Telecoms	0.90	1.07	1.10	1.09	1.04

Source: See Data Appendix available upon request from the authors.

Table 7.7 explains why the richest income class stands to gain the most from a poor distribution of the quasi-rents generated by the privatisations:

they are the largest owners of capital in the economy. In fact about 90 per cent of total capital was concentrated in the two highest income groups.

Table 7.8 shows that a large share of the returns and rents generated in infrastructure sectors would go abroad since 50 per cent of the ownership was foreign in electricity generation, gas and telecommunications. The public sector does not necessarily have a strong incentive to have an effective regulation of water and electricity distribution since it was a major owner of sector specific capital in these activities and, in the short run, it may stand to gain a large share of the quasi-rents generated in these sectors. Beyond that, taxes on profits still ensured an important share in their economic results.

Table 7.9 shows that the overall distribution of income improves as a result of the reform (negative sign of the Gini coefficient). The overall improvement is however six times larger when the regulators are effective and prices are 'walrasian', i.e. endogenously determined. The last two columns also show that the largest gains are for the poorest as indicated by the highest equivalent variation. But once more the distribution of gains is somewhat different when the regulators are not effective.

The poorest stand to gain the most from improvements in gas and electricity (major inputs in their consumption basket). They also stand to gain relatively more from improvements in water, although their main source of gain (access) is not modelled here. Finally the middle income class stands to gain the most from improvements in telecommunications, but only if the regulator is effective. Otherwise they end up paying a huge rent to the private operators of the services.

The calculation of the equivalent variation for each income group reveals that in general only improvements in firm efficiency and service quality tend to benefit every consumer group. In the other cases, the four poorest quintiles are worse off. The only exception is when bad regulators allow the utilities to benefit from the rent generated in the sector. This can be seen easily in the EV of the richest quintile: it is the only income group improving its welfare through changes in any of the indicators. In relative terms, the poorest tend to gain the most from efficiency and quality improvements and lose the most from improvements in labour productivity even if average labour income is higher. Finally, a good regulator leaves all income classes better off than a bad regulator.

Table 7.7   *Argentina: distribution of factor income per income classes,*
1993

	Composition (as % of total class income)			Shares (as % of total factor income)			
	Labour	Physical capital	Financial capital	Transfers	Labour	Capital	Total income
1 (poorest)	71.72	19.42	0.40	8.46	11.22	3.76	7.32
2	64.03	26.65	0.41	8.90	14.52	7.64	11.02
3	64.25	26.97	0.95	7.84	21.41	10.73	15.42
4	62.84	29.19	1.92	6.04	27.85	16.34	22.15
5 (richest)	28.86	61.00	5.73	4.41	25.00	61.51	44.07

Source: Chisari, Estache and Romero (1999).

Table 7.8   *Argentina: distribution of ownership of the infrastructure*
sectors, 1995

	Electricity generation	Electricity distribution	Gas	Water	Telecoms
Public sector	32.36	76.04	17.57	34.75	30.00
Foreign	49.66	15.29	50.51	17.36	51.42
Domestic	17.98	8.67	31.92	47.89	18.58

Source: See Data Appendix available upon request from the authors.

Table 7.9 Argentina: simulation results – decomposition of sector specific distributional effects

	Electricity distribution		Gas		Water		Telecoms		Total	
	p fixed	p flex	p fixed	p flex	p fixed	p flex	p fixed	p flex	p fixed	p flex
Gini	0.01	0	-0.05	-0.22	-0.06	-0.06	-0.06	0.07	-0.06	-0.24
EV for Income group 1 (poorest)	0.29	0.41	0.54	1	0.13	0.09	0.08	0.21	1.19	1.99
EV for Income group 5 (richest)	0.25	0.32	0.43	0.45	0.00	-0.01	0.19	0.35	1.02	1.30

Notes:
Gini and average factor income are expressed as percentage change over base year (1993). EV (equivalent variations) in terms of total income of the bracket.

Table 7.10 *Argentina: effects of changes of performance indicators on the distribution of income*

	Efficiency		Labour productivity		Quality	
	p fixed	*p flex*	*p fixed*	*p flex*	*p fixed*	*p flex*
Gini coefficient	better	much better	much worse	worse	better	much better
EV for Income Group 1 (poorest) to Income Group 4	better	much better	much worse	worse	better	much better
EV for Income Group 5 (richest)	better	much better	better	much better	better	much better
Average labour income	worse	better	better	much better	better	much better
Average capital income	better	much better	better	much better	better	much better

Source: Chisari, Estache and Romero (1999).

5.   MACROECONOMIC SHOCKS AND MICROECONOMIC REFORMS

After the reform was already in place, at the end of 1994 and early 1995, the so called 'Tequila effect' shocked the economy. Unemployment increased from 9.3 per cent in 1993 to over 18 per cent in 1995.

Since the utilities sectors often require high investments with long amortisation periods, tariffs tend to be very sensitive to changes in the cost of capital. Table 7.11 summarises the impact of a 2 per cent increase in international interest rates on the economy of Argentina and on the users of utilities services, after the implementation of the utilities reform and after all the efficiency gains were achieved.

The results remain consistent: with a better regulator, there was a definite advantage for Argentina as a whole. Negative effects from an interest rate shock extend to all income groups, particularly the middle class. But the consequences on the poorest sectors of the population can be alleviated with effective regulation. The main risk for the poorest and the middle-income classes comes from the strong adverse impact on investment and subsequently on employment. The upsurge in Argentina's unemployment rates in the 1990s is, to a large extent, a possible reflection of the 'tequila' and 'vodka' shocks compounded by the weakness of the internal financial market. From a distributional viewpoint, the adjusted Gini shows that under bad regulation income distribution worsens, but it still improves under good regulation.

Table 7.11   Argentina: simulation results – effects of a 2 per cent interest increase in the post-reform period

	Effects under:	
Indicators	Bad regulation	Good regulation
GDP	0.2	0.6
Industrial Product	-0.5	0.9
Investments/GDP	-1.5	-2.1
Rate of unemployment (absolute value)	13.6	11.1
EV for Income Group 1 (poorest)	-1.2	0.9
EV for Income Group 2	-1.5	0.0
EV for Income Group 3	-1.7	-0.7
EV for Income Group 4	-2.0	-0.7
EV for Income Group 5 (richest)	-1.3	-0.3
IGI	0.1	-0.3
IGIN	-0.5	0.2
Taxes/GDP	1.0	0.0
EV for government	4.9	1.1

Source: Own calculation. Changes in percentage with respect to base year.

The general equilibrium approach adopted here has allowed to us to isolate the effects of the utilities reform on the public and private sector respectively and to examine the distributional consequences of these effects. The main conclusions are that these reforms are good for the income levels of the country, that reforms have improved the fiscal situation of Argentina and have promoted, when capital markets have been stable, the competitiveness of the country. Reforms have led to greater efficiency and equity, but have created less fiscal revenue under a good regulatory regime than in a bad regime.

It is also clear that a better understanding of the full fiscal effects of reform is crucial to an assessment of its long-term sustainability. Since the public sector tends to gain in many ways from reform, reversibility on purely fiscal grounds is unlikely. More problematic is the weak incentive for governments worried about finances to adopt good regulation because stronger rents in regulated sectors would translate into significant additional revenue. Under good regulation, revenue gains in current net value are equivalent about 0.28 per cent of GDP compared to 1.23 per cent under bad regulation. The difference is significant, but still insufficient to compensate for the welfare loss imposed on consumers by bad regulation.

From a strictly distributional viewpoint, the conclusion emerging from the examination of the achievements of the utilities reform is comforting. The poorest families can benefit in the magnitude of about 50 per cent of their utilities bill. Globally, the EV for households is 54 per cent of their expenditures on utilities. The poorest groups would tend to benefit the most from improvements both in access and productivity.

Better results of privatised companies reduce the need for subsidies and increase revenue due to taxes on profits. In turn, this higher revenue is used to increase transfers to income brackets and the poor receive indirect benefits from those sources.

5. MICROECONOMIC REFORMS AND MACROECONOMIC PERFORMANCE: REGULATION AND TRADE RESULTS

We will now focus our attention on two questions, qualitative and quantitative respectively:

1. Is it possible that the regulatory mechanism, mainly the rule for adjusting tariffs, biases trade balance and the exchange rate?
2. If so, how important can biases be for a typical developing economy such as Argentina's?

There are two aspects that are relevant for addressing these questions: the relative weight of price flexibility with respect to domestic or foreign ownership on trade performance, and the comparative advantage of using more capital or covering the excess of marginal cost over tariff with the internal resources of the firm.

As mentioned in the introduction, regulatory issues are usually treated in partial equilibrium frameworks that ignore many of the indirect interactions of the regulated sectors with the rest of the economy; a key, yet underestimated, policy issue in the sector is the effect that the specific choice of the regulatory regime imposed on the private infrastructure operators has on the trade balance.[6] It seems indeed rational to expect that the recognition of the presence of a third party such as the rest of the world, exchanging goods and (capital) services with the regulated party, is likely to influence the optimal contract between the regulator and the regulated operator.[7]

While there are a few studies of the impact that the choice of the regulatory regime has on variables such as efficiency, equity or the fiscal balance, there are no studies of the interactions between the choice of the regulatory regime and the trade performance of a country.[8]

The main purpose of this section is to help close that gap by analysing the experience of Argentina, through simulations of a general equilibrium model built to assess the impact of regulatory regimes on the trade balance.[9]

The model needs to reflect the fact that traditional trade theory guides how we should expect factor rewards to respond to commodity price changes under given factor endowments and how sector outputs vary with factor endowments changes under constant factor prices. The model also needs to reflect the fact that factor mobility assumptions should influence price changes. Since this factor mobility is highly specific to the regulated industries, we need to model this specificity explicitly and hence we believe that a Ricardo-Viner framework provides a useful analytical framework to simulate policy changes. Our main concern is that comparative static effects can easily become undetermined when accounting for too many factors under the standard assumptions of the model. In particular, since we need to model the regulatory rule followed to determine prices in the infrastructure sectors, the net effect cannot be determined qualitatively directly. We thus suggest it should be assessed by adding up numerical (non-linear) impacts.

Let us focus in a simplified case, for which each sector uses two different categories of factors: one mobile, labour, and one non mobile, specific capital. There are four domestic sectors of production (activities): $I=\{1,2,N,R\}$, two of them are tradable sectors, $T=\{1,2\}$, and the rest are producers of goods and services that are not tradable; sector N produces services and sector R represents sectors under regulation.

In this version of the model, several sectors are included in each of the subsets. For example, R includes electricity, gas, telecommunication and transport; therefore the size of model is increased consistently to take into account the effects of changes in their relative prices.

We will focus our attention on the two questions already mentioned.

Table 7.12 presents the Social Accounting Matrix of an economy that replicates the main features of the Argentine economy as of 1997.[10] We have left aside financial transactions, as well as government and imperfections, such as unemployment. It presents the Social Accounting Matrix of the economy of our basic example.

Table 7.12   A SAM based on Argentina, 1997

	S1	S2	SN	SR	HH	RW
C1	13.2	-8.9	-0.2	-0.1	-1.2	-2.9
C2	-2.2	50.1	-8.0	-2.2	-28.6	-9.2
CN	-1.2	-9.0	82.8	-3.1	-69.5	
CR	-0.5	-4.5	-4.1	17.8	-8.7	
L	-2.3	-11.0	-31.2	-5.0	49.5	
K1	-7.1				7.1	
K2		-16.7			16.7	
KN			-39.3		39.3	
KR				-7.4	3.7	3.7
M1					-0.3	0.3
M2					-8.1	8.1

Source: Own calculation.

Columns represent agents and rows correspond to markets for goods or services. S1 and S2 are tradable sectors, SN stands for the non-tradable producer, while SR is our aggregate regulated industry. HH represents domestic households, and RW indicates the Rest of the World 'agent'. A positive entry represents a sale and a negative one corresponds to a purchase or payment of service; budget constraints oblige to balance when adding up the elements in a column. Balance must also be fulfilled when adding up elements in a row, in this case because a row represents a market and we are assuming that there is equilibrium in the benchmark. C1, C2, CN, and CR correspond to goods or services produced by tradable sectors, non-tradable and regulated industries, respectively. M1 and M2 are imports and L and K_i

stand for factors of production.

What the matrix does, after that purification, is to show the relative intensity in the use of factors, the burden given by the dividends to be paid abroad and the relative weight of the regulated sector in total GDP.

Regulated sectors represented about 12 per cent of total GDP and total dividends paid abroad were estimated as 3.7 per cent of GDP. We can see that Industry, Sector 2, was the heavier user of regulated sector products and services, followed by non-tradeable sectors. Ownership of regulated firms was not concentrated in foreign agents as we assumed in the example; in fact, the profit tax (35 per cent) itself explains why such assumption would not be tenable.

Table 7.13 presents the results of assuming a 25 per cent reduction in coefficient $a_{R,I}$, which is the quantity of regulated services needed to produce one unit of I, and which represents an improvement of quality of services in infrastructure.

Let us consider first the results of assuming that the production sectors are receiving the service or good with a better quality. Alternatively, this change could be interpreted as technological progress that reduces the regulated good-intensity of the economy. Notice that in any case, the regulated sector is losing relative efficiency compared to the rest of the economy and its relative rate of profit will fall, as well as the demand for the industry; that is the reason why it would be necessary to provide compensating action. Moreover, there will be increases in nominal wages due to scale effects in manufactures. Domestic welfare[11] improves anyhow, because the economy has a windfall gain in productivity. Column PL represents a conceptual exercise for a pure walrasian model without regulation. Prices are freely determined within the economic process and the results help us to understand what is going on in an economy under regulation. Columns PC and RR give the outcomes under price-cap and rate-of-return regulation, respectively.

A very interesting result is that domestic total welfare is not increased the most under PC, but under RR. The reason for this is that there is an efficiency gain obtained by the firm, but it is not allowed to keep it as part of its rate of return and it is fully transferred to domestic households and producers in the form of a price reduction. There is a pass-through from foreign agents to domestic agents.[12]

Exports performance exhibits dramatic differences: under PC exports must grow more than under RR, due to the reduction in the outflow of dividends. Long-run incentives to exports seem to be stronger under RR, since PN/PT is lower under RR than under PC.

We can advance the following conjecture (obtained from an example – though general, an example still) as a corollary of this discussion. PC gives incentives to improve efficiency; once obtained, the macroeconomic performance of the economy (particularly regarding the trade balance) could be satisfactory (because of the increase of exports). But though PC could give the impression of fostering relatively exports more than RR, that could simply be the result of a passive adjustment to movements in the capital account.

Table 7.13   *Reduction (25 per cent) in the economy requirements of the regulated good*

	PL	PC	RR
Domestic welfare	3.0	2.2	2.5
Wage rate	4.1	1.6	2.3
r_R [c]	-17.0	5.9	0.0
P_R [b]	-10.0	0.0	-2.7
Exchange rate [a]	0.7	1.4	1.2
Exports	-2.1	4.3	2.7
X / GDP (10%)	9.6	10.2	10.0
GDP	2.3	2.2	2.3

Notes:
Changes in percentage levels, except for X/GDP (benchmark in brackets). PL: walrasian model, PC: model with price-cap regulation, RR: model with rate-of-return regulation.
[a] Exchange rate: weighted average price ratio between non-tradables and tradables (PN/PT).
[b] P_R :price of the regulated service.
[c] r_R :total rate of return of the regulated service.

Source: Own calculation.

This raises the issue of whether the economy will be able to open new trade opportunities to cover the capital account deficit. In fact, relative prices favour exports more under RR and PL than under PC (PN/PT grow less and tradable sectors find domestic costs lower).

In this case, when productivity of the economy is improving but the regulated firm is left behind, the regulated price should fall; however there are monopolistic rents to protect and, therefore, we compute an increase in the mark-up (1+t), so that demand price remains at its initial level.

The efficiency gains in the regulated sector can be captured through reductions of a_{LR}, the coefficient that represents inputs requirements from the rest of the economy, or by reductions in labour requirements per unit of output. Table 7.14 shows the results of assuming a 25 per cent reduction of $a_{l,R}$

This is an internal gain of the regulated firm[13], normally expected as the result of a high-powered regulatory mechanism (price cap).

Exports do not augment in the same proportion under RR than under PC because dividends are smaller and the domestic propensity to import is less than one. PC is more demanding of a domestic effort to repay the initial investment in the privatised sectors; in fact, the required increments under PC are very significant for Argentina: around 9 per cent. This puts high pressure on the economy, not used to easily accessing international markets. The necessary increments under any of the rate-of-return adjustment mechanisms are much more modest, between 1 and 2 per cent.

Table 7.14   Argentina: simulation results – efficiency gains (25 per cent) within the regulated industry

	PL	PC	RR
Domestic welfare	1.7	0.9	1.9
Wage rate	1.6	-1.2	2.1
r_R c	4.4	29.3	0.0
P_R b	-9.4	0.0	-11.0
Exchange rate a	-1.1	-0.7	-1.1
Exports	2.4	9.3	1.2
X / GDP (10%)	10.1	10.7	10.0
GDP	1.8	1.8	1.7

Notes:
Changes in percentage levels, except for X/GDP (benchmark in brackets). PL: walrasian model, PC: model with price cap regulation, RR: model with rate-of-return regulation.
a Exchange rate: weighted average price ratio between non-tradables and tradables (PN/PT).
b P_R :price of the regulated service.
a r_R :total rate of return of the regulated service.

Source: Own calculation.

Though it is true that PC gives incentives for efficiency, from the point of view of welfare improvement and exports effort, the domestic society could have reasons to adopt a low-powered incentive scheme when the efficiency gains are expected within the privatised sector.

PC will give the highest improvement for domestic welfare, because there is an increase in domestic costs, especially the wage rate, and the increment of costs cannot be passed to customers; instead they are absorbed by shareholders reducing the flow of dividends abroad or increasing the inflow of 'subsidies' to the firm by their owners.

Accordingly, PL maximises the domestic welfare change when the economy is experiencing an improvement in efficiency (Table 7.14), but that is not true when the regulated sector is gaining efficiency (Table 7.15). In fact, in the second case, the RR regime (rate of return fixed in foreign currency) increases welfare more than PL because the excessive profits are transferred to domestic customers via a reduction of price.[14] Remember that we are quoting domestic welfare in the tables, and the proposition that welfare improves the most under flexible prices would be shown true if we added up domestic and foreign welfare.

7. PUBLIC SECTOR REFORM: SIMULATIONS FOR URUGUAY

This section presents the results of a Computable General Equilibrium model applied to Uruguay. The model simulations show that it is possible to increase welfare and savings for Uruguay by making infrastructure services more efficient; still higher gains of welfare are observed when those gains are transferred to prices. These additional gains duplicate the original ones.

The analysis addresses a question of special concern: how would public revenue and unemployment perform under such a reform? The exercises show that public sector finances are not necessarily jeopardised by a reform aimed at increasing efficiency and transferring those gains to prices. Additional revenue from increased activity levels (and corporate tax) compensates in excess the lost revenue due to high tariffs. This is an important result for Uruguay, since public sector companies contribute in a significant proportion to total government revenue; this also implies that social programmes undertaken by the government would not be in danger.

Additionally, the simulations show that, even in the short run, the rate of unemployment is reduced following a reform. Though part of the efficiency gains include reductions in labour requirements of state owned enterprises, efficiency gains allow increases in scale of operation of the economy that absorb the unemployed. Sensitivity exercises indicate that the short-run simulations underestimate the long-run gains. These illustrations do not encompass all the possible effects.

The influence of infrastructure provision could be exerted in more indirect ways influencing factor abundance. The availability of good communications, energy and sanitary services may increase the real wage and general wellbeing; this may help to retain human capital in the economy (an important issue for Uruguay), reducing wage costs for the firms. It is well known nowadays that one of the basic sources of growth is human capital availability.

The pattern of growth certainly determines different required infrastructure needs depending on, for example, comparative advantages in the country.

The data source for the CGE model is based on a Social Accounting Matrix (SAM) for Uruguay using information from 1997. Table 7.15 presents a schematic SAM summing up the main characteristics. In the SAM, the relations between sectors of production are taken from the Input-Output matrix. This matrix constitutes the basic transmission mechanism of the changes in public utilities. Therefore it is important to study in detail the use of public utilities services as productive inputs.

The analysis is based on our standard short-run CGE model. The model includes 22 sectors[15] that produce goods and services, two domestic aggregated consumers (Households and Government) and an aggregated consumer in the rest of the world. The economy is assumed to be small and open to trade with the rest of the world. National Accounts were adjusted to eliminate the problem of debt services, which tend to distort final effects. So, in this version, the trade account is balanced.

There are two factors: Capital is assumed to be sector specific, but Labour is mobile; further gains will be expected if capital is assumed to move responding to economic incentives (as we will see below) and if investments are included. It has been assumed that total labour supply is inelastic and constant real wages, so that a 16 per cent unemployment rate exists for the initial calibration. SOEs are assumed to contribute to government with net revenue of 2.73 per cent of GDP at market prices. There are four sectors of public utilities (electricity, water, transportation and telecommunications) and they represent about 13 per cent of GDP.

The first simulation is performed assuming efficiency gains of 10 per cent and 15 per cent in input requirements and labour productivity respectively in all the four public utilities sectors (these were taken from WB 2003 report). The second simulation compares the results when it is assumed that efficiency gains are obtained but they are not passed to tariffs, so that prices of public services are fixed at their initial nominal levels.

Table 7.16 presents the macroeconomic results of simulations 1 and 2. In simulation 1, Real GDP is increased by 1.82 per cent and welfare gain for households – measured by the Equivalent Variation – is equivalent to 1.5 per cent of GDP (about 1.8 per cent of household income). The government also gains a more modest percentage of GDP. Real GDP growth is considerably smaller in Simulation 2 than when tariffs are fully flexible, but the more important story is in distribution. Fixed tariffs absorb household welfare ains for efficiency enhancement.

The opposite is seen for the Government; a welfare index of the iovernment – measured by the Equivalent Variation, since it is treated as a rivate household – increases from 0.19 to 0.74 as a percentage of GDP.

Adding up public and private welfare, the net difference of the second mulation with respect to the first one is in the order of 0.94 per cent of iDP. That is, in both cases there is a gain but the first simulation shows a igher increase in welfare. This is important because the effects are assumed i be permanent. The rate of unemployment in the second case is higher ecause high tariffs prevent private sectors from expanding and absorbing ibour reductions in public utilities.

The increases in the rate of return of the public utilities are always above ie average for the economy and they experience a substantial growth when ist reductions are not passed to tariffs. In fact this sector captures the otential rate of return growth of the rest of the economy.

The water sector has the highest price reduction; this is a labour intensive ictor that is highly benefited by labour productivity improvements.

Input savings increase welfare and those gains are doubled when prices illy reflect cost reductions. The reason for this must be sought in the iisallocation of resources due to the distortion created by high tariffs.

Table 7.17 shows the macroeconomic impact of each sector. Most of the ital change is due to transport, followed by electricity. Water sector fficiency gains have a negative impact on electricity rate of return because lectricity is an important input (that is reduced) in water production inction. The null impact of the communication sector on export is due to the omplementation of two effects: the labour productivity increase has a ositive effect on exports which is offset by the input efficiency rise given ie import intensive technology. In addition to this reduced impact from elecommunication is due to its relatively small participation in Uruguay's iDP (2.11 per cent versus 4.65 per cent in Argentina). Since it is assumed iat savings in imported inputs are part of that efficiency enhancement, this iduces pressures on the trade account; however the result is sensitive to this ssumption. Privatisations or the adoption of new technological standards ould increase the propensity to use imported inputs, obliging the economy to icrease exports in order to compensate.

Figure 7.3 shows the combination of activity levels and rate of return for ach sector (excluding Public Utilities) after the Simulation 1, when fficiency and productivity gains are passed to tariffs. All the sectors benefit orm the efficiency improvement, but Food Production, Paper and Wood roducts and Metals and Mineral Products are clear winners. Some of these ectors are very important for Uruguay's exports.

is expected, those sectors that have the largest reduction in input

expenditures are those which have the largest increases (more than 1 p
cent) in their rate of return.

Electricity efficiency and productivity gains have an important effect c
electricity intensive sectors such as Minerals, Petroleum and Chemic
Products, Metals and Mineral Products and Services. Water, on the oth
hand, is not used intensively by any sector so there is no importai
expenditure reduction, and most of the price reduction only affec
households in a direct way. Transport's biggest input expenditure reductio
are found in heavy industry. Finally, as expected, Communication's bigge
impact is in trade and financial services.

It should be noted that this is a short-run estimate and therefore investme
misallocation costs are not computed. Additionally, gains in efficiency i
investment expenditures (how many units of capital stock are obtained fro
one unit of investment) are not computed, so the evaluation underestimat
full welfare improvement.

Fixed prices determine distortions that have consequences on resour
allocation and consequently on welfare. It illustrates the inefficienc
differential that is implicitly paid when utilities tariffs are used by th
government as a collecting device. Using infrastructure services to obtai
fiscal revenue is equivalent to imposing differentiated sales taxes.[16] It is we
known that indirect taxes are in general more distorting than direct taxes.[17]
is true that the public sector reduces the administrative costs of collectin
taxes but it is also certain that this increases welfare costs due to distortion
it is not known which is higher.[18] Moreover, though the government cou
use the proceeds for social programmes, the net effect for the poor of th
aid, financed with distortions, could be negative.

Summarising, this exercise confirms that: i) efficiency gains are beneficial f
the economy and welfare gains are permanent and significant, ii) those gai
are higher if tariffs are flexible and efficiency gains passed through
customers, as would be the result of competition in infrastructure servic
production, iii) the estimated gains are not negligible, and iv) unemploymen
is higher when tariffs do not fully reflect cost reductions.

Table 7.15 Schematic social accounting matrix for Uruguay as of 1997

		Expenditures			
	Sectors	Private consumption	Government consumption	Investment	Rest of the world
Revenues Sectors	Domestic input-output purchases matrix (US$10 963)	Domestic household purchases (US$15 000)	Gov. domestic purchases (US$2451)	Invest. domestic purchases (US$1555)	Exports (US$4203)
Rest of the world	Input-output imports (US$3096)	Household imports (US$493)	Gov. imports (US$178)	Investment imports (US$436)	
Government	Import Tax matrix (US$280) Factor taxes (US$1585) Indirect taxes (US$2600)	Import tax (US$115) Direct taxes paid by households (US$1538)	Import tax (US$10)	Import tax (US$80)	

Table 7.15   Continued

	Capital payments from pub. utilities (US$564)	
Households	Capital and labour payments net of taxes (US$15404)	Transfers from government (US$3280)
Investment	Private savings (US$1311)	Gov. savings (US$844)
		RoW savings (US$0)

Source: GTAP 5.3 and macroeconomic data from BCU.

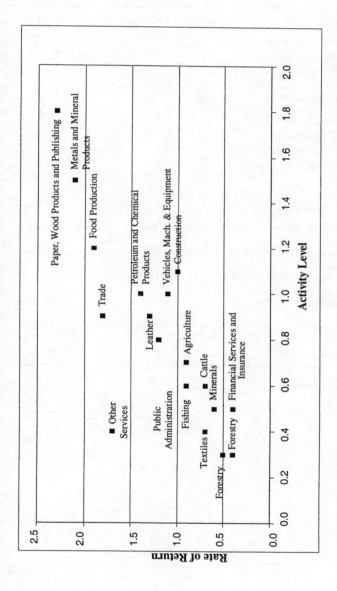

Figure 7.3   Activity levels and rate of return of Simulation 1(in percentage change)

Table 7.16   Uruguay: macroeconomic results of the Simulation 1 and 2

	Flexible prices	Fixed prices
GDP (% change)	1.82	0.57
Prices: IPC (% change)	-0.48	-0.02
• Electricity	-4.7	0
• Water	-10.7	0
• Transport	-5.9	0
• Communications	-3.8	0
Exports in US$ (% change)	0.5	-0.3
Rate of return (% change)	2.57	2.83
• Rest of the sectors	1.4	0
• Electricity	5.8	12.6
• Water	13.9	87.3
• Transport	11.7	23.8
• Communications	8.2	13.8
Real wage (% change)	0.04	0.00
Households welfare (as % of GDP)	1.50	0.00
Government welfare (as % of GDP)	0.19	0.74
Unemployment (16% benchmark)	15.50	18.10
Total welfare in US$	347.04	153.67
Total welfare % of GDP	1.68	0.74

Source: Own calculation.

Table 7.17   *Uruguay: macroeconomic results of the Simulation 1 (one sector at a time)*

	Electricity	Water	Transport	Comunic.
GDP (% change)	0.28	0.16	1.23	0.16
Prices: IPC (% change)	-0.04	-0.06	-0.37	-0.03
• Electricity	-5.0	-0.3	0.5	0
• Water	-1.7	-9.3	0	0
• Transport	0	0	-5.9	0
• Communications	0	0	0.1	-4
Exports in US$ (% change)	0.1	0.1	0.3	0.0
Rate of return (% change)	0.42	0.14	1.70	0.29
• Rest of the sectors	0.31	0.17	0.81	0.50
• Electricity	5.00	-0.40	1.10	0.00
• Water	1.90	11.20	0.30	0.10
• Transport	0.20	0.10	11.30	0.10
• Communications	0.20	0.10	0.50	7.20
Household welfare (as % of GDP)	0.25	0.08	1.00	0.17
Real wage (% change)	0.00	0.00	0.03	0.00
Government welfare (as % of GDP)	0.00	0.03	0.14	0.00
Unemployment (16% benchmark)	15.9	15.9	15.7	16
Total welfare in US$	51.4	24.1	233.7	34.3
Total welfare % of GDP	0.25	0.12	1.13	0.17

Source: Own calculation.

Table 7.18 *Long-run appraisal: simulation 1 and 2 if 30 per cent of capital is not sector specific*

	Simulation 1	Simulation 2
GDP (% change)	2.10	0.56
Prices: IPC (% change)	-0.56	-0.02
• Electricity	-4.36	0.00
• Water	-10.57	0.00
• Transport	-5.84	0.00
• Communications	-3.60	0.0
Exports in US$ (% change)	1.08	-0.31
Rate of return (% change)	3.37	3.84
• Electricity	6.47	12.5
• Water	14.18	87.4
• Transport	12.04	23.6
• Communications	8.57	13.8
Real wage (% change)	0.03	0
Household welfare (as % of GDP)	1.74	-0.17
Government welfare (as % of GDP)	0.24	0.49
Unemployment (16% benchmark)	14.9	18.0
Total Welfare in US$	409.0	66.99
Total Welfare % of GDP	1.98	0.32

Source: Own calculation.

8. CHOOSING THE EXTENT OF PRIVATE PARTICIPATION IN PUBLIC SERVICES

The case of Uruguay, discussed in the previous section, motivates further questions to CGE methodology: what determines the propensity to reduce or widen the extent of public ownership? Why has there been a tendency to privatise and concede public utilities during the early 1990s and tensions in the late 1990s? The answers to these questions depend both on macroeconomic and microeconomic considerations. And correct answers could also help to avoid or prevent inefficient reversals and frustrations that jeopardise reform processes.

On the microeconomic side, there are two prominent theories.[19] One emphasises the role of public ownership to resolve contractual problems and to influence the decisions of firms in certain sensitive issues for politicians; it s easier to control the decisions of the firm (on employment levels, for xample) when the company is under public ownership. The other focuses on 1e self exclusion of private sector under government opportunism; if taxes nd regulations are too unstable, the risk of arbitrariness discourages private nvestments, and public ownership is the only possibility.

Macro considerations have been concentrated in the need to control public eficits, obtaining revenues from privatisations and concessions, fostering ;rowth through efficiency enhancements and obtaining price reductions via a ompetitive environment.

One additional point to consider is the all-or-nothing character of the hoice. That is, are there gains from having private operators coexisting and ompeting with a public enterprise?

There are two aspects to take into account:

. Efficiency gains can be achieved with benchmarking, though in this case it is difficult to say whether benchmarking private operators or a mix of public/private is better.

!. Gains due to harder competition, though a similar observation applies and competition could prevail between private operators. In fact, having only private operators could alleviate the potential moral hazard of the public sector being involved simultaneously in operation and regulation.

An alternative perspective, that combines micro and macro arguments, is ;iven by general equilibrium models. Beyond short term increases in revenue or the governments, efficiency gains for the economy could justify a higher >resence of private sector.

General equilibrium gives a framework of consistency that impedes :ounting gains more than once, obliges the representation of budget :onstraints of all agents – including transfers – and gives net welfare results ifter taking into account changes in relative prices and factor rewards. In fact, :hanges in factor rewards could change expected gains of privatisations and ;overnment activity ... or not. And it is in the latter case where arguments in avour of private operation are stronger.

The objective of this chapter is to explore the rationality of the decision of :hoosing the implicit 'technologies' of private and public operators of itilities in an economy that has fiscal budget and trade balance equilibrium.

We do not consider either asymmetries of information or political >pportunism. They are certainly important elements to take into account, but t seems to be also relevant to focus on the core workings of the economy. What happens with relative prices and factor rewards after the privatisation or :oncession, net welfares gains and their distribution – even or not – the sensitivity of the decision to changes in fundamental parameters, like the cost >f capital, deserves deeper examination.

In broad terms, we will assume that the extreme cases of public an private operation have the following differences:

- Public enterprises show lower efficiency levels in the use c intermediate inputs and employment.
- This inefficiency implies that public enterprises must be subsidised and therefore, that taxes or prices of utilities services must be higher.
- This inefficiency is also present in the investment process: one unit o investment produces more units of capital installed under privat operation (or less units of investment are needed to compose one uni of capital).
- However the share of imported intermediate inputs is higher in th case of private operators, since new investments and methods ar complementary of inputs and services provided by the rest of th world.
- Capital reward of private operators in determined basically by its cos of opportunity in the rest of the world.

Given these elements, the typical choice will involve:

1. Taking into account that evidence tends to confirm that under publi hands inefficiencies are higher, that more resources will be necessary t operate utilities diverting them from other (valuable) activities, and tha subsidies will have to be covered with taxes or higher prices and that thi creates further inefficiencies in the allocation of resources.
2. Realising that though private operators are more efficient, productivity o capital in the rest of the world becomes a relevant benchmark as th minimum required reward for private capital, and that potential transfe of dividends abroad could put pressure on trade balance. The econom will enjoy higher efficiency and performance standards, but at the cost o having to devote more resources to export markets.

So the basic comparison can be reduced to the minimum cost choic between contributing to exports with local effort and consumption sacrific or accepting inefficiencies and the cost of misallocation of resources due t subsidisation. The intention is to attempt to give general equilibrium hints t the answers posed at the beginning of this section and to consider threshold for the cost of capital and public funds full costs that explain rational choices.

There are some provisos to take into consideration. The results must b examined both under full employment and unemployment; in the latter case the results will depend on the rule of indexation of wages. Unde unemployment, efficiency gains will be more important in obtainin increases in scales of operation that will influence welfare positively.

Asymmetries of information are not part of the model. It is true that they are a cornerstone of regulatory economics, but at this stage the differences of dealing with them under public or private operation will only add confusion to the results. In fact, especially under high-powered regimes, the capacity and willingness to deal with asymmetries of information will probably be higher under private hands and that would be a reason for recommending private ownership or operation. But what of the costs?

The analysis is based on a standard CGE model with regulation and service obligations, as presented in Section 2. So the economy must choose between: i) a local technology provided by the public enterprises, or ii) an updated – probably capital intensive – technology that uses mobile capital.

A fundamental difference between these technologies is that while capital is considered a sunk cost for public enterprises, it is not for private operators, though this condition can be relaxed. The idea is to compare the ongoing model – the public enterprises technology – with a new one, more demanding in terms of capital investments.

To simulate the model we will use a Social Accounting Matrix of reduced dimensions that captures the main characteristics of a developing economy, in terms of share of public services in GDP. There is a basic structure that will be specialised to consider the public and private technologies.

To keep the model within conceptual explorations, we constructed a small SAM that reflects acceptable proportions for a developing economy with relevant state owned enterprises participation. The SAM represents an initial condition, with prevalence of state-owned company technology. More than ever, this is 'a theoretical exploration using numbers', in the sense of Piggott and the model is a special case of the general system presented above.

Table 7.19 presents the SAM. The rows show markets and the columns budgetary constraints. Notice that the subsidy granted to the public utilities in government hands is represented as a positive entry of $12 973 in the corresponding column. H, PU, RW and G stand for Household, Public Utility and Rest of the World and Government, and L, K and FF for labour, specific capital and mobile capital respectively. M1 and M2 represent imports; in this version we do not have imports of intermediate goods to be used by industries.

The State Owned Enterprises (SOE) technology produces slightly more than 1 per cent of total sales of infrastructure services ($285 of $24 063), and receives a subsidy from the government of about 35 per cent of total costs. This subsidy is financed with a tax on household income.

Alternative technologies and model solutions

The first solution involves computing the initial subsidy that maintains the state owned company working at its observed levels whatever its inefficiency. Service obligations are met with the installed technology, less efficient in use of intermediate inputs and labour than the imported one. For the initial benchmark calibration we assume that L_R is used in fixed coefficients in the domestic state company, so that instead of (A 7.12) in the Appendix, we have the non negativity condition:

$$\Sigma a_{T,R} p_T + b_{N,R} p_N + a_{L,R} w - s \geq 0 .$$

The subsidy s is computed initially so that the excess of costs of state owned enterprise are compensated for and its production is equal to observed quantities. That is, s is determined to replicate given outputs of the SOE and of the Private Owned Company (POC); for example, if 70 per cent of total production is obtained from the state owned company, and the rest from the alternative technology, s will be computed to match those observed levels of production. The subsidy is financed with taxes on household income; this simulation assumes therefore that taxes do not create costs of distortion.

The alternative technology exhibits constant returns to scale, and uses domestic intermediate inputs and mobile capital (with the rest of the world) to produce the regulated good or service. For this technology we also assume fixed coefficients in this presentation, and the price is fixed at its cost of production:

$$\Sigma a^*_{T,R} p_T + b^*_{N,R} p_N + a^*_{L,R} w^* = p^*_R,$$

where the *) stands for the input coefficients of the mobile capital technology, and p^*_R is the price of the infrastructure service when produced with the imported standards.

It is assumed that the rate of profit is given at the level of the cost of opportunity of capital in the rest of the world, and that capital in the regulated sector is no longer sunk. It is an implicit cost-plus mechanism with a minimum rate of return given by the international productivity of capital. In this case K_R becomes a variable to be determined. The trade balance equilibrium condition becomes simply:

$$p_T x - p_m m = \pi_R + w^* K_R.$$

Given the initial subsidy s, the simulations explore the effects of assuming reductions in w^*. Changes in w^* are compensated for in order not to change relative prices of exports and imports. The model chooses the less costly between the internal cost of the subsidy and the alternative technology, to maximise welfare of the domestic household.

Table 7.19 SAM based on Uruguay, 1980

	Agriculture	Industry	Services	P.U. (old)	P.U. (new)	H	G	RW
Agriculture	26931	-18422	-377	-163	-2	-2058		-5909
Industry	-4479	100285	-16549	-4533	48	-55.76		-18916
Services	-2407	-18658	168206	-6381	-67	-140693		
P.U. (old)	-605	-5955	-5424	23778		-11794		
P.U. (new)	-7	-72	-66		285	-140		
L	-4832	-22636	-64477	-25675	-68	117688		
K	-14.6	-34542	-81313	0	0	130455		
FF					-100			100
Subsidy				12973			-12973	
Tax						-12973	12973	
M1						-732		732
M2						-23993		23993

Source: Own calculation.

Table 7.20 shows the results of three simulations. The first two explore threshold for the cost of mobile capital: which is the level of w^* such that th local public technology is substituted by the new imported technology? Th first scenario contemplates full substitution and the second, only partia Initially we calibrate the model so that 99 per cent of the total production c utilities is provided using the old technology and only 1 per cent with the ne mobile capital; we will say that full substitution occurs when thos percentages are reverted (we do not take 100 per cent to avoid potenti computational problems). It can be seen that a reduction of approximately 1 per cent in the rate of return of the rest of the world capital leads to a fu replacement, and about half of that reduction is needed to replace half of th share. Both simulations take as given the initial subsidy for the state owne enterprise.

However, it can be argued that the subsidy is conditional to th 'international price' of the service. In fact, though the infrastructure servic cannot be imported, mobile capital can be internalised to produc domestically. Therefore, the cost of one unit of service produced with th new technology puts an implicit cap on the domestic price of services. In th case, a reduction of w^* could be followed by further reductions in s, unles there is a quota or explicit ban on imports.

The subsidy s is an implicit rent of a sunk factor, and this explains why a endogenous subsidy will not necessarily lead to a substitution of th technology. That is why we consider the third simulation. Instead of reducin w^* we consider reductions in the subsidy s for a given level of the cost c mobile capital. Notice that in this case, the old SOE technology is full substituted when the subsidy is reduced by 15 per cent.

The results of reductions in the cost of mobile capital and in subsidie given to old public companies are shown as gains both in GDP and i households' welfare. The latter is computed as the Equivalent Variatior When the new technology is fully adopted, households enjoy welfare level that are equivalent to initial income increases of 5.6 per cent and 5 per cent.

It can be seen however that the new technology adoption is demanding fo the trade balance and requires additional export effort by the economy; thi effort is equivalent to w^*K_R since we assume that we are in a stationary state so that initial entry of capital $+K_R$ is compensated in the same period with a outflow $-K_R$; when the reimbursement of the principal encompasses severa periods, the stress on the forthcoming trade balances will be higher and th net effect will depend also on the gains obtained with the initial inflows anc the uses given to those funds.

Table 7.20 also alerts us to potential conflicts. Nominal and real wages fel in all scenarios; this is due to the need for rewarding mobile capital. Sinc labour is not mobile it must face – directly or indirectly – the costs o 'purchasing' the new technology.

It is important to remember that these simulations have been performed using non distortionary taxation and so we should expect faster substitution when taxes on subsets of goods are not charged, or when the tax structure is not even.

Lessons from the exercise

The simulations confirm that the choice of the technology to be used for servicing infrastructure depends on deep parameters of efficiency and costs.

It does not say why state owned companies may be more inefficient than private ones, but given those inefficiencies that create costs in terms of resources and distortions, the choice of the technology is not necessarily determined; it depends on the magnitude of waste and on the costs in the allocation of resources relative to the price of mobile capital (and implicitly on the export effort of the country). The model shows that there are plausible scenarios where the selection is not unique.

We have left aside additional characteristics related to the technologies that could favour one or the other. For example, corruption and passive deficit could lead to hyperinflation in a context of state owned enterprises, orchronic misallocation of resources reduce investments and destroy the base of capital of government companies. We have also not considered potential constraints on less developing countries' exports that could also increase significantly the cost of raising foreign currency to honour the payment of dividends to mobile capital.

We have not considered the possibility of using domestic capital to produce the service of infrastructure; the idea was to consider extreme cases that could give a confirmation of the basic intuition, and to check that that intuition was not rejected by general equilibrium effects.

Table 7.20   Simulations

	Simulation 1: Foreign capital price reduction until SOE production is replaced	Simulation 2: Foreign capital price reduction until half SOE production is replaced	Simulation 3 Domestic subsidy reduction until SOE production is replaced
GDP (% variation)	7.2	3.8	7.1
Agriculture	4.5	2.3	4.8
Industry	11.3	5.8	11.6
Services	6.6	3.4	6.5
Public utilities	3.5	2.4	2.5
Old tech. participation in public utilities production (benchmark 99%)	1%	50%	1%
New tech. participation in public utilities production (benchmark 1%)	99%	50%	99%
RPI (% variation)	-3.0	-1.6	-3.2
Agriculture	0.4	0.2	0.4
Industry	1.1	0.6	0.9
Services	-4.0	-2.2	-4.8
Public utilities	-8.8	-4.7	-4.4
Exports (% variation)	44.3	23.1	48.5
Imports (% variation)	5.6	2.8	5.0
Household welfare (% variation)	5.6	2.8	5
Foreign capital price (% variation)	-11.6	-6.2	0
Domestic subsidy (% variation)	-	-	-15.4
Rate of return (% variation)	6.1	3.1	5.2
Agriculture	5.4	2.8	5.6
Industry	15.7	8	15.2
Services	2.2	1	0.8

Source: Own calculation.

9. CONCLUDING REMARKS

In this chapter we have tried to show how microeconomic reforms with significant macroeconomic effects can be studied in the environment of a Computable General Equilibrium model. It is more than an interesting academic exercise.

Valuable policy measures are often blocked due to misunderstanding and uncertainty, mainly quantitative. When reforms are deep and structural, final relative prices are difficult to forecast and societies may opt for a minimum regret (i.e. status quo) solution.

Of course, CGE models had already been used with this aim, for example to study trade and fiscal reforms. The analysis presented above indicates that they can be fruitfully applied to the case of regulation, and on its effect on income distribution, trade balance and welfare.

APPENDIX

A. The structure of the simplified analytical model

In this section we will give a sketch of the model used for simulations.

Each activity produces only one commodity represented by $J=\{1,2,N,R\}$. We assume that the utility and production functions correspond to the traditional neoclassical version. However, production sectors are related through input-output transactions, which play an important role in understanding the net impact of regulation on the economy. Prices of tradable goods are determined by the rest of the world,[20] and domestic agents also import consumption goods that are imperfect substitutes of local production. Imports are not used for production.

Though it is natural to think that the production function of that sector should exhibit some economies of scale or sub-additivity, we assume that there are not non-convexities once specific capital is installed. This is a simplification with obvious theoretical costs, but it also contributes to the concentration of our effort in determining the impact of regulatory mechanisms and not on the properties of the production set.[21] The main focus of this analysis is in the short run, and when capital is installed the regulated sector is ex-post receiving a rent that compensates the initial investment; the alternative technology gives some hints on the long-run effects; in that case, we assume constant returns to scale (see Section 2).

Domestic household

There is only one domestic agent that makes the decision on the consumption plan and receives all factor rewards (except for the regulated firm) and profits. When income distribution matters, there are several agents and the matrix that crosses factor rewards and personal incomes is critical for results. Though we do not include government here, its action has been modelled and simulated in several of our applications.

The domestic agent maximises the utility function $u(c_1, c_2, c_N, c_R, m)$ subject to:

$$\sum_T p_T c_T + p_R c_R + p_N c_N + p_m m = w\overline{L} + \sum_{I/\{R\}} r_I \overline{K}_I + \theta \pi_R^* + \theta t p_R G(L_R, K_R) \quad \text{(A7.1)}$$

where θ is the share of domestic agents in profits of the regulated sector π_R^* and the last term corresponds to the compensatory transfer from domestic customers (t > 0) or to the firm from its shareholders (t < 0). In both cases, under price cap, t is computed so that $p_R = 1/\mu(1+t)$.

We obtain the familiar first order conditions for a maximum:

$$u'_{c_T}\big/u'_m = p_T/p_m \quad \text{(A7.2)}$$

$$u'_R\big/u'_m = p_R/p_m \quad \text{(A7.3)}$$

$$u'_N\big/u'_m = p_N/p_m \quad \text{(A7.4)}$$

c_T is consumption of domestic tradable goods, c_R is the consumption of goods and services under regulation and m are imports (a good produced abroad but not domestically) and p_T, p_R and p_m are their respective prices. w is the wage rate and r_I is the rate of return on capital in each sector. $\overline{L}$ and $\overline{K}$ represent the domestic agent endowments of labour and capital.

For simulations, consumers' utility function is modelled as a Cobb-Douglas between all goods except for retail trade which is assumed to be purchased in fixed proportions with the rest of the goods and services. The preferences of domestic agents are assumed to follow an Armington specification which implies no perfect substitutability in preferences between domestic and imported goods.[22]

Expenditures are distributed between domestic and imported consumption goods and investments. Goods and services of 'privatised' firms combine quantity and quality features but a change in quality is not necessarily associated with a change in the price of the service provided by the privatised firm. An increase in service failures increases cost for the buyer of services because the consumer needs to buy a higher number of physical units to reach the desired flow of services. This 'naïve' modelling approach allows, for instance, the modelling of costs of power losses or interruptions as a proportion of unit costs. Prices can be differentiated by income groups.

The budget constraint for each income group reflects total expenditures in goods and services as well as indirect taxes varying by the type of good and service, and direct taxes. Income sources are labour income in the private sector and in the public sector, and capital income in private firms; revenue from profits on domestic sales and sales abroad, and revenue from participation in the privatised firm redistributed in proportion to shares owned. Total capital wealth (physical plus financial) can be negative if the consumer group is in debt.[23] Families also get public sector transfers.

Domestic production

Y, H and G are the production function of the tradable, non-tradable and regulated sectors, respectively. We assume constant returns to scale in all cases.

Private firms are those for which there was no change in ownership or any major organisational change during the period covered by the study. They produce goods and services intended for intermediate and final consumption as well as export and investment. This differentiation is necessary to account properly for the differences in the tax treatment of the various destinations (for instance, exporters do not pay VAT and benefit from discounts on their gross income tax). There is no technological differentiation across these sectors. Exporters of goods are price-takers abroad and exports of services are price inelastic (i.e. they are constant). Non-tradeable prices are determined as solution variables and adjust with factor income until markets reach equilibrium. Credit requirements are constant per unit of output.

Quantities produced are obtained by combining intermediate inputs and value added in fixed proportions. Value added itself is obtained by combining labour and capital inputs in a CES production. The inter-industrial transactions requirements are proportional to total production and to exports respectively. Privatised goods and services are also proportional to output which is different from the assumption made for consumers where rationing could occur.[24] However, firms can be subject to adjustment in quality of services just as consumers are and hence can face differences in cost for the same service.[25] A quality improvement is equivalent to a cut in the absolute value of the input requirements. Remuneration includes total payments to capital and hence amortisation. This means that the savings and investment decisions are taken by households in the model.

Tradable sector   There is one firm that maximises profits in each tradable sector. The net price for the firm is the price to consumers less the cost of intermediate inputs.

$$\pi_T = \left[p_T - \sum_{J \neq T} a_{J,T} p_J - a_{R,T} p_R - a_{N,T} p_N \right] Y_T (L_T, K_T) - wL_T - \sum_T r_T K_T \quad \text{(A7.5)}$$

for every T=1,2 and where $a_{R,T}$ and $a_{T,R}$ are input-output coefficients also used to represent technical gains due to privatisation. A reduction in $a_{T,R}$ is an improvement of efficiency internal to the regulated firms, which reduces the requirement of intermediate inputs per unit of product. $a_{R,T}$ is a reduction of the requirement of regulated input per unit of tradeable output (due to a better performance of private operators).

Note that firms observe the incentive given by the net price after paying intermediate inputs costs. The maximum profit conditions are:

$$\left[p_T - \sum_{J \neq T} a_{J,T} p_J - a_{R,T} p_R - a_{N,T} p_N \right] Y_L = w \tag{A7.6}$$

$$\left[p_T - \sum_{J \neq T} a_{J,T} p_J - a_{R,T} p_R - a_{N,T} p_N \right] Y_K = r_T \tag{A7.7}$$

In both cases, the value of marginal product (corrected for intermediate costs) is equalised to the reward of the factor.

Non-tradeable sector

$$\pi_N = \left[p_N - \sum_T a_{T,N} p_T - a_{R,N} p_R \right] H(L_N, K_N) - w L_N - r_N K_N \tag{A7.8}$$

$$\left[p_N - \sum_T a_{T,N} p_T - a_{R,N} p_R \right] H_L = w \tag{A7.9}$$

$$\left[p_N - \sum_T a_{T,N} p_T - a_{R,N} p_R \right] H_N = r_N \tag{A7.10}$$

Regulated sector   As mentioned above, the regulated firm is treated as a neoclassical firm, and it behaves 'competitively' though there is no entry. Net price is obtained as the difference between the regulated price and intermediate cost.

$$\pi_R = \left[p_R - \sum_T a_{T,R} p_T - a_{N,R} p_N \right] G(L_R, K_R) - w L_R \tag{A7.11}$$

where K_R is given.

The total rate of return of this sector is $r_R = \pi_R / K_R$. The optimal condition for profits is:

$$\left[p_R - \sum_T a_{T,R} p_T - b_{N,R} p_N \right] G_L = w \tag{A7.12}$$

$a_{R,T}$ and $a_{T,R}$ are input-output coefficients used to represent technical gains due to privatisation. A reduction in $a_{T,R}$ is an improvement of efficiency internal to the regulated firms, which reduces the requirement of intermediate inputs per unit of product. $a_{R,T}$ is the requirement of regulated input per unit of tradeable output (due to better performance of private operators).

Privatised firms sell mostly to the domestic market, except for gas where some exports occur. With the exception of some differentiation due to regulation, service obligations or taxes according to their final users, each utility sector is assumed to sell a single product. Their profit function includes any subsidy that could be transferred by the public sector as differentiation of tariffs into retail, wholesale or commercial and residential as necessary. The quality variables are modelled as an improvement in the overall efficiency of the sector.

Outputs are limited by capacity and transmission constraints are incorporated through the value added function. The product of the privatised sector is also based on a fixed proportions production function for intermediate inputs and the value added function in the privatised sector is assumed to be Cobb-Douglas. This description of the technology of the private and privatised firms is key to modelling the changes in productivity, efficiency and quality. Price regulation in turn is modelled as RPI-x, where x is set to zero at the beginning of the contract.

Production abroad
The rest of the world produces substitutes for our exports and import goods, using a factor of production F.

$$\pi_m^* = p_m \alpha(F_m) - w^* F_m \tag{A7.13}$$

$$\pi_T^* = p_T \beta_T(F_T) - w^* F_T \tag{A7.14}$$

$$p_m \alpha' = w^* \tag{A7.15}$$

$$p_T \beta_T' = w^* \tag{A7.16}$$

$$m^s = \alpha(F_m) \tag{A7.17}$$

$$x^s = \beta_T(F_T) \tag{A7.18}$$

where π_m^* and π_T^* represent profits in the foreign industries that produce import goods and perfect substitutes of tradeables. w^*, the numeraire, is the wage rate of the only factor F used abroad.

F_m and F_T are factor quantities employed in the corresponding industries. The production functions: $\alpha(F_m)$ and $\beta_T(F_T)$ give the total supply in equations A7.16, A7.17 and A7.18. In the case of α' and β_T' constants, international terms of trade will be given by $p_T / p_m = \alpha / \beta_T$ (small economy assumption).

Foreign agents
Foreign consumers receive the rents of foreign factors, including capital installed in the regulated sector as well as profits in that sector. They maximise a utility function $v(x_T, m^*)$ that depends on the consumption of our tradeable goods and import goods. The budget condition is:

$$p_m m^* + p_T x_T = w^* \overline{F} + (1-\theta)\pi_R + \pi_m^* + \sum_T \pi_T^* + t p_R G(L_R, K_R)(1-\theta) \quad \text{(A7.19)}$$

The foreign agent receives profits and capital return of the regulated sector, as well as the rate of return F given by w^* and the proceedings of the mark-up factor. X_T are exports, that is, domestic tradeable goods bought by the foreign agent. The last term in equation A7.19 stands for the endogenous mark-up (positive) or internal subsidy (negative) computed as the difference between the benchmark tariff $1/\mu$ (as seen by customers) and P_R.

Consumers of the rest of the world exhibit Cobb-Douglas utility functions. They face a budget constraint in which revenues include payments from its share of capital in the privatised sectors.

Market equilibrium conditions

Equations A7.20 to A7.27 represent the equilibrium conditions for factors used domestically and A7.28 is the equilibrium condition for the foreign factor. Equations A7.25 to A7.27 correspond to equilibrium in markets for goods: regulated, non regulated and imports.

$$\overline{L} = L_1 + L_2 + L_R + L_N \tag{A7.20}$$

$$\overline{K}_T = K_T \quad (T=1,2) \tag{A7.21}$$

$$\overline{K}_N = K_N \tag{A7.22}$$

$$\overline{F} = F_m + \sum_T F_T \tag{A7.23}$$

$$G(L_R, K_R) + q_R = \sum_T a_{R,T} Y_T(L_T, K_T) + a_{R,N} H(L_N, K_N) + c_R \tag{A7.24}$$

$$Y_T(L_T, K_T) + x_T^s = a_{T,R} G(L_R, K_R) + a_{T,N} H(L_N, K_N) + c_T + x_T \tag{A7.25}$$

$$H(L_N, K_N) = \sum_T a_{N,T} Y_T(L_T, K_T) + a_{N,R} G(L_R, K_R) + c_N \tag{A7.26}$$

$$m^s = m + m^* \tag{A7.27}$$

The solution includes determining the endogenous mark-up to cover differences between the current tariff and the one defined in the regulation in the price-cap case, i.e.: t such that $p_R = 1/\mu(1+t)$, or to cover the difference between the current overall rate of return on capital in the regulated sector and its benchmark in the rate-of-return case, i.e.: t such that $\pi_R/K_R = w^*$.

Trade balance

We can now see how the relation between the mark-up factor (and its mechanism of adjustement) and the trade balance arises in the model. From1:

$$p_R c_R + \sum_{I/\{R\}} p_I c_I + p^* m = w\overline{L} + \sum_{I/\{R\}} r_I \overline{K}_I + \theta \pi_R + \theta t P_R G(L_R, K_R)$$

and since:

$$p_R c_R + \sum_{I/\{R\}} p_I c_I + px = w\overline{L} + \sum_{I/\{R\}} r_I \overline{K}_I + \pi_R + tP_R G(L_R, K_R)$$

we get

$$px - p^* m = (1 - \theta)[\pi_R + tp_R G(L_R, K_R)] \qquad (A7.28)$$

The left hand side is the trade balance and the right hand is the foreign share in regulated sector profits.[26] While this equation shows the interactions between the regulatory regime and the trade account, it may be too restrictive. In fact, domestic ownership is not sufficient to break the link between regulation and trade; domestic agents could reveal preferences for foreign assets or goods, and put pressure on the trade balance. On the other hand, foreign ownership is not necessarily a source of stress on trade surplus, for example, if profits are reinvested in the country. A more general model should include more elaboration on the domestic and foreign agent's portfolio and investment decisions.

How do the price-cap and cost-plus mechanisms work in this setting?

Basically, the endogenous tax on regulated goods consumption is a mark-up on sales and its proceedings are distributed between domestic and foreign owners of the firm according to their share in total assets.

Assume that the market price for the regulated firm were P_m and that this level were below the price-cap benchmark, given by w^*/μ, then the tax rate will be determined by:

$$t = (w^*/\mu P_m) - 1.$$

That is, we introduce an artificial tax system whose claimant is not the government, but the shareholders of the regulated firm.

If instead of a benchmark for price we have a benchmark for the rate of return on assets, the tax function is adjusted endogenously again; the tax rate will be determined using the equation:

$$(t\, P_m Q_R + \pi_R) = w^* K_R$$

which means that total dividends to shareholders (left hand of the equation) match exactly normal rate of return abroad (right hand), w^*.

These equations are added to the general equilibrium system, so that we have one more equation and one more unknown, the tax rate.

The proof of existence of equilibrium in this case could become an issue. Shoven and Whalley (1973) have already given a proof of existence for a general case when the claimant of the mark–up revenue is the government.

The natural requirement is that the mark-up function be homogenous of degree zero with respect to prices – see Ginsburgh and Keyzer (1997) for a summary of the approach. Our rules for determining the tax rate fulfil this condition.[27]

The tax could be negative if the market price is above the reference level $1/\mu$, or if the rate of return on assets, π_R/K_R is higher than w^*.

Government is not modelled here; in simulations it maximises social welfare including current collective goods produced with goods and services purchased, employment, credit (which can be domestic or international), retiree services and a proxy for future collective goods: public investment. Its utility function is a Leontief in which goods and services are combined in fixed proportions as a single input. Pensions, bonds services, investments, and current operative expenses are a constant proportion of total government income in this model. Its budget constraint is given by the sum of tax revenue, bonds and also revenue from their share of ownership in the 'privatised assets'.

Solution of the model using MPSGE

The solution of the model is obtained using the representation of General Equilibrium and using the Mixed Complementarity Approach – see Ferris and Pang (1997) for a survey of the mathematical method. The model is developed in the environment of GAMS/MPSGE developed by Tom Rutherford. MPSGE (Mathematical Programming System for General Equilibrium Analysis) was designed by T. Rutherford – see Rutherford (1999), among many other discussions of the subject – for solving Arrow-Debreu general equilibrium models. At present it can be used in interface with GAMS (see Brooke et al., 1992).

NOTES

1. If this assumption were not included, we would need to accept some form of rationing of customers (households or firms), and this will make the model much more complicated and ad hoc.
2. This section is based on Chisari, Estache and Romero (1999).
3. See Chisari, Estache and Romero (1999). In order to assess both the efficiency and distributional impacts of privatisation in electricity, gas, water and sanitation, and telecommunications services, we compare the economy of Argentina in 1993, the first year in which all the major privatisation had taken place, and in 1995, the last year for which data were available.
4. An earlier version of the model without detailed infrastructure accounts was presented in Chisari, and Romero (1996).
5. See Chisari et al. (1999) for the details on the data sources used to construct the SAM accounts.
6. Reformers had the choice between three main forms of regulation: a price cap, a cost plus or a hybrid regime. In most cases, reformers have chosen to try to promote incentives for efficiency in these sectors rather than to guarantee return through cost-plus regimes. In Latin America, according to a database put together on 954 concessions contracts awarded from

the mid 1980s to 2000, 56 per cent of the contracts were regulated under a price-cap regime, 20 per cent under rate-of-return regulation. For 24 per cent of the contract the regime is a hybrid one.

7. These optimal contracts are typically modelled in a Principal-Agent framework in the regulation literature. For an overview see for instance Laffont, J. J., and Tirole (1993).

8. Chisari et al (1999), and the papers included in Ugaz and Waddams (2003),

9. To some extent, a rule for determining the tariff can be modeled as a distortion that modifies optimal trade policy. We are leaving aside the financial and temporal considerations; in fact, it could happen that a rate-of-return regulation favoured a bigger initial inflow of foreign capital.

10. Considering the information available from National Accounts and Input-Output estimations.

11. The welfare changes are computed in terms of the equivalent variation as a percentage of household income.

12. Owners of the firm will not necessarily have incentives to introduce the efficiency gains, however.

13. Simulations considering efficiency loss of the same magnitude gave similar results but with the opposite sign.

14. They become implicit shareholders who have to cover also the increase in wage rate.

15. Agriculture, Cattle, Forestry, Fishing, Minerals, Food Production, Beverages and Tobacco, Textiles, Leather, Paper, Wood Products and Publishing, Petroleum and Chemical products, Metals and Mineral Products, Vehicles, Machinery and Equipment, Electricity, Water, Construction, Trade, Transport, Communications, Financial Services and Insurance, Other Services, Public Administration.

16. This reverses the traditional expected behaviour of public sector companies of keeping prices below costs.

17. It is interesting to take into account an observation from Galal et al. (1994): 'One must therefore ask, 'How much of the problem of public enterprises are due to state ownership and how much to their monopoly positions?'.

18. Some examples of this behaviour are in order from Report 25012: a) UTE (the electricity national company) generated a significant annual dividend to the state (US$75 million in 2001); b) fuel oil and gas oil are subsidised; c) in telecommunications, according to private operators opinion, there is a contradiction between the general message urging to 'open to competition' and significant pressure on public companies for obtaining revenue.

19. According to Esfahani and Ardakani (2004).

20. The 'small country assumption' in terms of Kehoe and Kehoe (1994).

21. Dierker et al. (1985) present an analysis of the existence of equilibrium when there are special pricing rules.

22. Although not necessary to ensure that the economy does not end up specialising, by assumption, the capital installed in the tradeable sectors cannot be reallocated.

23. An increase in the cost of debt leads to an increase in the supply of labour and a decrease in consumption by the indebted income classes.

24. Purchases of electricity in the wholesale market correspond to generation, purchases on the retail market correspond to distribution.

25. This assumes that there is no possibility of using 'home-made' substitutes for infrastructure services.

26. The trade balance must compensate the current account result. Notice that it is not influenced by entrance and exit of capital 'in the same period': the net impact is: $-r_R K_R$.

27. Whalley and Zhang (2002) have given examples of multiplicity of equilibria for general equilibrium models with taxes. Our functions do not respond to the forms they used in their examples, and we have explored multiplicity using sensitivity and have not found evidence.

REFERENCES

Brooke, A., D. Kendrick and A. Meeraus (1992), *GAMS: A User's Guide, Release 2.25*, Redwood City, California, Scientific Press.

Chisari, O. and C. Romero (1996), 'Distribucin del Ingreso, Asignacin de Recursos y Shocks Macroeconómicos', Serie Financiamento del Desarrollo, **36**, CEPAL, United Nations.

Chisari O.O., A. Estache and C. Romero (1999), 'Winners and Losers of Privatization and Regulation of Utilities: Lesson from a General Equilibrium Model of Argentina', *The World Bank Economic Review*, **13** (2), 357–378.

Dierker E., R. Guesnerie and W. Neuefeind (1985), 'General Equilibrium When Some Firms Follow Special Rules', *Econometrica*, **53** (6), 1369–1393.

Esfahani, H.S. and A.T. Ardakani (2004), *What Determines the Extent of Public Ownership?*, University of Illinois and University of Manchester conference on 'Regulation of Development and the Development of Regulation', Illinois.

Ferris M.C. and J.S. Pang (1997), 'Engineering and Economic Applications of Complementarity Problems', SIAM *Review*, **39** (4), 669–713.

Galal, A. and M. Shirley (1994), 'Does Privatization Deliver? Highlight from a World Bank Conference', EDI Development Studies.

Ginsburgh V. and M. Keyzer (1997), *The Structure of Applied General Equilibrium Models*, Cambridge MA: The MIT Press.

Kehoe P.J. and T.J. Kehoe (1994), 'A Primer on Static Applied General Equilibrium Models', *Federal Reserve of Minneapolis Quarterly Review*, **18** (1).

Laffont, J. J. and Tirole, J. (1003), 'A Theory of Incentives in Procurement and Regulation, Cambridge Mass, MIT Press.

Rutherford T. (1999), 'Applied General Equilibrium Modeling with MPSGE as a GAMS Subsystem: An Overview of the Modeling Framework and Syntax', *Computational Economics*, **14** (1–2).

Shoven J.B. and J. Whalley (1973), 'General Equilibrium With Taxes: A Computational Procedure and an Existence Proof', *The Review of Economic Studies*, **40** (4), 475–489.

Ugaz, C. and C. Waddams (2003), *Utility Privatization and Regulation: A Fair Deal for Consumers?*, Cheltenham: Edward Elgar Publishing.

Whalley J. and S. Zhang (2002), 'Tax Induced Multiple Equilibria', mimeo, University of Western Ontario, May.

8. The effectiveness of competition policy in Argentina, Chile and Peru during the 1990s

Paula Margaretic, Maria Fernanda Martínez and Diego Petrecolla

1. INTRODUCTION

During the last decade, there has been an increasing concern about the importance of competition policy as a mean to increase efficiency in the allocation of resources and the supply and variety of goods and services. Competition between firms provides powerful incentives for cost minimisation and technological improvements and also contributes to create an environment where firms can develop, encouraging free enterprises in the best interests of users and consumers.

Both competition policy and regulation are public instruments that aim at improving the functioning of the market. Competition defence attempts to prevent firms from abusing their dominant position or colluding, and prevents mergers and concentration that can facilitate such conduct. Competition policy and regulation are complementary policies which require an effective coordination between them.

During the 1990s the Latin American region has experienced an extended process of structural reforms, including privatisation, deregulation and in particular the implementation of competition laws. All these major changes required an active role from the State. However different models of competition agencies were created within the region. These differences can be related to the particular necessities and peculiarities of the different countries. In such a context many questions arise. For example, how do structural reforms affect competition policy in Latin America? What was the impact of competition law on the different markets? Have the different models of competition that have been implemented been effective in the fulfillment of their objectives? Is there any significant difference between the alternatives? Which are the problems that a competition agency has to tackle in order to reach its aims? These questions are addressed in this chapter.

The goal of this chapter is to develop a methodology to classify the different models of competition agencies that were created in Latin America during the 1990s. This taxonomy requires an analysis of whether the agency is independent or not, whether the agency controls mergers or not and whether the final decision is made at the judiciary level or at the administrative level.

The main objective is to determine if there is any relationship between these characteristics and the model of competition agency adopted; in other words, is there a particular type of agency that tends to be more effective than others in pursuing anticompetitive conducts. In order to measure this effectiveness, we construct partial productivity indexes to compare and contrast the different agencies.

We also define some measure of output generated by each agency based on the partial productivity indexes and try to evaluate the use of resources and the significance that structural and environmental variables have on the output of each agency. The chapter relates these indexes to the requirement of resources and factors such as the size of the economy, the degree of openness of the economy and the functions of the agencies. The methodology provides an interesting approach that aims at improving the quantitative analysis of competition issues and increasing the information a regulator or a policy maker should rely on in order to assess the implications of any political decision.

The chapter is structured as follows. In the second section we present a description of the different legal frameworks and competitive environments of the countries under analysis. We consider Argentina, Peru and Chile. The objective is to identify their major attributes and compare and contrast them, in order to shed light on their advantages and weaknesses. The section concludes with a comparative chart. The third section presents principal cases where the competition law has been implemented that might help to compare the different agencies in a qualitative and quantitative way. In the fourth section, we try to estimate the relationship between the different models of competition agencies and their enforcement capacities, as well as their impact on the market. The aim is to assess whether there is any statistical relationship between the taxonomy of agencies and their effectiveness in the improvement of the competitive environment. Finally, section five presents the conclusions.

2.   DESCRIPTION OF THE COMPETITION FRAMEWORK OF THE COUNTRIES SELECTED

2.1   Argentina

2.1.1   The Competition Law

In 1980 Argentina initiated its modern competition policy, with the creation of the Competition Act N° 22.262. Since then, the National Commission for Competition Defence – CNDC[1] has enforced Argentinean Competition Law.

However, in 1999 Law N° 22.262 was replaced by Act 25.156 which basically completed and improved the former Act by: i) introducing ex ante review and authorisation of mergers and acquisitions, ii) giving the competition authority full jurisdiction on competition issues in every sector of the economy and iii) ordering the setting up of the National Tribunal for Competition Defence – TNDC[2] as an independent body to enforce the law within the Ministry of Economy. The Amendment of the Law aimed at increasing the enforcing power of the Antitrust Agency and also introduced merger control as a preventive tool in the fight against cartels to minimise costs to all parties.

Law N° 25156 constitutes the legal framework to enforce the competition policy. It regulates the agreements and anti-competitive practices that restrain the markets, as well as the abuse of dominant position. Even though the Law establishes the creation of TNDC, the CNDC is still in charge of enforcing the Competition Law.

CNDC is the agency that performs the investigations, which end up in reports and recommendations based on the legal and economic antitrust principles. Both mergers and antitrust investigations are subject to the antitrust analysis performed by the CNDC. The agency also advocates for competition, issuing non-binding recommendations on competition matters to other governmental agencies.

The CNDC nowadays reports to the Technical Co-ordination Secretariat of the Ministry of Economy and Production.[3] The main functions and faculties of the TNDC are the following:

- Conduct market investigations in order to determine if there is any anticompetitive practice taking place. An investigation can be opened by a formal complaint or an initiative of the Tribunal.
- Ask for information and conduct public enquiries, using investigative techniques, enquiries and dawn raids to gather evidence that justify the decisions taken.
- Impose sanctions. The amendment of the Law increased the Agency´s capacity to impose sanctions and measures to re-establish competition in any market.

- Provide pro-competitive recommendations, promoting its advocacy role.
- Participate in the Negotiation of International Treaties and Collective Agreements that related to competition issues.
- Encourage agreement between parties.

Some major legal innovations on the competition framework took place during 2001, when the new Competition Act 25.156 was complemented by Decree 89/2001 and amended by Decree 396/2001. Decree 89/2001 defined the necessary proceedings for the creation of the aforementioned TNDC and regulated some aspects concerning the notification of mergers and acquisitions to the authority. Additionally, it incorporated the Competition, Deregulation and Consumer Defence Secretariat as an enforcement authority, giving exaggerated influence on the investigations. In particular, the Decree allowed the Secretariat to participate in any instance of an investigation, which contradicted the independence principle of the Tribunal.

Decree 396/2001 amended the volume of sales threshold by which mergers and acquisitions must be notified to CNDC in order to avoid notification and investigation of minor operations. In turn, Decree 89/2001 was complemented by Resolutions N° 40[4] and N° 164.[5]

Regarding mergers, Article 6° of the Law 25.156 defines an operation of 'economic concentration' as changes in control over one or more undertakings, through the following transactions: a) mergers between undertakings, b) acquisitions of a business, c) acquisitions of shares or any other rights related to shares or debt giving any kind of influence over the firm issuing those shares or debt, when that acquisitions gives the buyer control or substantial influence over an undertaking, and d) any other agreement or transaction that transfers, de jure or de facto, to a person or an economic group the assets of an undertaking or gives a determinative influence over ordinary or extraordinary business decisions.

Article 8° of the Act and its implementing regulation, Decree 89/2001, establish that operations falling within Article 6° must be notified when the total turnover of the acquiring and target group of companies exceed the amount of pesos $200 million within Argentina. Economic concentrations must be notified before or within a week after the conclusion of the agreement, or the announcement of the public bid, or the acquisition of a controlling interest.[6] There is no adjustment of the thresholds. Any adjustment would only be possible by a change in the law.

Article 7° of the Act (with modifications according to Decree N° 396/01) sets the substantive standard for assessing a merger. It prohibits economic concentrations, which have as object or effect a restriction, or distortion of competition in a way that may result against the general economic interest.

This provision can be understood as implying an SLC Test (substantial lessening to competition).

Article 13° of the Act states that the Competition Authority must decide on a notified operation within the term of forty-five (45) working days after the date of the notification. Article 14° states that if that the term elapses without a resolution, the notified operation must be automatically considered authorised. There have never been mergers tacitly authorised according to Article 14. Regarding the relationship between competition policy and regulation, Law N° 25156 derogates any competition faculty to other public office and centralises it within TNDC.

2.1.2   The Competition Authority

As already mentioned, the Amendment of the Law aimed at increasing the enforcement power of the Agency in order to increase its effectiveness and widen its scope, including all the sectors of the economy. It created the National Tribunal for Competition Defence – TNDC as an independent body to enforce the law within the Ministry of Economy. The TNDC, however, has not been created yet.

At the moment, the CNDC is in charge of enforcing the Law. It reports to the Technical Co-ordination Secretariat of the Ministry of Economy and Production. Its decisions are non-binding recommendations, reported to the Secretariat, which takes the final decisions about anticompetitive conducts and mergers and acquisitions, based on CNDC technical reports. Nevertheless, final decisions generally follow CNDC's recommendations. This decision process clearly reduces the effectiveness of the measures taken, as there is a probability that the reports produced by the CNDC are not followed by the Secretariat. Additionally, it generates significant transactions costs.

The CNDC consists of a President and four Commissioners, who are advised by a Chief Economist and a Chief Attorney and a staff of approximately 35 lawyers and economists or accountants.

In turn, TNDC will be constituted by seven members, to be appointed by the President of the Republic after a selection process, involving a public contest, which includes examinations and interviews before a special jury. According to the new Act, the jury is composed of representatives of each branch of the government and of remarkable academic bodies.[7] The special jury was constituted in December 2002 and the selection process of the candidates has already begun.

The Members of the Tribunal serve for six years and can be re-elected indefinitely by the former procedure. The renewal of the Tribunal will be undertaken on a partial basis: three members will change after three years and the remaining four will change three years later. They can be removed from their functions only by the jury and by a majority.

2.1.3   Some preliminary conclusions concerning the Competition Agency in Argentina

Even though the amendment of the law aimed at increasing the enforcement power of the Antitrust Agency, the evidence considered allows us to argue that those objectives are not being fulfilled at the present time. Firstly, the National Tribunal has not been established and the CNDC remains in charge of enforcing the Law. As already mentioned, the functions of the Commission, as well as its structure, reveal major drawbacks that need to be remedied in the shorter term. This task has been postponed, which damages the authorities' reputation to fulfil its proposed objectives.

Secondly, successive amendments to the Law have reduced its effectiveness in the enforcement of the competition framework, such as the introduction of a greater role for the Secretariat during any investigation, and the changes to the thresholds required to notify a concentration operation.

2.2   Peru

2.2.1   The legal framework

The Constitution of Peru, dated from 1993, establishes that one of the government functions is to encourage free competition, prohibiting the abuse of a dominant position and the existence of monopolies (Article 61).

Prior to 1991, there was no law that properly defined anticompetitive practices. Legislative Decree N° 701 gave the basis for an Anticompetitive Law. The purpose of the Law was to eliminate monopolistic practices that control and restrict free competition in the production and commercialisation of goods and services, encouraging free enterprises in the best interests of users and consumers.

In Article 3°, it is settled that '... any acts or conduct related to economic activities constituting an abuse of a dominant position[8] in the market or limiting, restricting or distorting the free competition,[9] in such a way that damages the general economic interest in the national territory are forbidden and will be punished'.

The Antitrust Agency in charge of enforcing the competition Law is the National Institute of Free Competition and Intellectual Property Rights Protection (INDECOPI). The list of restricted practices includes horizontal and vertical practices and the criteria followed by INDECOPI is the rule of reason. However the Tribunal follows the per se rule as well as the rule of reason. In cases concerning abuse of dominant position or collusive practices between competitors, the general criterion followed is the rule of reason, while the per se rule is used for price agreements, market separation and collusion in public auctions.

The Antitrust Law in Peru does not include merger control. This is rationalised on the basis that is that the Competition Law regulates firm conducts but not the structure of the industries. However, there is one exception to the above rule, which is the electricity sector. This sector, as well as telecommunications, differs from the rest of the sectors of the economy and is worthy of separate analysis.

The electricity sector in Peru initiated major economic reforms in 1992, including privatisation and deregulation. The regulatory and legal framework since then set the rules for the granting of concessions in a competitive environment. New rules for the fixing of tariffs and market entry were established. In this context, the former public enterprises were vertically divided in the following units: generation, transmission and distribution. Private investment was encouraged. Generation was considered as a competitive market, prior to authorisation or concession by the public regulator.

Regarding public institutions participating in this market, the activities of co-ordination of energy distribution, fixing of tariffs, general regulation, fiscalisation and competition were divided between different governmental agencies. In respect of competition, INDECOPI was in charge of enforcing the Competition Law in the sector. As mentioned before, this is the only sector where the Competition Agency has power to control mergers. Law N° 26876 defines the Antitrust and Antioligopoly Law for the Electricity Sector. Its Article 1 defines that 'both types, vertical or horizontal mergers that will take place on generation and/or transmission and/or distribution activities of the electric energy will be subject to a prior permission procedure... in order to avoid acts of concentration that tends to diminish, lessen, damage or prevent competition and the free concurrence in the markets of the activities mentioned before or on the related markets'.

Article 3 establishes that all the concentration operations that, directly or indirectly, involve companies that develop activities of generation and/or transmission and/or distribution of electrical energy that account previous or afterwards, in a joint or separate way, a market share equal or greater to 15 per cent in the cases of horizontal concentration have to request permission. In the case of acts of vertical concentration, they have to notify all operations that involve, directly or indirectly, companies that account previous or afterwards a market share equal or greater to 5 per cent of any of the involved markets.

Therefore only in the electricity sector is there an explicit intention by the state to prevent any concentration in the market that might potentially affect competition and worsen consumers and/or users welfare. This contradicts the general criteria through which the impact of competition policy is only ex post, and at the same time, introduces asymmetries in the legal framework.

The second sector that needs to be analysed is telecommunications. In this sector it is not INDECOPI but OSIPTEL, an institution in charge of enforcing the Competition Law. Additionally, OSIPTEL regulates the market. The Decrees N° 701 and 702 give power to INDECOPI to enforce the Law in general, and to OSIPTEL in particular, in telecommunications. This again raises a question about the existence of asymmetry between the different sectors, which also reduces the effectiveness in the enforcement of the antitrust framework. OSIPTEL can formulate non-binding guidelines for the sector and it is also in charge of preventing anticompetitive practices, and can impose sanctions to firms that operate in the telecommunication sector. Regarding the legal framework for the sector, the criteria is that in the first instance the specific norms must be applied and must be complementary to the general competition rules. In other words, through the application of the general legal framework of competition it is possible to remedy competitive problems that are not dealt properly in the specific norm. However, the previous criteria mean that the application of the law is not uniform across all sectors and therefore contradicts the principle of specialisation in the public function.

2.2.2 The Competition Agency

In 1992, Law N° 25868 created the National Institute of Free Competition and Intellectual Property Rights Protection (INDECOPI). INDECOPI is in charge of enforcing the Competition Law (Decree 701 and its Amendments). It is organised into four bodies: the Directory, the Functional Units, the Area of Economic Research and the Administration. The Functional Units are the Unit of Free Competition and the Unit of Property Rights that together constitute the Tribunal of Free Competition and Intellectual Property.

The Free Competition Unit is divided into:

* the Commission of Consumer Protection;
* the Commission of Fair Trade;
* the Commission of Free Competition;
* the Commission of Dumping and Subsidies Repression;
* the Commission of Free Access to Markets; and
* the Commission of Technical and Commercial Registrations.

INDECOPI depends on the Ministry of Industry, Tourism, Integration and International Commercial Negotiations. It is a body with technical, economic and administrative autonomy and its Commissions are technically and functional autonomous.

The Directory is the highest body and it is integrated by three members, two representatives of the Industry Ministry and one representative of the Ministry of Economy. They are elected by the Executive Power.

The Unit of Free Competition and the Unit of Property Rights (which constitute The Tribunal of Free Competition and Intellectual Property) receive and deal with the appeals to the decisions taken by each INDECOPI Commission. The Unit of Free Competition is integrated by six members and the Unit of Property Rights by four, elected by proposals from the Directory and approved by the Ministry of Industry. Members of each Commission are elected by the Directory for a non-determined period.

Regarding the decisions taken by each of the units, the administrative role is finished once the Tribunal of Free Competition and Intellectual Property has made its decision. Only then can the decision be appealed to the Judiciary Power.

The Commission of Free Competition can impose sanctions and emit cautionary measures. Regarding sanctions, the severity of them depends on the following:

* the scope and characteristics of the anticompetitive conduct;
* the size of the market;
* the market share of the firm(s); and
* the effect on competitors, consumers and users and the duration of the practice.

2.2.3 Some preliminary conclusions concerning the Competition Authority in Peru

Several points need to be highlighted to assess the efficacy of the Antitrust Agency to enforce the Competition Law. Firstly, there is a lack of a unique Antitrust Agency with uniform attributes in all sectors in which competition activities are concentrated in a centralised agency. As mentioned before, in telecommunications, it is not INDECOPI but OSIPTEL who is in charge of enforcing the Competition Law with respect to telecommunications. The fact that the application of the law is not uniform to all the sectors contradicts the principle of specialisation in the public function, which says that the Antitrust Agency should be competent in all the sectors, while the sectoral regulators should have only responsibilities related to economic regulation in the particular markets. However, in the case of OSIPTEL, it acts as a sectoral regulator and also has competition responsibilities. This distorts the markets and reduces the effectiveness of the competition policy.

Secondly, there is a degree of overlapping of functions between the different government agencies. There are a diversity of institutions dealing with the activities of co-ordination of energy distribution, fixing tariffs, general regulation, fiscalisation and competition. The lack of a clear delimitation of responsibilities also damages the effectiveness of the competition policy.

Thirdly, the asymmetry between sectors is also worth highlighting. The legal competition framework does not contemplate merger controls. However, there is one sector in which vertical or horizontal mergers has to be subject to a prior permission procedure in order to avoid acts of concentration that tends to diminish, lessen, damage or prevent competition. This is the electricity sector.

Fourthly, during the 1990s there has been a process of deregulation and private capital growth that has altered the competitive environment in many markets and, in particular, markets where there are natural monopolies. In this context, the lack of a competition authority able to analyse the impact on competition of this concentration process remains a serious drawback.

Fifthly, there is an insufficient level of autonomy for the Antitrust Agency. On the one hand, members of the Commission and Tribunals are elected by Executive Power, and thus lack enough independence. On the other hand, the decisions taken are non-binding. For instance, OSIPTEL can formulate non-binding guidelines for the sector and is also in charge of preventing anticompetitive practices. This again reduces the effectiveness and impact of any determination. Decisions taken by the Commission are initially given to the Tribunal for appeal in order to complete the administrative role and only then do they go to the Justice.

Finally, the coexistence of numerous institutions and complex procedures to enforce the law also damages the enforcement power of any Antitrust Agency.

2.3   Chile

2.3.1   The legal framework

Chile's current competition law was adopted in 1973, but was amended in November of 2003 in Chilean Law No. 19.911. This created a new Competition Tribunal and introduced a number of other reforms.

Article 1 of the law contains a very broad prohibition of acts or agreements'…'attempting to restrain free competition in business activities …'. This ban is a criminal provision, but the law's civil aspects predominate. As amplified by Article 2's illustrative list of behaviours deemed to tend to restrain free competition and Article 6's passing reference to '…any abuse incurred by whosoever monopolises a business activity…'.

Article 1's ban is the basis for all enforcement actions, whether they involve horizontal agreements, vertical agreements, monopolisation (abuse of dominant position), mergers, or unfair competition. Both the generality and the criminal nature of the initial ban are consistent with the view that the law was based on the United States' Sherman Antitrust Act. Chile is primarily a civil law jurisdiction.

Article 2 is an illustrative list of anticompetitive arrangements. It sets out five specific categories of 'actions or agreements' covered by Article 1. The first, third, and fourth categories are standard; but the second and fifth are unusual. The categories include actions or agreements that relate to the ollowing:

* the distribution of quotas and reduction or suspensions of production;
* transportation;
* trade or distribution, such as imposing quotas, allocating territories, or exclusive distribution;
* determining prices of goods or services; and
* the freedom to work, unionise and bargain.

There is some continuing uncertainty about the legal effect of Article 2. In he early years, as Resolving Acts showed, the Prosecutor's Office and the Commissions apparently took the position that Article 2 was not merely .llustrative of conduct that tends to restrain free competition, but a declaration hat the listed forms of conduct are always illegal. That approach justified the condemnation of non-price vertical restraints without consideration of efficiencies or market power.

The competition institutions no longer take that approach with respect to vertical restraints, and this has been interpreted by some as a recognition that Article 2: (a) is merely illustrative of conduct that can violate Article 1, and herefore (b) does not establish or authorise the application of a different egal standard. This argument implies that Article 2 does not authorise per se reatment of any competition law violations, including hard core cartels, resale price maintenance, and unfair competition.

Competition officials generally take the position that hard core cartels are illegal per se, basing this position on either Article 2 or on a flexible interpretation of Article 1. The argument based on Article 1 seems significantly more persuasive. The amendments proposed, as part of the pro-growth agenda, will revise the list in Article 2 to drop the two unusual items and to set forth more precise descriptions of the covered conduct. The agenda mentions:

(a)   explicit or implicit agreements or collusive practices whose object is to fix resale or buying prices, limit production, or allocate zones or quotas;
(b)   the abuse of a dominant position by an enterprise or group of enterprises with a common owner by fixing buying or selling prices, tying arrangements, allocation of markets or quotas, or other similar conducts; and
(c)   predatory practices to gain or increase a dominant position.

The amendment appears to drop nonprice vertical restraints from the list. If Article 2 is the law's authorisation for use of the per se rule, dropping nonprice vertical restraints codifies the current practice of using rule of reason analysis to assess such agreements. However, the new language does not answer the important and long-running question of whether Article justifies subjecting the listed forms of conduct to the per se rule.

Article 1's ban applies to all individuals, to all enterprises (regardless of state ownership), and in some circumstances to government ministries or other agencies.[10]

2.3.2 The Competition Agency

Chile's current competition law – the 'Law for the Defence of Free Competition' – was adopted in December of 1973.

The 1973 law created a tripartite institutional framework – an enforcement agency (the Prosecutor's Office[11]), a special tribunal (the Antitrust Commission[12]), and a number of largely advisory Preventative Commissions[13] (one central and several regional). Proposed amendment would replace, in part, the Antitrust and Preventative Commissions with an independent Antitrust Tribunal.

The Antitrust Commission (or Resolving Commission) is the highest body in the Chilean competition system. Its nature is that of a special court. It is not an organic part of the judiciary, but is chaired by a judge from the Supreme Court and is subject to the Court's supervision. Its other member are Chiefs of Service from the Economy and Treasury Ministries, a law school dean, and a dean of an economics department.

The Commission's main function is to decide on cases brought by either the Prosecutor's Office or private complainants. When a case is initiated by a private complaint, the Prosecutor's Office may choose whether to participate as a party, though the Commission can ask the Office for a report. In addition, the Commission may (but rarely does) open an investigation on its own initiative, and it may in appropriate cases call upon police assistance in 'lock-forcing' and executing search warrants. It also decides appeals concerning the Prosecutor's information requests and the Preventative Commissions' decisions. It has the broadest remedial powers; its remedies may involve fines, cease and desist orders, dissolving or restructuring businesses, and disqualifying individuals from holding office in professional and trade associations.

The Preventative Commissions are the most unusual element in Chile's institutional structure. Often described as consultative organs, these Commissions were charged with answering questions and determining how individuals, firms, and government entities had to deal with activities that restrict competition.

Chilean Law No. 19.911, published on 14 November 2003, amends the prior competition law by creating a new Competition Tribunal and introducing a number of other reforms. As proposed, the Tribunal is an independent entity that has judicial powers but is not formally part of the judiciary. It has five members. The President of the Tribunal, who must be a lawyer with at least ten years of experience in the competition law field, will be appointed by the President of the Republic from a list of five nominees established by the Supreme Court through a public contest. The other members (two lawyers and two economists) will be chosen as follows: one lawyer and one economist will be chosen by the President from a list of three nominees established by the Central Bank (Council of Governors), also through a public contest.

Other changes clarify how particular types of anticompetitive conduct should be considered and ban 'unfair competition' only when the conduct is intended to gain, maintain, or increase a dominant position. The law now provides a limited 'settlement' procedure. Imprisonment is eliminated as a sanction, but the amount of fines is raised to US$10 million (20 UTA). The head of the competition enforcement entity, the National Economic Prosecutor, is given new powers, including the authority to sign agreements with domestic agencies and foreign entities.

The Commission also has other, less judicial powers. Sometimes an investigation by the Prosecutor's Office does not lead to a legal challenge, but rather to a report that discusses competitive conditions in a market and urges the Commission to propose the modification or abolition of laws or regulations that are creating competition problems. Also, in addition to issuing binding orders to entities found to have violated the law, the Commission may issue 'general instructions' – binding rules that direct all members of an industry to act in particular ways in order to avoid restraining free competition.

In addition, the Antitrust Commission currently plays a role in determining when the normal competition rules do not apply, though the new law proposes to abolish this system. A 'well-founded positive report' by the Antitrust Commission is required before the state may confer a monopoly on a private party or authorise a conduct prohibited by the competition law.

2.3.3   Some preliminary conclusions concerning the Competition Authority in Chile

The competition institutions' cautious approach seems to have helped facilitate the gradual acceptance of competition enforcement. But the tradition of caution, including an apparent reluctance to find violations and to impose fines, has in part reflected a view in Chile that economic offences against the public are not serious and that the costs of monopoly may not exceed the costs of competition law enforcement.

In order to improve decisions, it is necessary to clarify legal standards introducing guidelines or policy statements. There is much uncertainty on basic issues such as the means of defining markets, evaluating dominance or market power, assessing the legality of a vertical restraint, and even the standard applicable to cartels.

Chile's very broad ban on acts or agreements that attempt to restrain free competition provides a sufficient basis for a full range of competition enforcement. A significant number of basic substantive issues appear to be unresolved. In the early years, agreements within the categories of Article 2 were essentially illegal per se. Through time, there has been an increasing use of economic principles, which meant moving away from rules per se to the rule of reason. However, simultaneous to this process, much uncertainty has been introduced in terms of the decisions taken.

At the same time, competition policy has had an increasing role in the regulation of public utility services; the telecommunications and electricity sectors for example, are not authorised to set tariffs unless the Commission has found the market to be competitive. A Commission ruling that local telephony services were not competitive laid out six provisions aimed at creating a genuinely competitive market.

On the other hand, mergers have evidently got increased attention in the last few years. Competition officials observe that in Chile's very open economy there are few anticompetitive mergers and that in recent years, at least, the potentially problematic mergers have been reviewed. Some of Chile's most important recent merger cases have involved the acquisition of firms operating in infrastructure sectors such as telecommunications and electricity. The cases constitute an important part of Chile's overall regulatory approach to those markets. Until recently, however, it appears that Chile has never had a significant merger control programme except in infrastructure industries.

3.　PARTIAL PRODUCTIVITY INDEXES FOR MEASURING THE EFFECTIVENESS OF COMPETITION POLICY

The objective of this section is to develop some partial productivity indexes that capture the effectiveness of the antitrust agencies to enforce the competition law and allow us to compare the different agencies. So far the evaluation of competition policy has been based on qualitative analysis and not much has been done on the estimation or quantification of the effectiveness in the enforcement of the competition law.

We are conscious that the analysis is partial and only focuses on some of the important factors. We are aware of the caveats of this approach: it is biased and dependent on the particular ratios that we construct and analyse. Furthermore, the chapter does not aim at providing a broad assessment of the role and effectiveness of competition policy in each of the countries. This would require a general equilibrium analysis, which exceeds the scope of the present chapter. Additionally, it would require us to take into account other nportant dimensions of the country that might affect the development of the ompetition policy.

Besides developing indexes, we complement the analysis with the onstruction of technological frontiers. We believe that this methodology rovides an interesting approach that aims at improving the quantitative nalysis on competition issues and increasing the information a regulator or a olicy maker should rely on in order to assess and strengthen the role of ompetition policy. We will also discuss further extensions to the present nethodology that might enrich the analysis.

Performance indicators can be separated into two main categories: a) roductivity indicators and b) frontier estimates. In our case efficiency is efined as the capacity of the competition agency to obtain the maximum roduct at the minimum costs. It includes two aspects: productive and echnical efficiency and it deals with the input requirements and the llocation of resources. Outputs produced by each agency can be measured s the number of procedures finished per year, the number of procedures with resolution per year, and the number of sanctions imposed per year. Iowever, considering only this information would provide a biased ssessment of the importance and magnitude of these figures. To avoid this ve proceed to scale them by factors such as the number of procedures nitiated each year or the number of employees.

In this context, it is also important to distinguish the activities or functions ach agency performs. Each Competition Authority deals with conduct cases nd, when appropriate, merger control. Therefore, we present some lternatives of partial productivity indexes distinguishing conduct cases and nergers. We commenced by presenting the evolution of conduct cases of ach agency per year. As it is shown, the evolution is quite dissimilar etween agencies. We distinguish between the number of cases solved, the umber of cases where fines were imposed, and the evolution of cases that vere considered non-problematic in terms of their effect on competition. In ne case of Chile, the number of procedures includes decisions such as the greement between parties. In this case, the data has been estimated through a letailed internet search to find an approximation of the total number of cases.

The following points can be emphasised from Table 8.1:

- In Argentina during the first years, a small number of leading cases were solved. The Competition Commission increased the number of procedures completed each year, but not with a constant pattern.
- Chile has a better performance in terms of the number of procedures initiated each year relative to the set of countries considered. What remains to be answered is the real significance of cases solved.
- Peru has the highest proportion of fines to total cases solved throughout the period.

Using the information gathered for 2002, indexes were derived on th following basis:

* the number of cases to total budget of each Agency;
* budget per employee;
* the number of cases solved per employee during a year; and
* the number of fines to total cases solved during a year.

The information is provided for the year 2002.

The Argentinean and Chilean agencies can be described as small agencie in terms of personnel. However, in terms of budget, the Chilean agency i proportionately bigger than its Argentinean counterpart.[14] This is confirme by the index budget per employee. Regarding Peru, it is important t emphasise that the number of employees and the budget includes not only th Competition Tribunal but also the rest of the tribunals. Therefore, in thi respect they are not comparable. The lack of proper disclosure of the dat also raises a derived concern about the effectiveness of the agency to fulfil it functions.

Considering only the information on 'cases solved to budget' and 'case solved per employee' one can assess that the Argentinian Agency is relativel more efficient in concluding a determined number of cases with its give resources. However, it must be borne in mind that we are using only tw indexes to assess the relative efficiency of each agency.

As discussed, in the case of Peru, the figures for employee and the budge include not only the Competition Tribunal but also the rest of Tribunals. Thi must be properly taken into account in order to interpret the results obtainec Regarding the data for cases solved, on the contrary, we present in Table 8. only the number of cases for anticompetitive activities. In order to addres this issue, we present the same information in Table 8.3, with a modificatio to the number of cases solved. The aim is to get a better assessment, i possible, of the level of efficiency of the agency, considering differen alternatives concerning the segmentation of functions. The first alternative i to consider the total number of cases of all the Tribunals instead of thos corresponding only to competition. Table 8.3 includes the total number o cases of INDECOPI, which amounts to 302 cases solved in 2002.*In thi context, the figure for cases solved per employee amounts to 1.12.*[15]

Table 8.1 Evolution of number of conduct cases, 1990–2003

		1990–5	1996	1997	1998	1999	2000	2001	2002	2003
Argentina[a]	Solved	23	8	24	32	17	15	20	32	39
	Fined	7	2	3	3	3	2	3	2	4
	Destimation	13	12	13	26	13	12	17	30	34
	Agreement	3	1	1	3	1	1	0	0	1
Peru[b]	Solved	53´	14	17	9	6	3	8	12	8
	Fined	18´	5	6	3	2	1	3	4	3
	Desestimation	35´	9	11	6	4	2	5	8	5
Chile	Solved	245	40	31	31	35	51	47	40	40
	Fined	136	3	0	3	1	2	3	2	2
	Desestimation	98	16	12	12	14	20	19	16	16
	Conditioned	11	21	19	16	20	29	25	22	22

Notes:
[a] The total number of conduct cases were only defined by the National Commission for Competition Defence for leading cases.
[b] Resolution of cases by 'Commission of Free Competition'. (´) Years 1993 to 1995.

Source: Authors' calculations.

Comparing the figures in Table 8.4 it appears that Peru tends to specialis in the resolution of cases regarding unfair competition, while Chil concentrates most of its resources on vertical arrangements. The distributio of conduct cases appears to show a greater variety in Argentina.

Table 8.5 shows the evolution of merger cases for the period 1990–2003. It appears that Argentina conducts mainly merger controls. The Amendme of the Law in 1999 gave attribution to the Tribunal of Competition to condu ex ante merger control as a preventive tool in the fight against cartels. As ca be seen, since 1999 there has been a major increase in the number of merger analysed. However, a number of legal innovations were also introduced afte 2001, which implied, among other things, an increase in the threshold fc operations to notify. This more strict requirement explains the relativ reduction in the number of mergers controlled in the last years. It appear that, on average, Argentina's merger control policy has had a mor significant impact on markets than is the case in the other countries. Peru' legal system does not have ex ante merger control, with the exception of th electricity sector. The lack of a uniform policy between sectors is anothe caveat of the system and at the same time raises a concern regarding th effectiveness of the antitrust agency to enforce the competition law. In th case of Chile, the Antitrust Agency is allowed to control mergers. Howeve the evidence considered seems to indicate that the impact on markets is nc very significant.

Having analysed both conduct cases and mergers, it is important t emphasise that the former analysis maybe biased. Another approach can b used in order to shed more light on the main features that characterise eac agency. This second approach consists of further analysing some of the mai cases that each agency has dealt with during the period of reference Analysing the most significant cases will allow us to derive conclusion regarding the scope and the impact that each agency's decisions have o markets. Additionally, it also contributes to assessing the effectiveness o each agency's functions. This is accomplished by examining the main case where each competition agency has imposed sanctions during the perio 1996 to 2004. To do this, we construct two indexes, distinguishing betwee antitrust resolutions (horizontal arrangements, vertical arrangements dominance and unfair competition) and merger resolutions.

Table 8.2 Selected indexes, 2002

Year	Personnel	Budget (1)	Cases solved	Cases solved/ Budget	Budget per employee	Cases solved per employee	Fines to total cases
Argentina	42	830	32	3.9	20	0.76	0.06
Peru	268[a]	9094[a]	12	n/a	34	n/a	0.33
Chile[b]	54	2224	47	2.1	41	0.87	0.05

Notes:

(1) Expressed in thousands of US$.

[a] Includes all the Tribunals. It is not possible to provide the information only for the Tribunal of Competition.

[b] Information for 2001.

Source: Authors' calculations.

Table 8.3 Modified selected indexes, 2002

Year	Personnel	Budget (1)	Cases solved	Cases solved/ Budget	Budget per employee	Cases solved per employee	Fines to total cases
Argentina	42	830	32	3.9	20	0.76	0.06
Peru	268[a]	9094[a]	302[a]	3.3	34	1.12	0.33
Chile[b]	54	2224	47	2.1	41	0.87	0.06

Notes:

(1) Expressed in thousands of US$.

[a] Includes all the Tribunals. It is not possible to provide the information only for the Tribunal of Competition..

[b] Information for 2001.

Source: Authors' calculations.

Table 8.4   Distribution of conduct cases

Conduct	Argentina [a]	%	Chile [b]	%	Peru [c]	%
Horizontal arrangements	30	18	35	10	51	4
Vertical arrangements	21	13	143	41	53	4
Other monopoly conducts	73	43	73	21	24	2
Mergers	29	17	13	4	11	1
Unfair competition	15	9	88	25	1.130	89
Total cases	168	100	352	100	1.269	100

Notes:
[a] Years 1990 to 2001.
[b] Years 1996 to 2004.
[c] Years 1993 to 2003.

Source: Authors' calculations.

Table 8.5   Evolution of number of merger cases, 1990–2003

		1990–95	1996	1997	1998	1999	2000	2001	2002	2003
Argentina	Total	0	0	0	0	39	156	37	26	29
	Denied	0	0	0	0	0	1	0	1	1
	Conditioned	0	0	0	0	1	6	0	1	32
	Authorised	0	0	0	0	37	150	37	24	31
Peru *	Total	0	0	0	0	1	0	0	0	0
	Denied	0	0	0	0	0	0	0	0	0
	Conditioned	0	0	0	0	1	0	0	0	0
	Authorised	0	0	0	0	0	0	0	0	0
Chile	Total	7	0	1	7	1	0	0	2	2
	Denied	1	0	0	3	0	0	0	0	0
	Conditioned	1	0	0	1	0	0	0	2	0
	Authorised	5	0	1	3	1	0	0	0	2

Notes:
* Includes only one merger in the Electricity Sector.

Source: Authors' calculations.

As seen in Table 8.6, the total amount of fines is very heterogeneous between countries because, in part, competition institutions and legal systems are very dissimilar. In Argentina these fines represented – for the three first leading cases – US$110.823 million, in Chile penalties were around US$1.100 million, and in Peru US$6.3 million. These fines were imposed on the leading companies in each country for anticompetitive practices, including agreements and abuses of their dominant position. As a consequence they provide an indication of the relevance and impact of decisions taken by the Commissions in competitive matters.

In Argentina the cases involved important economic sectors. For example in 2000, the first case in Table 8.6 was a recommendation by the Commission to impose a fine of US$109.6 million on YPF-REPSOL S.A, which is the leading oil and gas company. The defendant was found responsible of abusing its dominant position in the propane gas market and of artificially increasing their prices.[16]

Relative to the set of countries analysed, competition institutions in Chile play an active role in infrastructure and service sectors. As we show in Table 8.6, the Antitrust Commission found CTC S.A. (a telecom company) guilty of fixing predatory pricing, and imposed a sanction of US$514,000.[17] Additionally, in the air transport sector, the Resolving Commission found that Lan Chile Airlines S.A. had sought to drive a new competitor out of the market by predatorily lowering its prices on the one route in which it competed with the new entrant, and imposed a fine of US$328,000.

In Peru between 1993 to 2003, out of the 130 proceedings, only one resulted in a significant penalty of US$6.085 million in the market of poultry farming. This was an isolated case considering Peruvian jurisprudence. The conduct sanctioned was an agreement over prices among poultry producers during 1996. In addition to fines, in all the cases mentioned, injunctions were imposed in order to restore competitive conditions.

In order to assess the effectiveness and impact of competition law enforcement we consider two indexes: the ratio of fines to profits earned by each company and the share each fine has on the maximum penalty available, shown in table 8.5. There is a wide variety and severity in the amount of fines imposed. It should be noted that as a result of the investigation, the economic impact of these penalties differ among countries and companies. This variety in the degree of indicators gives evidence to the lack of a clear pattern of competition goals during the 1990s. As it was shown, the number and the amount of fines tend to confirm the apparent reluctance of Chile's and Peru's competition agencies and legal systems to impose sanctions.

In Chile, the Prosecutor's Office is allowed to impose criminal sanctions for violations of the competition law, but this does not occur in practice. The maximum fine was approximately US$230 000, but fines are rare and seldom reach this maximum. In fact, during the 30 years of competition enforcement, fines have been imposed in only 73 cases. Since 2004, there have been amendments to the legal framework in Chile, for example Law N° 19.911 amends the previous competition law by:

- the creation of a new Antitrust Tribunal – Competition Tribunal, and
- the imposition of fines up to an amount equivalent to 20 000 'annual tax units' to be paid to the Treasury (approximately US$10 million).

It is also important to analyse conduct fines compared to the maximum penalties available within the legal system. In this case, Argentina imposed average fines that were approximately 60 per cent of the maximum amount, Chile 54 per cent, while Peru was the worst performer with 13 per cent.

In order to compare data from the three agencies, we calculate an Index for conduct fined cases for each country (ICFC)[18] based on the ratio of fines to gross technical profits and fines to maximum fine. The aim is to assess the ability of the Agencies to enforce competition law in the markets during the period of reference and compare between them. Furthermore, we measure the impact of each agency's decision by the numerical value of the index. As a consequence, the higher the index number, the better the performance.

A comparison between countries suggests that the performance of Argentina and Chile is better than Peru. The main difference between the first two is that Chile tends to impose less significant sanctions, while Argentina tends to impose high-impact fines in leading cases.

However, in addition to the above results it is instinctive to examine the wider dimensions regarding the importance that each agency has in the regulatory and legal framework. In this sense, during the 1990s the Chilean agency had considerable influence on public monopoly utilities. Peru's Commission also played a prominent role in litigations among market players or customers, as well as between municipalities and public bodies. The role the competition agency has played in Argentina has varied through time, and has been influenced by the political cycle.

To conclude, the process of competition law implementation has not been homogeneous among countries during the 1990s. Chile and Peru appear to have had a more active role in regulatory issues than in the design of effective sanction systems, such as the introduction of investigative tools. On the other hand, Argentina has efficiently imposed sanctions in a limited set of cases and probably with a higher impact.

We continue to follow the same analysis for merger controls through analysing the main cases conducted by each competition agency for the period 1996 to 2004.

Table 8.6   First three conduct fined cases, 1996–2004

Country	Company	Economic sector	Conduct	Fine (US$ million)	Fine (US$)/ gross technical profits	Fine (US$)/ maximum fine
Argentina	YPF SA – REPSOL	Gas and oil	Abuse of dominant position	109 644	6%	100%
	Tele Red Imagen SA (TRISA), Televisión Satelital Codificada SA (TSCSA)	TV transmission	Abuse of dominant position. Price discrimination	1,059	n/a	80%
	YPF SA - REPSOL	Gas and oil	Abuse of dominant position	120	Insignif- icant	Insign- ificant
Chile	CTC Comunicaciones Móviles Startel SA	Telecommun ications	Dominance Predation prices	514	1%	100%
	Lan Chile Airlines SA	Airline	Price agreements	328	Insignif- icant	60%
	Falabella SACI	Supermarket chain trade retailer	Barriers to entry	257	1%	1.3%
Peru	Asociacion Perúana de Avicultura and 20 companies	Poultry farming	Dominance Predation prices	6,085	n/a	30%
	KLM, Lufthansa e Iberia	Airlines	Barriers to entry	149	n/a	5.5%
	El Pacífico Perúano, Suiza Compañía de Seguros, etc.	Insurance companies	Price agreements	72	44%	3%

Notes:
* In Argentina the maximum fine imposed varies between US$150 million and US$10 000 (Law 25.156 and 22.262). ** In Chile the maximum fine imposed was around 10 000 UTM (approximately US$500 000). In 2004 the maximum fine imposed increased to 20 000 UTA (approximately US$10 million). ***In Peru fines were calculated and based on resolutions of the 'Free Competition Commission'. In all cases gross technical profits were informed by each country's Stock Exchange.

Source: Own elaboration.

Table 8.7   Index of conduct fined cases (ICFC), 1996–2004

ICFC	Argentina	Chile	Peru
1996–2004	93%	82%	42%

Source: Authors' calculations.

The legal framework varies significantly between these countries, not only in strictly legal terms but in the economic consideration over whether or not mergers would generate efficiencies in the economy. It should be noted that the antitrust law in Peru does not include merger control. Competition law focuses on firm conduct but not the structure of the industries except in the case of the electricity sector. Mergers in Argentina are dealt with through new legislation introduced in 1999 which provided for ex ante review and authorisation of mergers and acquisitions and gave the competition authority full jurisdiction on competition issues in every sector of the economy.

In Argentina two mergers were denied by the Competition Commission and had considerable impact. They were Correo Argentino SA – OCA SA (postal services market) – and LAPA SA – Aeropuertos Argentina 2000 (air transportation and airport management). In Chile only one case in the telecommunications sector was denied (see Table 8.8).

A point to highlight is that liberalisation of the economy, together with the privatisation (electricity, telecommunications, transport and other infrastructure) during the 1990s, seems to have generated new challenges in the agencies' merger-related tasks. In this sense, Chile and Peru participated in the Enersis SA and Endesa SA merger process. As a consequence the competition institutions began playing a more active role in some infrastructure sectors, even though the legal framework does not include merger control (see Table 8.9 for an index of activity in this area). This raises a concern about the asymmetries within each of the legal frameworks, which has a consequence for the effectiveness of each agency's enforcement of competition law.

Table 8.8   Main merger operations, 1996–2004

Country	Company	Result
Argentina	Correo Argentino SA (CASA) and Sociedad Anónima Organización Coordinadora Argentina (OCA)	Merger – negative
	LAPA's acquisition by Aeropuertos Argentina AA – 2000	Merger – negative
	Ambev (Brahma) – Quilmas	Merger conditional
Chile	CTC Comunicaciones Móviles Startel SA and VTR SA	Merger – negative
	Enersis SA and Endesa Chile	Merger conditional
	Banco Santander Hispano and BSCH	Merger conditional
Peru	Eléctrica Cabo Blanco SA, Generadores Perú SA, Generalima SA, Inversiones Distrilima SA.	Merger conditional

Source: Authors' calculations.

Table 8.9   Index merger cases (IMC), 1996–2004

IMC	Argentina	Chile	Peru
1996–2004	83%	67%	17%

Source: Authors' calculations.

4.   EMPIRICAL ESTIMATION OF THE EFFECTIVENESS OF COMPETITION POLICY

In this section, we proceed to estimate the relationship between the different models of competition agencies and their enforcement capacities, as well as their impact on the market. The aim is to assess whether there is any statistical relationship between the taxonomy of agencies and their effectiveness in the improvement of the competitive environment.

Performance indicators can be separated into two main categories: a) productivity indicators and b) frontier estimates. We have presented in the last section some partial productivity indexes, which required us to define some outputs 'produced' by each agency. One of the main conclusions derived was that on average, and based on the information provided by those indexes, Argentina performed best across a range of dimensions considered.

In this section we proceed to evaluate the use of resources and the significance that structural and environmental variables have on the output of each agency. The aim is to assess conclusions reached in the previous section. It must be repeated that the present quantitative analysis has many drawbacks, such as data limitations and, therefore, the analysis is only illustrative.

With the introduction of yardstick competition for the regulation of natural monopolies, there has been an increasingly interest in developing standardised performance indicators.[19] These indicators have been used by regulators to assess the absolute and relative performance of regulated utilities.[20] In this context, one of the main instruments to measure the efficiency of a firm or an institution in general is the efficiency frontier. Efficiency measures were originally introduced by Farrell in 1957. Below we discuss the main features of the efficiency frontier literature in order to provide the basic guidelines to understand and interpret the results presented in this chapter.

Technological frontier studies can be classified according to their specification and estimation methodologies. Focusing on specification, the problem can be viewed from two different approaches: the production function and the cost function. The production function shows the output as a function of inputs, while the cost function shows the total cost of production as a function, of output and input prices. We construct a production function, and in doing so there is an implicit choice regarding the type of efficiency to estimate. There are basically two possibilities: theoretically defined production function (based on engineering knowledge of the process of the industry) and an empirical function constructed on estimates based on observed data. The usual practice for regulatory purposes is to analyse individual performance in relation with best-observed practice rather than comparing with an ideal practice (which is generally unobtainable). In this work, we will consider that the efficient production function is represented by the best-observed practice among the firms in the sample. Regarding the alternative estimation methods, both production and cost functions estimates can be obtained using statistical or mathematical programming methods.[21]

Once a decision is made on which type of frontier, costs or production, is going to be estimated, and which technique, statistical or mathematical programming, is to be used, the following step is to decide on whether a deterministic or stochastic frontier is to be used. If a deterministic approach is chosen, all observed difference between a particular firm and the frontier is attributed to inefficiency, ignoring the possibility that the performance of a firm might be affected not only by its own efficiency but also by factors beyond its control (such as adverse climate conditions).[22]

The deterministic frontier production function model with panel data is written as

$$Yit = \beta 0 + X'it\ \beta + \varepsilon it,$$

where Yit is the output of decision making unit (DMU, hereafter) i (i=1, 2,...,N) at time t (t=1,2,...,T), Xit is the corresponding matrix of k inputs and β is a kX1 vector of unknown parameters to be estimated. The error term is specified as εit Technical efficiency accounts for those factors that can be controlled by the DMU, and can be defined as the discrepancy between a DMU's actual output and its potential output. The level of technical efficiency of DMU i in period t is obtained as

$$EFit = \exp(-uit).$$

The measure of productive efficiency adopts values between zero and one, with one denoting a firm that is 100 per cent efficient. These measures are defined under the assumption that the production frontier or efficient production function is known.

We apply this approach to measure and compare the performance of the antitrust agencies. We are implicitly assuming that the approach conducted by regulators when analysing the performance of regulated firms can be replicated to compare the performance of public agencies.

The approach consists of constructing a frontier and evaluating the efficiency of each institution as the distance from the observed practice to that empirical frontier formed by the best practice. We are focusing on relative efficiency, based on the data set used for the estimation. As already mentioned, we are analysing the performance of three agencies: Argentina, Chile and Peru, for eight years (1996–2003). There are some alternatives regarding the way to treat the data: one possibility is to consider each year separately, estimate cross section sets and then evaluate the rate of variation of the scores between years and through the different agencies. Another possibility is to consider each observation independently, construct a panel set with all the observations and estimate the efficiency score of each agency for each year as the distance between the observed practice to the one that builds the frontier, given a particular environment. The advantage of this last approach is that by considering all the information together in a panel set, we increase the efficiency of the estimated coefficients. This is the approach that we follow in the present chapter.

We estimate the efficiency of each agency based on a production function. A production function relates the maximum amount of output that can be obtained, given some resources. To measure the efficiency of them, we apply econometric techniques. We suppose that the level of efficiency is constant through the period of reference. Thus, we obtain one efficiency score for each of the agencies considered for the whole set of years. Additionally, we discuss and consider the role of the environment in the development of each agency, and therefore in the level of efficiency at which they operate. In particular, we analyse the role of the legal framework in the level of efficiency.

Firstly, we discuss the possible alternatives for outputs generated by an agency. Secondly, we discuss which factors help to control and contribute to the explanation of the variability between outputs. Finally, we show the results of the estimations and present the conclusions.

4.1   Dependent variable

As dependent variable we consider the total number of procedures finished by each agency per year, including conduct cases and mergers. We do not distinguish between conduct cases and mergers. The availability and quality of the data considered explain in part the selection of the variables. We also attempt to use the total number of fines (including sanctions and some kind of conditioning) imposed by each agency per year.

4.2   Control variables

The paper relates these indexes to the requirement of resources and environmental factors such as:

- Size of the agency. This is measured by the evolution of the number of employers in each agency. Additionally, we consider the yearly budget assigned to each agency needed to develop competition policy.
- Size of the economy. We use the real GDP of the current period or the variation of GDP in order to capture the influence of the business cycle.
- Functions of the agencies. We include two dummy variables to capture whether the agency controls mergers or not (named as d1 with d1 = 1 if there is ex ante merger control) and whether the agency has enforcement powers in all the sectors of the economy (named as d2).

The size of the economy and the functions of each agency are defined as environmental variables. We include these variables in order to capture the factors that each agency does not fully control but nevertheless affect their performance. Starting with an over parameterised model, the methodology adopts a stepwise procedure in order to reach a final specification that fulfills desirable statistical properties, including parsimonious. A production function was constructed in order to measure the performance of each agency. We define output as the total amount of cases solved. Regarding inputs, we include the number of employees in each agency.

The results of the estimations of the model selected are presented in Table 8.10 below. We attempted other specifications including variables such as the yearly budget. However, the inclusion of the budget proved to be statistically insignificant in explaining the variability of the total number of cases solved among the agencies.[23]

In the final specification, we include environmental variable d1 in order to capture merger control. We also consider d2 and the evolution of GDP. This last variable is not significant to explain the variability of total cases. Regarding the first two variables, including d2 instead of d1 does not significantly alter the results and the main conclusions derived.

The following tables show the specification of the basic model and the results of the estimations. We estimate a fixed effect panel data for the whole period. We also tried a random effect model, but the results were not better than the fixed effects model.[24]

In this specification, we consider one product and only one input (labour intensive production function). The main features of the estimation are as follows:

- Labour is significant in explaining the variability of total cases. The sign of the coefficient is the one expected in theory.
- The model has an adequate global adjustment.
- Since all the variables are expressed in logarithms, the coefficients can be interpreted as elasticities.

- The substitution of the evolution of the number of fines as a dependen variable did not improve global adjustment.

Table 8.10   Production function: fixed effect model I – panel

ln(cases)	Coef.	Std.	Err.	Z
ln(emp)	1.73	0.38	4.52	0.00
_cons	-4.19	1.63	-2.56	0.02
sigma_u	29.13			
sigma_e	0.46			

Notes:
R-sq: within = 0.5608   Obs per group: min = 5
between = 0.9986   avg = 6.7
overall = 0.3751   max = 7

Source: Authors' calculations.

In the Table 8.11 we present a variation to the basic model where we include d1 as another regressor. With this specification the global adjustment is adequate. Even though the value of the coefficients vary, the efficiency scores and the ranking between agencies derived from this specification do not significantly change. Stability of coefficients and of the efficiency scores is highly desirable as a property and thus reinforces the robustness of the results of the model selected.

Table 8.11   Production function: fixed effect model II – panel

ln(cases)	Coef.	Std.	Err.	T
ln(emp)	1.22	0.50	2.43	0.03
d1	0.67	0.44	1.51	0.15
_cons	-2.33	2.00	-1.16	0.26
sigma_u	2.02			
sigma_e	0.44			

Notes:
R-sq: within=0.6188   Obs per group min=5
between= 0.971   avg=6.7
overall= 0.199   max=8

Source: Authors' calculation.

Having described the specifications and the estimation results of the basic model and its alternative, in Table 8.12 we present the mean of the efficiency scores derived from the production functions. One point to highlight is that the means of both models are comparable and quite similar. The standard deviation is also relatively similar between them. Additionally, in Table 8.13 we present the efficiency scores for each of the agencies considered and the ranking between them for both models.

As already mentioned, a score of 1 is interpreted as a 100 per cent efficient agency within the set of antitrust agencies considered. However, it is important to emphasise that the conclusion derived in both models is that the Argentinean agency is the relatively more efficient agency. Frontier estimation is sensitive to the number of observations and furthermore to the quality of the data used to conduct the analysis. In other words, it is highly sensitive to the presence of outliers and badly measured variables. Thus, the discussion about data availability, data deficiencies and the assumptions made to obtain each figure are particularly relevant when deriving the conclusions.

Table 8.12   Efficiency scores for the selected model

Scores	Obs	Mean	Std. Dev
Model 1	20	0.57	0.44
Model 2	20	0.55	0.43

Source: Own elaboration.

Table 8.13   Efficiency scores and rankings

	Model 1		Model 2	
Agency	Score	Ranking	Score	Ranking
Argentina	1	1	1	1
Chile	0.02	2	0.05	2
Peru	0.66	3	0.57	3

Source: Authors' calculations.

In addition, we evaluate some indicators of efficiency. In this case, we consider the investigations solved to presented investigations during a year. We aim to analyse which factors contribute to explain the variability of the ratio of sanctions to total cases. In this case, we estimate a random effect model for the period. In addition, a fixed effect model was estimated. The Hausman test was performed to prove the consistency of the fixed effect model coefficients compared with random effect ones. At a 5 per cent level of significance, the hypothesis that the coefficients of fixed effect model are equal to those of random effect model could be rejected, providing evidence in favour of the random effect model. Table 8.14 shows the results of the estimation.

The methodology provides an interesting approach that aims at improving the quantitative analysis of competition issues and increases the information a regulator or a policy maker should rely on in order to assess and strengthen the role of competition policy.

However, one caveat of this approach is the fact that we are only considering data at the national level, with the limitations it has in terms of the conclusions. Sectoral information will significantly enrich the analysis, allowing to distinction between the impact competition policy has on each sector.

Table 8.14   Impact of agencies: random effect model – panel

ln(sanc/cases)	Coef.	Std.	Err.	z
ln(emp)	0.84	0.19	4.31	0.00
_cons	- 8.84	1.60	-5.54	0.00
sigma_u	0.00			
sigma_e	0.61			

Notes:
R-sq: within = 0.0486   Obs per group: min = 6
       between = 0.9999   avg = 6.7
       overall = 0.5075   max = 7

Source: Authors' calculations.

5. CONCLUSIONS

During the 1990s, a large number of regulations were eliminated in Latin America, fostering economic competition and market transparency. Large investments in industries lead to more issues relating to cartels and monopolies.

As a result, competition institutions in Argentina, Chile and Perú have been active but with different levels of success in competition advocacy concerning: the abuse of dominant positions, vertical arrangements and infrastructure industry monopolies. The effects were not extensive and systematic enough to maximise and guarantee competition in all markets.

In fact, if we analyse all case resolutions by the competition agencies in each country, we realise that in the leading cases where fines were imposed, most seem to have been more a consequence of erratic decisions made by a government and the agencies than as a result of a systematic effort in the fight against cartels. It is furthermore important to point out that on average the three countries considered have only 18 per cent conduct fined cases over total cases from 1996 to 2002.

If we analyse Antitrust Resolutions during the 1990s, it appears that the process of competition law implementation has not been homogeneous among countries with respect to the significance and the impact of fines imposed on different companies and sectors, as well as the legal framework.

During the 1990s, there has been an extended process of amendments to the legal frameworks in Latin American economies. The majority of them have aimed to increase the capacity of each competition agency to enforce the law, such as the creation of the Tribunal of Competition both in Argentina and in Chile, the derogation of competition attributes in other institutions, the introduction of new investigative tools, and clearer definition of responsibilities in competition matters. However, other changes in the legal framework have gone in the opposite direction, in terms of their enforcement capacities, such as the modifications since 2001 in Argentina's thresholds. In any case, in all three countries considered, there is more scope for further reforms that will increase competition in markets. These include the introduction of leniency programmes, advocacy functions and greater independence.

In relation to merger control, the differences among agencies are significant. Argentina and Chile conduct ex ante merger controls. On the contrary, and with the exception of one sector (electricity) the competition authority does not control merger operations. In this case, vertical or horizontal mergers have to be subject to a prior permission in order to avoid acts of concentration that tends to diminish competition.

In terms of autonomy, competition agencies in Peru and Argentina give non-binding resolutions to the Secretariat, which reduces the effectiveness of the decisions taken. In the case of Chile, Law No. 19.911 (2003) amended the previous competition law by creating a new Competition Tribunal as an independent entity with judicial powers. The decisions taken by the Tribunal can be appealed through the Supreme Court.

It is argued that competition policy should be applied to all sectors of the economy while regulation ought to be specific to each sector. This economic principle will maximise the efficiency of the agencies responsible for enforcing the law. In this regard, and based on the information and data considered, we believe that Chile has been relatively successful in the fulfilment of this requirement. In fact, the capacity to develop as a consultancy unit for the specific regulators in infrastructure sectors has increased through time. This process has been accomplished with major innovations and amendments to the legal framework. In the case of Argentina, through the introduction of law N° 25156 and its amendments, the legal framework reduced the competition responsibilities of other agencies and institutions, and concentrated them in the competition agency. However, in practice, through the period of reference, there have been a very small number of cases in which this attribution has been exercised by the

Competition Commission. Finally, in the case of Perú there is not a clear definition of responsibilities in this regard. In the electricity sector, there are a diversity of institutions dealing with the co-ordination of energy distribution, fixing tariffs, general regulation, fiscal and competition matters. The lack of a clear delimitation of responsibilities damages the effectiveness of the competition policy.

In relation to Peru, it is worth highlighting the lack of a unique antitrust agency with uniform attributes in all sectors; the competition functions are not centralised in one agency. As discussed earlier, in telecommunications it is not INDECOPI but OSIPTEL that is in charge of enforcing the competition law. OSIPTEL is therefore a sectoral regulator with responsibilities for competition. This distorts the markets and reduces the effectiveness of the competition policy. In this case, there are also some overlapping of functions between the different government agencies.

In terms of the quantitative analysis, we provided different partial productivity indexes that aimed to capture the effectiveness of the enforcement of competition law by antitrust agencies. We were able to make comparisons between the different agencies. The results indicated that Argentinean and Chilean agencies can be described as small agencies in terms of personnel, however, in terms of the budget, the Chilean agency is proportionately larger than its Argentinean counterpart.

Considering indexes representing the 'cases solved in relation to the budget' and 'cases solved per employee' it is easy to see that the Argentinean agency is relatively more efficient in completing cases.

Regarding the information concerning fines to total cases solved, it seems that Peru imposes considerably more sanctions than the rest of the agencies under analysis. However, this does not necessarily indicate the real impact that these fines have on markets.

The comparison between countries on the evolution of fines imposed and their impact on markets permits us to conclude that the performance of Argentina and Chile is better than Peru. The main difference between the first two is that Chile tends to impose less significant sanctions, while Argentina imposes high-impact fines in leading cases.

Finally, we applied the frontier estimation approach to measure and compare the performance of the antitrust agencies. We implicitly assumed that the approach conducted by regulators when analysing the performance of regulated firms can be replicated in order to compare the performance of public agencies. We tested whether the conclusions derived for partial productivity measures were valid when a broader analysis using production frontiers was applied. In the final specification of the model, we concluded that personnel explain the variability of total cases and that models have an adequate global adjustment. Regarding the efficiency scores obtained from the models, the means are comparable and quite similar. The standard deviation is also relatively similar between them. Through the frontier estimation, we concluded that Argentina has the relatively most efficient agency than Chile and Peru. It is important, however, to emphasise that the conclusions derived from both models are subject to data limitations. Frontier estimation is sensitive to the number of observations and furthermore to the quality of the data used to conduct the analysis. The presence of outliers and poorly measured variables is significant and needs to be dealt with.

Finally, it must be said that the drawbacks and limitations of the information considered serve to emphasise the importance of adequate data sets in order to make comparisons and increase the information that policy makers need to take their decisions.

NOTES

1. Comisión Nacional de Defensa de la Competencia, in Spanish.
2. Tribunal Nacional de Defensa de la Competencia, in Spanish.
3. Until June 2003 CNDC reported to the Competition, Deregulation and Consumer Defence Secretariat (SDCyCD), which in turn was under the Ministry of Production. The new government has created the aforementioned Technical Co-ordination Secretariat to which the CNDC and the Consumer Defence Agency directly reports. In turn, the Secretariat reports directly to the Ministry of Economy and Production, which resulted from the merger of former Economy and Production Ministries.
4. *Resolution SCDyDC N° 40/01* 'Guidelines for the Notification of Economic Concentration Operations' establishes the formalities and procedures that shall be observed by notifying Parties. There are three different forms. Forms F1 and F2 are standardised forms for simple and complex operations, respectively. Form F3 is a customised form for the particular case, issued by the Commission to obtain detailed information in very complex cases.
5. *Resolution SCDyDC N° 164/01,* ('Guidelines for Controlling Economic Concentration Operations') sets the economic methodology for assessing the competitive impact of a merger. The 'Guidelines' focuses on horizontal mergers, but it also has a short reference to assessment of vertical and conglomerate mergers.
6. The Act contemplates in Article 10 hypothesis where the transaction is not subject to notification. Those particular cases are: a) acquisition of a company where the buyer previously owned more than 50 per cent of the shares; b) acquisitions of bonds, debentures, shares without voting rights or debts issued by companies; c) acquisition of a single company by a single foreign company, which previously did not own assets or shares of companies operating in Argentina and d) acquisition of a company in bankruptcy, with no activity during the last year. Also there is a final e) exemption, which takes place when an operation involved companies under the notification threshold, but the amount of the contract and the value of the assets acquired, absorbed, transferred or controlled do not each one exceed the amount of Pesos $20 million. This exception is only valid if it is not the case that: a) in the previous twelve (12) months there has been operations that in the aggregate exceed the amount of Pesos $20 million, or b) in the previous thirty six (36) months there have been operations that in the aggregate exceed the amount of Pesos $60 million. In both a) and b) cases, operations must be referred to the same market.
7. Accordingly to the Act, the Jury has been constituted by the General Attorney of the Government, the Secretariat for Trade, Industry and Mining of the Ministry of Economy, the Presidents of both High and Low Congress Chambers Committees for Trade, the

President of the National Court for Appeals on commercial subjects and the Presidents of both the National Academy of Economics and the National Academy of Law.

8. Article 5° defines abuse of dominant position in the market as a situation in which one or several companies being in a dominant position act unduly in order to obtain benefits and cause damages to third parties, which would not have been possible if such dominant position did not exist. Therefore, it refers to a situation where a firm or a set of them can act independently without taking into account its or their competitors, due to factors such as significant market shares, the attributes of supply and demand, barriers to entry, technological developments, etc.

9. Regarding restrictive practices affecting free competition, the Decree defines them as those practices such as agreements, decisions, recommendations, parallel actions or agreed practices among companies that restrict, impede or falsify, or may restrict, impede or falsify, competition.

10. There are no express exclusions in the competition law. As in other countries, statutory monopolies do exist and there are instances when laws (such as those governing intellectual property) grant exclusive rights. Since possession of a monopoly is not a violation, these laws do not actually create exclusions, as long as abuse of the monopoly or exclusive right is subject to the law. In Chile, this is generally, and perhaps universally, the case. For example, Chile accords the usual kinds of intellectual property rights, and also provides that anticompetitive use of those rights can be penalised under the competition law. Chile's Constitution provides that the state is the sole owner of all mines, regardless of who owns the surface land; this includes ownership of the right to explore for and exploit liquid and gaseous hydrocarbons. It appears, however, that the competition law would apply if the state acted to abuse its monopoly.

11. Fiscalía Nacional Económica, in Spanish.

12. Comisión Resolutiva, in Spanish.

13. Comisión Preventiva, in Spanish.

14. A point to highlight is the Argentinian budget was calculated in dollars before the economic crisis and a substantial devaluation of exchange rate at the end of 2001. In this sense budget may not be representative of an average budget for this Commission.

15. Implicitly it is assumed that the distribution of cases dealt between the different departments is constant which is a caveat of the approach.

16. Due to the price differences and access to gas connections in Argentina a large proportion of propane gas is used by poor consumers (residential, commercial and others).

17. Chile's telecommunications industry has been privatised. To a large extent, the industry is owned by foreign companies. The telecoms law states that providers may generally set the price for their services, except for access charges which are always fixed. Other prices may be fixed if the Antitrust Commission finds that competitive conditions do not exist. In practice, this means that Chile's telecom regulator sets tariffs for local fixed telephony (pursuant to Antitrust Commission rulings) and for access charges in the mobile market. Only access prices can be fixed, and long distance charges are free by law.

18. The Index Conduct Fined Cases is used to measure agencies' performance and it is calculated as follows:
    - Σ [0.5 . (A_i . (US\$ Fine/ US\$ Gross Profits)$_i$)+ 0.5 . (A_i . (Total Fine US\$/ Maximun Fine)$_i$)]
    - i (Number of Cases)= 1 to 3. Years 1996 to 2004.
    - A_i ε to [0,1]. This parameter indicates the relevance of the company that was fined. In all the cases it was assumed that A_i=1, because each company is the largest or one of the most significant in that sector, in terms of market share.

19. Modern regulatory regimes are focused on improving technical efficiency through incentive mechanisms. Among these, yardstick competition is a must. Yardstick competition, originally proposed by Shleifer (1985) requires the horizontal separation of some of the stages of the natural monopoly industries in order to obtain comparative information on relative efficiency levels. This information can then be used to set up tariffs for the regulated companies allowing some efficiency gains to be passed on to consumers and preserving at the same time incentives for the firms to reduce their own costs.

The principles of yardstick competition are quite simple, consisting in defining prices, revenues and quality standards based not on data of the own company, as this would eliminate all incentives to improve efficiency, but on the average of a sample of comparable companies. In other words, the regulator acting as the principal prefers to have several agents in order to reduce the existing asymmetry of information. In exchange for this superior knowledge some economies of scale and or scope are lost when the activity is separated into different units. Efficiency measures are an important tool for regulators, showing how much a firm can raise its output without using more inputs.

20. This requires developing objective measures to screen the functioning and the operation of the different natural monopolies through time in order to promote competition, give incentives to cost minimisation and ensure that, eventually, users benefit from these cost reductions.

21. Non-statistical methods estimate frontiers (which can be parametric or non-parametric) without assumptions on the form of the distribution of the error term. The estimates as a result have no statistical properties, making it impossible to test hypothesis. In the case of estimates using mathematical programming, the frontier can or cannot be specified as a parametric function of inputs (obviously, statistical methods are always parametric). The main advantage of non-parametric methods (also known as Data Envelope Analysis or DEA for short) is that no a priori functional form is imposed on the data. The main disadvantage is that to estimate the frontier it uses only a subset of the available data (those actually determining the frontier), while the rest of the observations are ignored.

22. An additional disadvantage of deterministic estimates is the high sensitivity to outliers. A single outlier observation can have strong effects on the results. Moreover, increasing the size of the sample cannot solve the problems associated with the outlier problem. The estimation of deterministic frontiers assumes a one-sided error term, implying that it is possible to define exactly the minimum necessary cost to produce a given level of output. Therefore, the actual cost is given by the minimum cost plus an inefficiency term (which by definition is equal or greater than zero). Clearly, the underlying assumption is that all external events which might affect the cost function are the same (and with equal intensity) for all firms.

23. In this regard, the quality deficiency of the data might contribute to explaining the non significance of this variable.

24. For a regression such as: $y_{it} = a + x_{it} * B + u_i + e_{it}$, this model assumes that $E(u_i)=E(e_{it})$ $=0$; $E(e_{it}^2) = \sigma^2_e$; $E(u_i)=\sigma^2_u$; $E(e_{it} u_j) =0$ for all i, j and t; $E(e_{it} e_{js}) =0$ if $t \neq s$ or $i\neq j$ and $E(u_i u_j) =0$ if $j \neq i$.

BIBLIOGRAPHY

Charnes, A., W. Cooper and E. Rhodes (1978), 'Measuring the Efficiency of Decision Making Units', *European Journal of Operational Research*, **2** (6), 429–444.

Green, W. (1993), 'The Econometric Approach to Efficiency Analysis', in H.O. Fried, C.A. Knox Lovell and S.S. Schmidt (eds), *The Measurement of Productive Efficiency*, Oxford: Oxford University Press.

Huettner, D. and J. Landon (1977), 'Electric Utilities: Scale Economies and Diseconomies', *Southern Economic Journal*, **44** (4), 883.

Hunt-McCool, J. and R. Warren (1993), 'Earnings Frontiers and Labour Market Efficiency', in H.O. Fried, C.A. Knox and S.S. Schmidt (eds), *The Measurement of Productive Efficiency*, Oxford: Oxford University Press.

Lovell, C. (1993), 'Production Frontiers and Productive Efficiency', in H.O. Fried, C.A. Knox and S.S. Schmidt (eds), *The Measurement of Productive Efficiency*, Oxford: Oxford University Press.

Mackerron, G. (1999), 'Current Developments and Problems of Electricity Regulation in the European Union and the United Kingdom', mimeo.

Petrecolla, D. (2000), 'Defensa de la Competencia', in *Enoikos,* **17**, Buenos Aires, 49–52.

Petrecolla, D. and L. Soto (1999), 'La ley de Defensa de la Competencia: su Aplicación en Casos Recientes', in *La Regulación de la Competencia y de los Servicios Públicos: Teoría y Experiencia Argentina Reciente,* Fiel, Buenos Aires, 91–111.

Petrecolla, D. and C. Ruzzier (2003), 'Problemas de Defensa de la Competencia en Sectores de Infraestructura en la Argentina', *Temas Grupo Editorial S.R.L,* Buenos Aires.

Rodríguez Pardina, M. and M. Rossi (1999), 'Efficiency Measures and Regulation: An Illustration of the Gas Distribution Sector in Argentina', mimeo.

Rodriguez Pardina, M. Rossi and C. Ruzzier (June 1999), 'Consistency Conditions: Efficiency Measures for the Electricity Distribution Sector in South America', mimeo.

Rossi, M. (2000), 'Technical Change and Efficiency Measures: The Post-Privatisation in the Gas Distribution Sector in Argentina', mimeo.

Schmidt, P. and R. Sickles (1984), 'Production Frontiers and Panel Data', *Journal of Business and Economic Statistics,* **2** (4), 367–374.

Shleifer, A. (1985), 'A Theory of Yardstick Competition', *Rand Journal of Economics,* **16** (3), 319–328.

Winslow, T. (2004). 'Competition Law and Policy in Chile', a peer review (OECD), *Energy Economic Transition.*

Index